GRADE LEVEL
K-12

A Systemwide Approach to Leadership

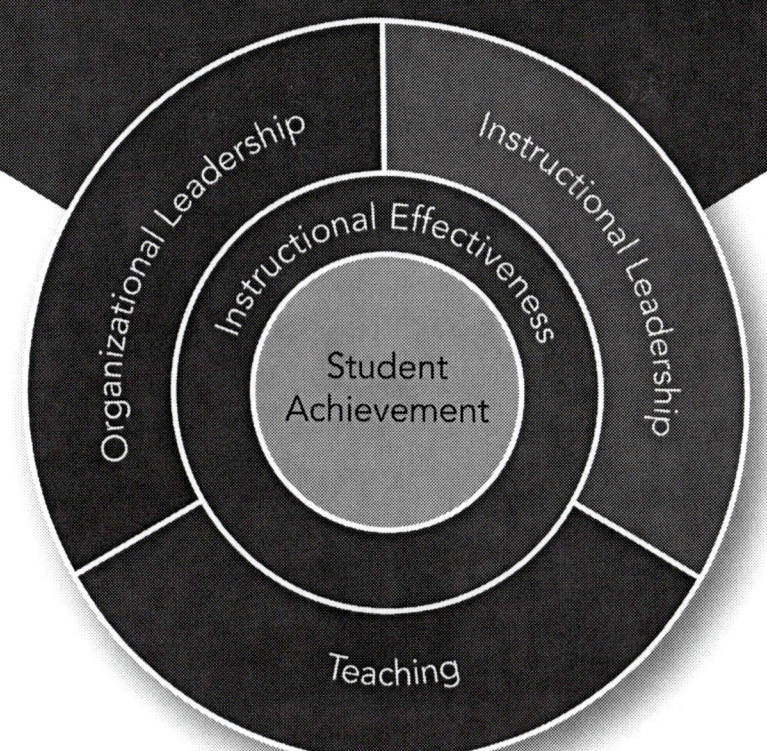

- Organizational Leadership
- Instructional Leadership
- Instructional Effectiveness
- Student Achievement
- Teaching

International Center for Leadership in Education

RIGOROUS LEARNING FOR ALL STUDENTS

Acknowledgment

The International Center for Leadership in Education wishes to thank
Dr. Paul Ezen for his contributions to this book.

No part of this publication may be reproduced in whole or in part, or stored in a retrieval system, or transmitted in any form or by any means, electronic, mechanical, photocopying, recording, or otherwise, without written permission of the publisher.

Copyright © 2012 by International Center for Leadership in Education, Inc.

All rights reserved.

Published by International Center for
Leadership in Education, Inc.

Printed in the U.S.A.

ISBN-1-935300-81-4

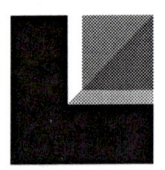

International Center for Leadership in Education, Inc.
1587 Route 146
Rexford, New York 12148
(518) 399-2776
info@LeaderEd.com

Contents

Overview 1

1. **The Daggett System for Effective Instruction** 5
   Converging Challenges 5
   It Takes a System, Not Just a Teacher 6
   Daggett System for Effective Instruction 6
   Summary 8
   Reflection Activity 9

2. **Using the DSEI to Drive Leadership** 11
   Organizational Leadership 12
   Instructional Leadership 13
   Summary 15
   Reflection Activity 15

3. **Setting High Expectations and a Vision as a Transformational Leader** 17
   Lessons About Leadership 17
   Transformational Leadership 29
   Context 48
   Target 49
   Practices 49
   Creating a Shared Vision 57
   Case Study of A.B. Combs Leadership Magnet Elementary School 63
   Summary 68
   Reflection Activity 68

© International Center for Leadership in Education

4. Instructional Leadership...69
Using Instructional Leadership to Address Challenges...69
Creating a Context for Instructional Leadership...72
Commitment to 21st Century Learning...93
Target for Instructional Leadership...97
Management Practices...111
Data-Driven Instructional Leadership...118
Educators' Need for Data...119
Collecting and Analyzing Student Data...125
Cultural Practices...132
Supplemental Instructional Time...136
Summary...142
Reflection Activity...142

5. Leadership Through Empowerment...145
Defining Leadership...145
Total Leadership...146
Leadership Turnover...146
Components of Leadership Through Empowerment...147
The Role of Courage in Empowerment...153
Creativity and Empowerment...162
Transformational Leadership and Empowerment...163
Getting Everyone on Board...166
Vital Factors: Self-Knowledge, Philosophy, Mission, and Vision...167
Mindfulness, Self-Knowledge, and Empowerment...170
Philosophy...171
When "No" Is the Answer...175
Conflict Resolution and Decision Making...178
School Boards and Policy Issues...181
Data Is King...182
Meaningful Conversations That Lead to Empowerment...183
A Constructivist Approach to Meetings...185
Making Empowerment Possible...186
Inspiration Is Not Transferable...189
Revisiting the Key Questions...190
A Summary of the Power of Empowerment...192
Summary...194
Reflection Activity...194

6. **Leadership Skills for a Positive School Climate** **197**
   Climate and Relationships 197
   Bending the Rules: Some True Stories 202
   Situational Adaptations 203
   Empowerment and Trust 204
   Attributes of Leaders Associated with Positive School Climate 206
   Collecting Qualitative Data 211
   Summary 212
   Reflection Activity 212

7. **Leadership and Community Engagement** **215**
   Who Is the Community? 215
   Engaging Parents. 220
   Empowering Community Groups 239
   Empowering the Business Community 244
   Some Interesting Approaches to Engagement. 245
   Summary 250
   Reflection Activity 251

8. **Focus on the Future** **253**

Appendix **257**

Overview

The Daggett System for Effective Instruction

The Daggett System for Effective Instruction (DSEI) provides a coherent focus across the entire education organization on the development and support of instructional effectiveness to improve student achievement. Whereas traditional teaching frameworks are teacher-focused and consider what teachers should do to deliver instruction, DSEI is student-focused and considers what the entire educational system should do to facilitate learning. It is a subtle but important difference based on current research and understanding about teaching and learning.

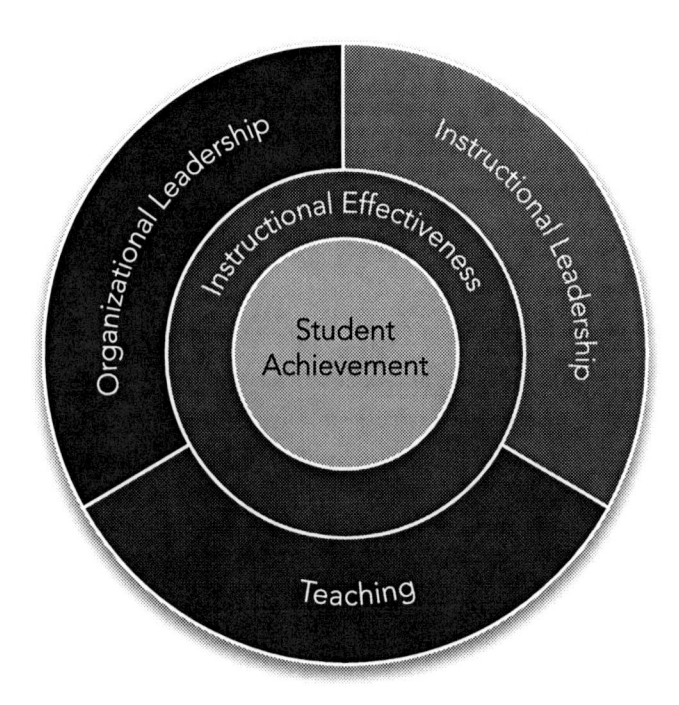

A Systemwide Approach to Leadership

The three parts of DSEI are illustrated here. The following are the critical functions of each part of the system. Think about where you, as a professional educator, fit into this system.

Six Elements of Organizational Leadership

- Create a culture of high expectations.
- Create a shared vision.
- Build leadership capacity.
- Align organizational structures and systems to vision.
- Align teacher/administrator selection, support, and evaluation.
- Support decision making with data systems.

Five Elements of Instructional Leadership

- Use research to establish urgency for higher expectations.
- Align curriculum to standards.
- Integrate literacy and math across all content areas.
- Facilitate data-driven decision making to inform instruction.
- Provide opportunities for focused professional collaboration and growth.

Six Elements of Teaching

- Embrace rigorous and relevant expectations for all students.
- Build strong relationships with students.
- Possess depth of content knowledge and make it relevant to students.
- Facilitate rigorous and relevant instruction based on how students learn.
- Demonstrate expertise in use of instructional strategies, technology, and best practices.
- Use assessments to guide and differentiate instruction.

When all parts of the system are working together efficiently, teachers receive the support they need, and students are successfully prepared for college, careers, and citizenship.

Using DSEI to Drive Leadership

The focus of this book is on the role of leadership and the ways in which organizational leadership and instructional leadership together can increase student achievement. From kindergarten through high school, the entire system must be involved and engaged to make this happen. Once leadership addresses all segments of the system and a plan is in place, the learning environment can focus on meeting the needs of all students.

Chapter 1: The Daggett System for Effective Instruction

Chapter 1 provides an introduction to DSEI and the reasons, rationale, and research that support its premises.

Chapter 2: Using DSEI to Drive Leadership

Chapter 2 takes an in-depth look at the leadership segments of DSEI and how the elements of leadership drive increased student achievement.

Chapter 3: Setting High Expectations and a Vision as a Transformational Leader

Chapter 3 discusses the qualities and practices of transformational leadership. The Transformational Leadership Framework model is described, and situational leadership in each quadrant is described.

Chapter 4: Instructional Leadership

Chapter 4 looks at the role of instructional leadership and how it is used to address a variety of challenges in the school setting. The concepts of context, target, and practices are discussed. Chapter 4 also emphasizes the importance of data-driven decisions in instructional leadership.

Chapter 5: Leadership Through Empowerment

Chapter 5 describes the importance using empowerment to build the leadership capacity of the school community. The role of transformational leadership in empowering others is explained. The benefits of having many empowered leaders in a school community are identified and discussed.

Chapter 6: Leadership Skills for a Positive School Climate

Chapter 6 explains the importance of a positive school climate and the role that school leaders play in establishing this type of climate.

Chapter 7: Leadership and Community Engagement

Chapter 7 describes the role of the school leadership in engaging parents, community groups, and the business community. The benefits of engaging the school community — which is an important stakeholder in any school's success — are discussed.

Chapter 8: Focus on the Future

Chapter 8 summarizes the major points about transformational leadership and why it is so important to the future of education.

Appendix

The Appendix contains references that readers can use to learn more about transformational leadership.

Chapter 1

The Daggett System for Effective Instruction

Converging Challenges

As Western nations struggle to recover their economic equilibriums following the financial crisis of 2008, China and India are leveraging their size and human capital to become global economic powerhouses. Emerging economies such as Vietnam, Argentina, Brazil, Indonesia, and Panama are increasingly capable of winning greater shares of international business. The ability to compete in the interconnected global economy is primarily leveraged by technical innovation and a highly skilled workforce. A more rigorous and more applied curriculum is needed to drive both levers.

While our schools are working hard at improving, the reality is that the rest of the world is changing even faster, leaving a growing gap. In an effort to close the gap, state-supported initiatives for raising standards and measuring student achievement will require schools to change what and how they teach. The "fewer, clearer, higher" Common Core State Standards (CCSS), anchored by the "next generation assessments" (NGA), will raise the bar for most states to help ensure that every student is challenged to achieve and succeed. Proficiency levels will be set higher. Assessment will measure not just what students know but also what they can *do* with that knowledge. Most schools involved with Race to the Top (RttT) initiatives will need awareness building, planning, time, and support to realize the mandatory 2014–2015 implementation dates of the new learning expectations represented by the CCSS and NGA.

A Systemwide Approach to Leadership

These challenges are driving a greater focus on accountability and a growing demand for proof of effectiveness and efficiency in public education. If *No Child Left Behind*'s Adequate Yearly Progress (AYP) provision laid accountability for results on the backs of principals, today's education policy, including measures such as growth models and teacher effectiveness evaluations, is shifting the burden of accountability to teachers.

It Takes a System, Not Just a Teacher

Research supports what most of us see as common sense: What goes on between the teacher and each student is central to high-level learning. Effective teaching is not the end goal, however; it is the means to an end: student achievement.

Nevertheless, all teaching is more effective when it is effectively supported. Achieving the goal of improving instruction requires a supportive and aligned system. Stated another way: Although effective teaching is essential, it is not sufficient to maximize achievement for all students. This understanding of the need for an organization-wide commitment is at the heart of the DSEI.

Daggett System for Effective Instruction

For decades, the International Center has been an active observer of and participant in education reform. The International Center's "on the ground" work with schools has reinforced the view that it takes an entire system to develop, maintain, and enhance effective instruction. Teachers must be supported by instructional leadership and organizational leadership.

The DSEI has been significantly informed by:

- **Observing and disseminating best practices.** This is the result of the International Center's 20 years of assisting leadership and teachers, as well as identifying, studying, and showcasing America's most successful schools — including its CCSSO-co-sponsored Bill & Melinda Gates Foundation-funded research on thousands of America's most effective and most rapidly improving exemplar schools and school districts — at the annual Model Schools Conference and other events.
- **Current and past research.** This has been conducted by some of the most respected thought-leaders in K–12 education, as described previously.

At the same time, the DSEI departs from some of the existing models and frameworks for teaching in several significant ways.

Traditional Teaching Frameworks	DSEI
What teachers should do	What the entire system should do
Teacher-focused	Student-focused
Teachers deliver instruction	Teachers facilitate learning
Vision is set by top leaders	Vision is built more inclusively
Define vision primarily in terms of academic measures	Define vision as strong academics and personal skills and the ability to apply them
Rigid structures support adult needs	Flexible structures support student needs
Focus on teaching	Focus on learning

Other models are excellent guides and tools for what they choose to focus upon, primarily teachers' professional development, mastery of content, and use of instructional strategies.

By comparison, DSEI's most distinguishing attributes include:

- focus on coherence and alignment at the system/organization level
- focus on instructional leadership grounded in a broad base of analysis and meta-analysis research on instructional effectiveness
- balancing effectiveness with considerations of efficiency (e.g., affordability)
- best practices drawn from partnering with model schools

DSEI leverages more than the teacher in the classroom. It emphasizes vertical alignment (with organizational systems and structures and with instructional leadership) and horizontal alignment (with teaching colleagues and classroom resources) as keys to success. Because teachers are the most powerful influence on instruction, the entire system needs to be focused on making teachers effective. Therefore, DSEI provides a coherent focus across an entire education system: Organizational Leadership, Instructional Leadership, and Teaching.

A Systemwide Approach to Leadership

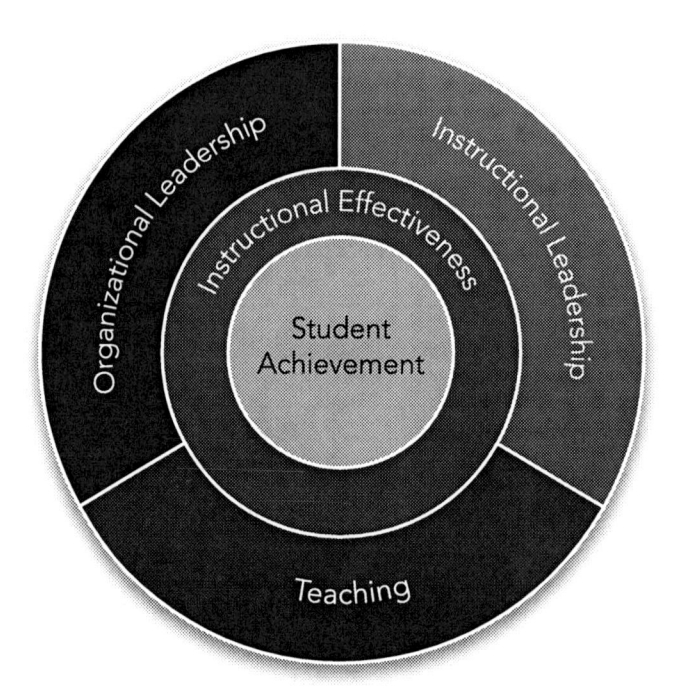

Summary

DSEI is more than an approach to enhancing instruction and instructional capacity. It is a way of thinking about what we believe about children, schools, and learning that has coalesced at a critical time in American education — a time when standards, assessments, accountability, and teacher evaluation systems are intersecting with budgets, the global economy, technological innovation, "wired kids," and public policy debates.

DSEI builds upon the ideas, inspirations, practices, and research of others, including the best research and meta-analysis on effective instruction and the years of collective experience that International Center staff, consultants, and thought-leaders have accumulated and harvested from thousands of American schools. DSEI recognizes the primacy and immeasurable value of great teachers and great teaching and strives to align education systems and functions with what teachers need to be the best support to learners. It does so not only by looking at teachers but also by looking beyond the classroom to inspire leadership at all levels in support of instruction. DSEI empowers all educators to tackle the challenges with a sense of practical urgency and a buoyant sense of the possible.

DSEI is a way to transform a traditional system into one that better supports all teachers and more fully prepares every student for college, careers, and citizenship.

Reflection Activity

1. Reflect on DSEI's philosophy that "It takes a system, not just a teacher." Identify a professional experience you have had that reinforces the validity of this statement. Discuss this experience and reflect on the experiences shared by others.
2. Examine the shape of the DSEI model. Write a short statement that explains how the circular shape of the model reflects the inherent focus of DSEI on student achievement.

Chapter 2

Using the DSEI to Drive Leadership

The DSEI focuses on a systems approach to transforming learning environments. This book focuses on leading schools through changes that are highly effective and on targeting increasing student achievement. The book examines five key areas of leadership and how these areas drive change:

- Setting High Expectations and a Vision as a Transformational Leader
- Instructional Leadership
- Leadership Through Empowerment
- Leadership Skills for a Positive School Climate
- Leadership and Community Engagement

As we develop an understanding of these key areas, we will focus on the two segments of DSEI that directly relate to leadership: Organizational Leadership and Instructional Leadership. These two segments move the system toward a coherent pathway that enables teachers to see the district's focus and purpose in all that drives the change. The information below details the elements of these two segments.

Organizational Leadership

Organizational leadership is a function, not just a person. It involves a mentality, structure, focus, and commitment to create the environment in which learning is optimized. Six elements of organizational leadership are listed below.

Create a culture of high expectations. The culture must communicate and encompass these areas:

- **Why**: the challenges of changing demographics; a wired and tech-savvy generation of students growing up in a digital world; a global economy in which the United States must innovate and compete
- **To Whom**: students, staff, and community stakeholders
- **How**: through active and ongoing communications and messaging at staff development events, community forums, business roundtables, and so on

Create a shared vision. Culture needs to be embedded in goals and action plans focused on instructional effectiveness that all stakeholders can understand, contribute to, and commit to. The Learning Criteria is a broad, holistic framework of variables that help establish a common definition of *success*, not just for students as scholars but also as future workers, citizens, consumers, and parents.

Build leadership capacity. Organizational leadership needs to enhance existing leaders and identify and cultivate the development of emerging, future leaders. Doing so broadens the leadership capacity of the organization immediately and paves the way for continuous development and growth of new leaders.

Align organizational structures and systems to vision. Once culture, mission, and distributed and empowered leadership are established, organizational leadership needs to:

- decide which external impediments to instructional effectiveness can be changed or compensated for and which are beyond the control of the education organization
- ensure that enabling conditions and structures to support instructional effectiveness are in place
- identify which factors impacting effective instruction are most effective and efficient

Using the International Center's Effectiveness and Efficiency Framework, DSEI extends the data and research on effectiveness provided by Hattie and others to accomplish those tasks. It allows decision-makers to consider the broader perspective of how to prioritize initiatives related to enhancing instructional effectiveness according to what can reasonably be impacted and then to examine both effectiveness and efficiency. For example, by using the Effectiveness and Efficiency Framework to analyze several of Hattie's factors, one can determine that not only are they effective but also that they make efficient use of resources (that is, provide the highest "return-on-investment").

Align teacher/administrator selection, support, and evaluation. Organizational leadership's role is to adopt "talent management" systems for recruitment, retention, development, and evaluation that are understood, broad-based, focused on instructional effectiveness, and aligned horizontally and vertically among all individuals who support instructional effectiveness and student achievement. These systems must also reinforce the instructional vision of the organization for all staff.

Support decision making with data systems. Organizational leadership needs to ensure that a data system is used to inform and enhance instructional effectiveness. This includes building "data literacy" among all stakeholders as well as emphasizing the importance of data-driven decision making.

Instructional Leadership

Instructional leadership is directly focused on instructional effectiveness and, ultimately, student achievement. Instructional leadership can support teachers through a variety of people, functions, and means:

- district and regional instructional leadership
- principals, assistant principals
- department chairs
- expert teachers, counselors, social workers
- mentor teachers, teacher coaches, teaching peers/team leaders

The instructional leadership segment of DSEI concentrates on five overarching elements:

Use research to establish urgency for higher expectations. The first job of instructional leadership is to reinforce the vision set forth by organizational leadership. To do so, instructional leadership must offer "proof statements" to staff, students, and stakeholders in the form of research and authoritative testimony that corroborate the urgent need for improvement in student achievement. The International Center's National Essential Skills Study and its research on reading and math proficiency levels involving the Lexile Framework® for Reading and Quantile Framework for Mathematics are examples of such indicators. Instructional leaders also need to see themselves as the key change-agents in raising standards and expectations.

Align curriculum to standards. Instructional leaders also need to prepare teachers for the new types of instruction and formative assessment that are at the core of CCSS and the related assessments. To bridge the gap between the current state tests and the new assessments, the International Center's Next Navigator supports instructional leaders and teachers in planning instruction that prepares students for these requirements.

Integrate literacy and math across all content areas. Literacy and math are essential for success in college and careers and are therefore consistent with the CCSS, with special emphasis in the English language arts standards placed on text complexity and nonfiction transactional reading and writing. The CCSS also emphasizes the practical applications of literacy. All teachers at all grades and across all subjects need to assume responsibility for this heightened emphasis on broad-based literacy development. Similarly, the CCSS focuses on what it calls "Standards of Mathematical Practice," which consist of process standards (such as problem solving, reasoning, and proof) and "strands of mathematical proficiency" (including adaptive reasoning, strategic competence, conceptual understanding, procedural fluency, and productive disposition). Therefore, Instructional Leadership must ensure the integration and application of literacy and math standards across all curricula.

Facilitate data-driven decision making to inform instruction. To meet the needs of diverse learners, teachers must use data to measure student growth and to inform and differentiate instruction. Achieving this goal will involve both providing teachers with a clearer understanding of student data and applying that understanding to actionable instruction and interventions.

Provide opportunities for focused professional collaboration and growth. The research conducted by Hattie and others clearly shows the importance of teacher selection and development and of a continuous cycle of evaluation and support. Race to the Top (RttT) and pending federal education legislation mandate the availability of quality and sustained professional development, in part as an underpinning of the new emphasis on teacher performance evaluation systems.

Professional development is one of the cornerstone "Four Assurances" in RttT: "Recruiting, developing, rewarding, and retaining effective teachers and principals, especially where they are most needed." And rightly so: With an effect factor of .62 (the equivalent of approximately 1.24 years of growth) on Hattie's scale, professional development also clearly is a high-impact — and cost-effective — approach to improving instructional effectiveness for student achievement.

Summary

The DSEI assists us in setting parameters for schools and districts so that they can maximize collaboration within the organization in order to increase student achievement and teacher growth. This is why the organizational leadership and instructional leadership segments are so important in our work. This book describes and provides leadership-focused ideas and materials that support leaders as they drive toward increased student achievement.

Reflection Activity

1. Think about organizational leadership and instructional leadership. In what ways are they similar? In what ways are they different?
2. How does the implementation of CCSS and related assessments bring the role of leadership to the forefront?

Chapter 3

Setting High Expectations and a Vision as a Transformational Leader

Lessons About Leadership

Simply defined, good leadership is a process of guiding people to go places that they probably would not have gone to on their own. Leadership is change: change of goals, direction, practice, work, or values. Deliberate changes in people's behavior are difficult to accomplish, and this is the challenge of leadership.

Leadership is not a rigid list of practices that can be applied with predictable results, for any action or decision can elicit very different emotional responses from different individuals. Effective leadership involves recognizing what works, when it works, and with whom it works. Successful leaders must understand their own personal strengths and inclinations in order to work with others effectively. For example, good leaders learn to control their emotions and how to use their own behaviors to motivate and inspire passion in others.

A Systemwide Approach to Leadership

The idea that leaders are essential to the quality of schools and school improvement seems obvious, but school leaders still seek practical perspectives to guide them through the demands of their challenging jobs. At the same time, schools and districts seek definitive guidance about how to identify and support effective leaders. DSEI, which clearly defines the roles and overarching elements of Organizational Leadership and Instructional Leadership, can be used to address these issues. The application of DSEI can help individual leaders, schools, and districts utilize and assess leadership to improve student achievement. Hattie's meta-research confirms the importance of a leadership-focused school culture on student outcomes. (Hattie, John, *Visible Learning*)

Discussions and debates about school leadership raise theoretical questions such as these:

- Are all managers leaders?
- Are leadership skills innate, or acquired?
- Which is more effective for leadership development: formal education, or on-the-job experience?
- Which is better for school improvement: keeping the same leader, or changing leaders?
- Is teacher leadership a nicety, or a necessity?

Such questions reflect a common misconception about leadership — namely, that its effectiveness depends solely upon the character traits, training, skills, and behaviors of individual leaders. Superintendents, principals, and teachers all provide leadership, and their individual qualities and skills do influence their effectiveness as leaders; however, school leadership must be judged on how well an organization functions.

Leadership is like a lighted match. A match needs certain chemicals and friction to ignite a flame, but the flame alone will not accomplish much. The match's effectiveness depends greatly on what happens when the flame is applied. The flame can provide beneficial things, such as heat, or it can be the source of devastating things, such as a forest fire. So it is with leadership: How it is used in its surroundings is what is most important. Application determines effectiveness.

In recent years, one strand of leadership research, discussion, and policy research has focused on the evolution of the school leader's current roles to (1) build a curriculum around CCSS or individual state standards, (2) analyze student achievement data and plan improvement strategies, (3) develop and support teachers in ways that promote

Chapter 3: Setting High Expectations and a Vision as a Transformational Leader

student learning, and (4) transform schools into more effective organizations to improve learning for all students. This is a new role for leaders, requiring new skills.

In 1996, the Council of Chief State School Officers led the creation of Interstate School Leaders Licensure Consortium (ISLLC). These were revised in 2008 and provide a set of common expectations for the knowledge, skills, and dispositions of school leaders, grounded in principles of teaching and learning. More than 40 states have adopted the ISLLC standards (or a slight variation thereof) in their administrative certification program requirements. (National Policy Board for Educational Administration (NPBEA) Educational Leadership Policy Standards. ISLLC, 2008. http://www.ccsso.org/content/pdfs/introduction_elps_isllc2008.pdf)

Lists such as ISLLC standards help state policy makers and universities develop leadership certification programs, but these lists do not help leaders handle the daily challenges of leading school improvement. While it is necessary to redefine the qualities required of school leaders, simply identifying and acquiring skills and knowledge is not sufficient.

Another strand of research correlates student achievement with characteristics of school leaders, such as experience, consistent core values, high expectations, communicating a vision, perceived fairness, and trust. For example, Robert Marzano's meta-research identifies 21 responsibilities that correlate with increasing student achievement. While this list of responsibilities looks appealing, it is lengthy, and it does not clearly inform school leaders which responsibilities to focus on in dealing with specific problems or overall issues. For example, it does not answer such questions as whether a school leader should use involvement in instruction or teacher input (two different responsibilities) to deal with poor student engagement in the classroom. Furthermore, correlation does not mean causation, and focusing on a long list of responsibilities may not guide leaders through a specific problem or challenge. (Marzano, R.J., Waters, T., and McNulty, *School Leadership That Works: From Research to Results*)

Historically, leadership studies have suggested that school leaders have been able to succeed simply by carrying out the directives of central administrators. Some districts still try to succeed this way, developing rigid policies and procedures that they expect school leaders to implement with absolute fidelity. However, this dictatorial approach is not enough to meet today's challenges.

These days, school leaders must embrace a more complex leadership role. Since every school is unique, a standardized set of procedures cannot possibly address the needs of all. New challenges crop up every day, each requiring leadership action. School leaders must be able to do more than merely follow a procedure book or apply a general district policy. But, again, what does effective leadership look like, and how can districts find and support leaders who will guide their schools to success? (Perez, Milstein, Wood, and Jacquez, *How to Turn a School Around: What Principals Can Do*)

The need for leadership is clear, but improving leadership and assisting those who take on leadership roles demands more than prescribing preparation standards or listing job responsibilities. Leadership is the application of specific skills and abilities coupled with insights about organizational dynamics and human behavior. In schools, leaders must have a clear understanding of and passion for student needs and aspirations, and they must be capable of defining and supporting the work required to address those needs.

To accomplish this essential work, leaders need a flexible framework for leadership action, one they can use to attend to daily challenges while keeping the school community moving toward the ambitious goal of improving student achievement. Such a framework should not be a mere list; it should be a straightforward model that allows leaders to draw upon their talents and experience to lead a school community successfully. It should engage school leaders to evaluate their decisions and work continually to improve instruction and student learning. The International Center for Leadership in Education's Transformational Leadership Framework provides such a practical model for educators.

The Transformational Leadership Framework reflects the latest thinking about what constitutes effective leadership. In particular, research conducted in three fields has provided insight for education leadership: (1) science, especially recent brain research and social scientific observation; (2) business; and (3) education, especially practices in rapidly improving schools. We will examine leadership lessons from these three areas on the following pages.

Lessons from Brain and Social-Science Research

Are leaders born, or made? Advances in technology and social-science research techniques provide evidence that the answer to that age-old question is a little bit of both.

Brains and Behavior

Over the last two decades, neuroscience has provided scientists with tremendous insight about learning and behavior. Advanced computer analyses of brain activity have enabled neuroscientists to develop an increasing body of evidence linking the physiology of the brain with the cognitive, emotional, and behavioral mind. This research has helped inform teaching and learning, and it can lead to a better understanding of school leadership practices and how they relate to school change.

Social scientists' observations of human behavior and relationships also have contributed to the study of effective management and leadership. The technological capabilities of neuroscience now make it possible not only to observe human behavior but also to see which areas of the brain are active while those behaviors are occurring. As this type of research continues to evolve, opportunities to augment the understanding of human behavior and motivation will increase. Already, the traditional understanding of the connections among motivation, action, and relationships is being challenged. Such advances will have positive impacts on education and leadership.

Neuroleadership is an emerging interdisciplinary field that combines cognitive neuroscience and social science to explore the neurological basis of leadership and management practices. The objective is to improve leadership effectiveness within institutions and organizations by developing a scientific model for leadership development, taking into account the physiology of the brain and its relationship to the mind. (Ringleb, Al, and Rock, David, "The Emerging Field of NeuroLeadership")

Neuroscientific research has helped dispel many myths about leadership, as in these examples:

- **Myth:** Adult brains are fully developed and do not change.
- **Reality:** A human brain has plasticity. It is able to create new neural connections throughout an individual's life, allowing a person to learn novel ideas and obtain new knowledge at any age.

- **Myth:** A combination of incentives and threats — so-called "carrots" and "sticks" — will change behavior.
- **Reality:** Change efforts based solely on stimuli rarely succeed in creating long-term change. Repeatedly rehearsing a behavior is essential for change to occur.

- **Myth:** People who respond to proposed changes with great emotion are cognitively weak.
- **Reality:** Change is difficult because it triggers biological/chemical sensations of discomfort in the brain. Changes in an organization can cause individuals to feel real pain. This physiologically driven emotional response occurs uniquely in humans and is not correlated to cognitive capacity.

- **Myth:** Some people are more suited than others to the stresses of leadership.
- **Reality:** While the nuances of brain function are unique to each individual, the process is essentially the same across individuals. Rational behavior develops over time through the development of the frontal lobes. A person who demonstrates a strong aptitude for rational thought and emotional control has, through practice, developed the frontal lobes, which dominate the brain's more emotional limbic center.

Social Chemistry

The human brain is a social organ that compels us to seek relationships. When we see or are in the presence of other people — even if we do not speak to them, hear them, or touch them — our brains react. Infants exhibit signs of this brain reaction early on, when they respond to their parents' facial expressions or mimic sounds or body movements. These types of brain functions form the foundation of learning.

When we experience positive relationships, our brains produce chemicals that generate pleasurable feelings. When relationships are bad, however, the brain produces different chemicals, and the resulting emotional pain may be experienced as acutely as an actual physical blow. These negative feelings may lead to undesirable behaviors or other unexpected outcomes. (Rock, David, "Managing with the Brain in Mind")

When a school or district makes a decision that will increase class size, reassign teachers to new schools, or impose additional testing on students, teachers often are expected to accept the change without comment or complaint. They may be told that they must comply because the change is part of the job. Authoritarian edicts, however, elicit feelings of social isolation and a sense of helplessness, and these feelings create chemical and emotional responses in the brain. Teachers in these situations may become disenchanted and disengaged. They may feel that their good work is going unrecognized or underappreciated. These typical human responses are partially the product of natural reactions in the socially driven human brain. The trouble is that these chemical reactions — and the resulting negative feelings — carry over into behavior.

In education, this can result in teachers' putting forth minimum effort to meet the requirements of their positions. The feelings may carry over into their spoken language, body language, and actions with others, notably students. In turn, negative brain reactions are triggered in students, degrading their attitudes and efforts. Thus, what seemed like a simple decision or action by a school or district instead kicks off a downward spiral that translates into an unpleasant environment and poor student achievement. Research shows that what may be equated with poor character or willfulness, however, is actually a natural manifestation of chemical processes in the brain. One person's actions activate chemical reactions in others' brains, which can trigger a range of thoughts and emotions that are controlled by the more emotional part of the brain.

The social aspect of the brain explains why people respond so positively to compliments from others. We all crave recognition, some reassurance that we are important. We join groups for the sense of comfort in social situations. We seek nurturing relationships by creating families or by cultivating friendships. Social feedback is an important brain stimulant. Rewards and feedback spark strong positive brain responses. This is why one of a leader's most important tasks is providing feedback and encouragement to those whom he or she leads. (Lieberman, Matthew D., "Social Cognitive Neuroscience: A Review of Core Processes")

Some social cognitive neuroscientists argue persuasively that the need to belong is as basic a human need as sleeping, eating, and breathing. Consistent with this viewpoint, academic and business communities acknowledge that the need for employees to work as team players is so strong nowadays that many organizations resist hiring individuals who cannot or do not want to work with others.

Understanding the neuroscience behind the physiological aspects of leadership helps leaders to:

- make decisions and solve problems
- collaborate with and influence others
- cope with stress and pressure
- facilitate change successfully
- work at maximum potential

As researchers discover more about the human brain, they increasingly find that effective leadership involves a complex interaction of many elements, including brain chemistry and activity, analytical thought, emotional reaction, the power of images and symbols, the strength of perceptions versus reality, an understanding of the power of personal relationships, and the contagion of passion and humor. To be successful, a leader cannot separate his or her actions from the reactions of the people in an organization.

Lessons from Business

Effective school leadership must address some conditions that are unique to education, but other types of organizations, particularly successful businesses, offer many leadership lessons.

The XYZs of Leadership

In the 1960s, American social psychologist Douglas McGregor proposed that there are two fundamental approaches to managing people in business; he called them Theory X and Theory Y. Theory X reflects an authoritarian management style. Many managers employ this approach, with poor results. Theory X is predicated on these beliefs:

- The average person dislikes work and will avoid it if possible.
- People must be forced — with the threat of punishment — to work toward organizational objectives.
- The average person prefers to be directed, avoids responsibility, is relatively unambitious, and seeks security above all else.

In contrast, Theory Y is characterized by a participative management style. Enlightened managers tend to use Theory Y, which usually produces better results, encourages stronger performance, and allows people to grow and develop. Theory Y makes these assumptions:

- Effort in work is as natural as it is in leisure.
- People will demonstrate self-control and self-direction in the pursuit of organizational objectives, without external control or the threat of punishment.
- A commitment to objectives is a function of rewards associated with personal achievement.
- People usually accept, and often seek, responsibility.
- The capacity to use a high degree of imagination, ingenuity, and creativity in solving organizational problems is widely, not narrowly, distributed in the population.
- In industry, the intellectual potential of the average person is not used fully.

Although more recent studies challenge their simplicity, Theory X and Theory Y are still among the most frequently used models in human resources management. They endure as basic guidance for leaders who wish to develop a positive management style and leadership techniques. (McGregor, Douglas, *The Human Side of the Enterprise* and "Theory X and Theory Y")

One newer philosophy, Theory Z, was developed by William Ouchi, a professor of management at UCLA. Theory Z advocates combining the best elements of Theory Y with those of modern Japanese management, which assumes that workers are loyal to the organization and interested in working in teams. Managers who use a Theory Z style place a great deal of trust in their employees and offer them a large amount of freedom. (Ouchi, William G., *Theory Z*)

While McGregor's theories mainly focus on management and motivation from the managerial and organizational perspectives, Theory Z advocates for greater reliance on the attitudes and responsibilities of workers. Moreover, Theory Z considers the dynamics of work performance and leadership action throughout an organization rather than through the traditional top-down approach.

Authority and Influence

Joseph Rost, professor emeritus of leadership studies at the University of San Diego School of Education, offers one of the best analyses of business leadership and management styles in *Leadership for the Twenty-First Century*. To gain a historical perspective of leadership and management, Rost conducted an extensive literature review, including an analysis of much of the work written between 1930 and 1990. (Rost, Joseph, *Leadership for the Twenty-First Century*)

Rost's work is important in the field of leadership studies because it traces the evolution of leadership based upon the social, technological, and economic changes that have occurred in business. The fundamental purposes of business have remained the same; however, the culture and patterns of interactions among individuals within business organizations have changed markedly, reflecting societal changes.

The primary distinction that Rost makes between "management" and "leadership" is that leadership is an influence relationship whereas management is an authority relationship. The differences between these kinds of relationships have to do with the use of coercion and the directionality of relationships. Rost concludes that the 20th century was dominated by an "industrial paradigm" that defined leadership as "good management," characterized by "an authoritarian relationship between a manager and subordinates." In this model, coercion is used regularly, and subordinates respond to authoritative directives.

A Systemwide Approach to Leadership

While there may be some democratic relationships between managers and subordinates, the fundamental relationship is top-down.

In contrast, the 21st century has seen the rise of a "post-industrial paradigm," in which leadership is an influence relationship among leaders and followers in pursuit of mutual purposes. In this model, coercion is rarely used. Leaders use authority to guide rather than to dictate. As a result, leadership is an interactive network of relationships that exist across all levels of an organization, and it is multidirectional: top-down, bottom-up, and peer-to-peer.

Rost's Comparison of Management and Leadership

Management	Leadership
Authority relationship	Influence relationship
Managers and subordinates	Leaders and followers
Top-down relationships	Multidirectional relationships

Leadership Practices

Jim Kouzes and Barry Posner, co-authors of the award-winning bestseller *The Leadership Challenge*, provide one of the best current analyses of leadership practices in business. In 2008, they completed the extremely ambitious analysis of 950,000 responses to the Leadership Practices Inventory. The inventory involved 80,000 self-assessments by business leaders, plus 870,000 assessments of those leaders by individuals who know them. Based on the surveys, Kouzes and Posner developed a list of ten top leadership lessons. (Kouzes, James, and Posner, Barry, *The Leadership Challenge*)

1. **Leadership is everyone's business.** Leadership is not a position but a practice among many people within the organization. Leadership is a series of practices that are accomplished by many people at every level of the organization. In military units, an effective squad leader will challenge a small team to work together to accomplish a mission. Throughout a corporate organization, leadership actions are taken at every level. In customer service, for example, each employee who has direct contact with customers must have the support to take appropriate leadership actions to meet customer needs.

2. **Credibility is the foundation.** One of the most noted characteristics of good leadership is a strong sense of trust in the individual who is a leader. A leader's behavior and actions create a sense of credibility (or lack of it) throughout

the organization. Followers are more likely to support an individual when they trust that he or she is credible and when they believe in his or her goals, values, and commitment to the organization.

3. **Personal values drive commitment.** People expect leaders to stand up for their beliefs. If a leader is only talking about an organization's goals and not demonstrating a commitment to them through his or her actions, then others are less likely to be supportive.

4. **You either lead by example, or you don't lead at all.** People make judgments about their leaders based on the actions they see. Leaders who do not set a strong positive example or who are not willing to take on the same responsibilities and tasks as others within the organization will be perceived as weak or false. Effective leaders are good role models.

5. **Looking forward is a leadership prerequisite.** People expect leaders to have a sense of direction and a vision. Followers are skeptical of leaders who do not have a strong vision of how to move an organization to a positive future. Strong leaders need to be forward-thinking people and confident about what can be accomplished.

6. **It is not just the leader's vision.** In the healthiest organizations, it is not only about the leader having the most powerful and optimistic vision. All members of the organization must embrace and support the vision. The actions of the leader should inspire every member of the organization to see his or her role in the outcome. Effective leaders inspire a shared vision and create a culture in which each individual aspires to a positive vision for success.

7. **Challenge provides the opportunity for greatness.** The best examples of outstanding leadership are forged through successful resolution of a challenge. Great leadership emerges when there are opportunities to work cooperatively to overcome significant challenges.

8. **Leaders are team players.** No leader in history ever accomplished an extraordinary feat alone. Leaders must build a sense of trust among members of the organization and must show a strong commitment to accomplish the common vision. They must demonstrate their dedication through a willingness to work as hard as everybody else to achieve the goals.

9. **Leadership is a relationship.** Leadership is a connection between those who choose to lead and those who choose to follow. Exemplary leaders spend time building and nurturing relationships based upon mutual respect and caring. The very best leaders know that their job is to make others feel powerful, not simply to acquire power for themselves.

10. **Caring is at the heart of leadership.** The best leaders are not cold and detached from other people in an organization; rather, they constantly think about people and how the organization's activities will affect individuals personally. A sense of caring does not prevent leaders from making difficult decisions, but it helps guide them. Caring is at the heart of building relationships, and relationships are at the heart of strong leadership.

Lessons from Rapidly Improving Schools

Since its inception, the International Center has worked with or examined the work of thousands of schools that have achieved sustainable change. The annual Model Schools Conference and collaboration with the Successful Practices Network — a network for schools to share ideas, feedback, and strategies — have enabled extensive examination of the characteristics of rapidly improving schools. One of the most consistent findings is that strong leadership — leadership that is future-focused, persistent, and distributed throughout the organization — is at the center of successful and sustainable school improvement.

Over the years, various school improvement groups have identified many rapidly improving schools. Typically, each of these schools has been led by a charismatic individual who introduced a vision that raised expectations, who created or introduced the innovations necessary to achieve the vision, and who was able to build a consensus of followers willing to take risks. In this model, the leadership of a specific individual made the difference, and it is easy to identify the essential leadership characteristics that facilitated the change, such as vision, communication skills, passion, people skills, willingness to take risks, and persistence.

The problem with this model is that it is difficult to sustain improvement when change is based on the leadership qualities and skills of a single individual. Sustaining school leadership is tremendously challenging, for even charismatic school leaders move on or retire. Many schools that were exemplars of innovation a decade ago are no longer models.

Leaders must adapt to constantly changing conditions. For example, the simple act of assigning a group of teachers to plan a student recognition celebration can have different consequences in different settings. In a school with a highly collaborative staff, for example, the request may be a simple task that requires a committee to meet a few times to get the project rolling; but in a school struggling with contentious contract negotiations, the assignment could be met with protest and grievance.

In rapidly improving schools, there are subtle differences in leadership styles. Certainly each leader in these schools has an impact on the school culture, and the school community would identify the leader's encouragement and support as integral to success. But while some of these leaders seem to possess endless stores of energy and to be involved in any and all activities, others serve more as delegators, with assistant principals, team leaders, and school staff assuming greater responsibility in making decisions, solving problems, and taking action. Both types of leaders are successful; however, simply trying to replicate either or both styles is less likely to result in long-term, sustainable school improvement.

A wide range of definitions, theories, notions, and ideals attempt to address the question of what makes a leader effective. Many models exist, but few can be applied practically. Education leaders need a framework that can guide them as they develop the plans, practices, and systems that will lead to rapid and sustainable change, including improvements in student performance. Remember that judging the effectiveness of leadership depends more on looking at school performance than at an individual leader's behavior.

A careful study of current research from the fields of neuroscience and social science, along with a review of historical and contemporary lessons from the business world and observation and analysis of best practices from successful schools, has resulted in valuable insights into the kind of leadership that yields the best results. What has been learned is unique from much of what the existing literature about school leadership describes. The Transformational Leadership Framework applies that learning.

Transformational Leadership

There is no single prescriptive model that will guarantee sound leadership. Therefore, effective school leaders need an adaptable framework for leadership action that can guide problem solving, decision making, and planning. More than a list of good practices, a useful framework helps lay the foundation for leaders to develop mental models that help them apply their talents and experience effectively.

A mental model is like a really good city map: It enables one to navigate quickly and easily when the way — or required action or decision — is clear, or it reveals possible alternatives when there is an obstacle. Professional development in mental models introduces a framework, provides concrete examples, and encourages patterns of reflective thought and conversations to act consistently.

Certain assumptions about leadership, such as the following, define the context for a workable school leadership model:

- Leadership is about relationships.
- Leadership is not just about individuals who fill traditional leadership positions. Leadership in schools should include faculty, staff, and students.
- As leaders learn from their experiences, their leadership capacity continues to grow.
- There is no single or fixed "proper procedure" for performing a leadership task in every situation.
- The environment and circumstances significantly influence leadership action in any given situation.
- Not everyone in a school will automatically work to improve the organization and student learning. It is the responsibility of leadership to always be alert for individuals who will undermine the potential for success.

Defining Transformational Leadership

School leadership is not a position; it is a *disposition* for taking action. When leadership is considered a position, a leader is judged upon the decisions he or she makes. When leadership is considered a disposition, it is judged upon the actions taken in the school community. Effective school leaders broaden the definition of *leadership* in their schools to include the many staff members and student leaders whose efforts further progress toward a common vision.

Transformational leadership is the collaborative responsibility for taking action to reach future-oriented goals while meeting the intellectual, emotional, and physical needs of each student.

Transformational leaders are:

- flexible and able to adapt to the school environment
- able to analyze the leadership characteristics of their school
- knowledgeable about where their school community is and where it needs to move to
- able to develop and articulate a vision about the future needs of students to ensure that all stakeholders are using the same language about leadership in the school
- able to work with people in a manner that ignites their passions, talents, and desires to attain a shared vision

The Transformational Leadership Framework

Just as we must prepare students to be 21st century learners, so we must prepare adults to be 21st century leaders. The International Center's Rigor/Relevance Framework helps teachers quantify the level of their instruction and make progress toward providing students with the highest level of learning, described as Quadrant D.

Rigor/Relevance Framework®

Knowledge Taxonomy (vertical axis):
- 6 Evaluation
- 5 Synthesis
- 4 Analysis
- 3 Application
- 2 Comprehension
- 1 Knowledge/Awareness

Quadrants: C, D (Adaptation), A, B

Application Model (horizontal axis):
1. Knowledge in one discipline
2. Apply in discipline
3. Apply across disciplines
4. Apply to real-world predictable situations
5. Apply to real-world unpredictable situations

© International Center for Leadership in Education

A Systemwide Approach to Leadership

In 2001 Bloom's Knowledge Taxonomy was updated and revised by Lorin Anderson, a student of Bloom's, and David Krathwohl, a colleague, to reflect the movement to standards-based curricula and assessment. Nouns in Bloom's original model were changed to verb forms (for example, *knowledge* to *remembering* and *comprehension* to *understanding*) and slightly reordered. We believe that the original Bloom's Taxonomy as shown in our Rigor/Relevance Framework clearly describes expectations for Quadrants A, B, C, and D. The revised Bloom's elevates the importance of Quadrants B and D and indicates how 21st century lessons should be built. We regard both the original and revised taxonomies as necessary and important.

Like its instructional counterpart, the Transformational Leadership Framework is divided into four sections, or quadrants. The framework is set along the vertical Knowledge continuum and the horizontal Application continuum. The level of individual leadership is identified in each quadrant.

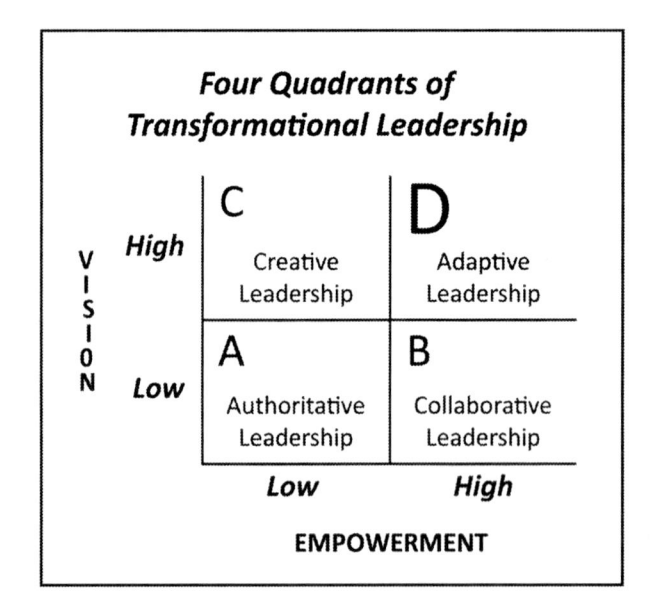

Four Quadrants of Transformational Leadership

VISION		Low EMPOWERMENT	High
High		C — Creative Leadership	D — Adaptive Leadership
Low		A — Authoritative Leadership	B — Collaborative Leadership

In the context of the Transformational Leadership Framework, *vision* involves raising the level of thinking about what is important in a school. At a low level of the vision continuum, leaders acquire understanding of school practices and the management of day-to-day tasks. Moving to higher levels allows leaders to imagine and anticipate the future: What skills will students need in order to be successful in the future? Are there programs and services that could be added to help students realize their potential? These are the types of reflective questions that leaders ask at high levels of the continuum in order to create a vision for rigorous and relevant student achievement. Schools reach high levels of leadership when all staff members acquire a thorough knowledge of school goals and student aspirations.

High-knowledge leaders recognize that a current strategy may not be the best or most effective practice. They are willing to take risks and innovate. These leaders keep part of their attention on the distant horizon of sustained long-term improvement and constantly seek creative solutions.

Leadership *empowerment*, the Transformational Leadership Framework's horizontal continuum, describes the action and style of leadership. At low levels, leaders execute leadership practices singularly, making decisions and solving day-to-day problems on their own. At higher levels, leadership empowerment shifts from the actions of a single leader or small leadership team to leadership that is distributed throughout the school community. Staff, faculty, and students are empowered to participate in leadership and a collective sense of responsibility and ownership emerges.

The skill sets along the vision and empowerment continuums can be organized according to the framework's four quadrants and the corresponding levels of leadership they represent. The aspects of leadership in each quadrant are discussed in detail on pages 37–45.

Leadership decisions and actions occur across all quadrants, but it is at the intersection of high vision and high empowerment that transformational leadership emerges. Ultimately, transformational leadership is the most desirable and the most reliably associated with effective schools.

Building Toward Transformational Leadership

Becoming a transformational leader is a process. Operating in Quadrant D requires not only an awareness of how the many components of effective leadership fit together but also the ability to draw upon the elements of each quadrant to deliver the most suitable decision or action. A transformational leader applies different elements of leadership as appropriate. For example, when there are safety or security threats that demand quick, authoritative action, a transformational leader employs a Quadrant A approach.

A Systemwide Approach to Leadership

As a leader shifts to consistent use of a Quadrant D approach, an organizational culture of leadership will begin to emerge. At that point, staff members will be able to understand more clearly the leader's role in decision making as well as their own as part of the leadership structure. Once this culture is established, leaders must be careful to avoid complacency. Sometimes a leader becomes too comfortable with the effectiveness of the organization and slips back into Quadrant A leadership. If the Quadrant D culture has been cultivated well, however, all staff will share in the responsibility of maintaining it.

The shift to transformational leadership begins when a leader understands the positive impacts that a highly inclusive and collaborative environment can have on student and school performance. To start, leaders should consider the ways in which they can increase the empowerment across all levels of the organization. On the framework, this is represented by movement from Quadrants A and C to Quadrants B and D — a shift that is characterized by increasing both staff and student leadership. At the highest levels of leadership, students take significant responsibility for their actions. Practices related to teacher leadership are consistent with moving organizational leadership to Quadrants B and D.

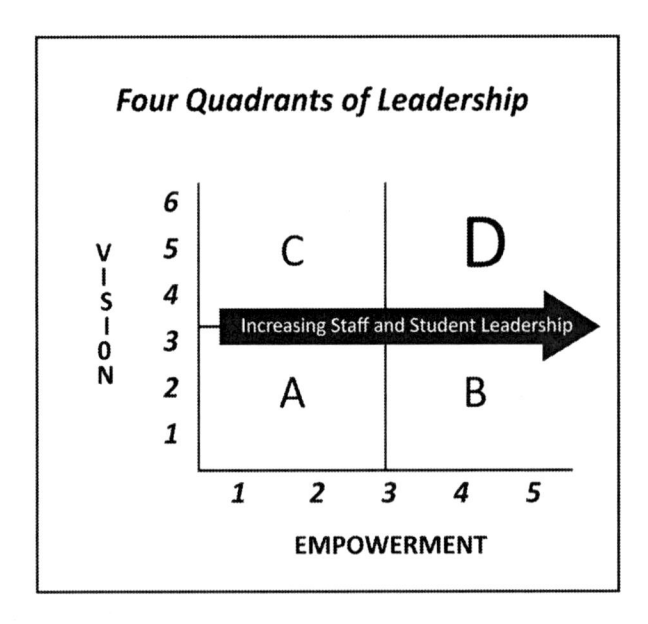

Four Quadrants of Leadership

	Empowerment 1–2	Empowerment 3–5
Vision 3–6	C	D
Vision 1–2	A	B

Increasing Staff and Student Leadership →

Chapter 3: Setting High Expectations and a Vision as a Transformational Leader

Building Leadership Capacity

Increasing the level of leadership horizontally on the Transformational Leadership Framework is about empowering staff and students to take responsibility and initiate actions. One way to do this is to create specific leadership teams around groups of students or specific school functions, which increases opportunities for both staff and student leadership. For example, many high-performing high schools use 9th-grade academies to ease the transition into high school and to ensure that students are supported for success — through personalized learning, intervention, and other structures — from the start. These academies are managed by leadership teams that consist of older students and staff who have responsibility for decision making and problem solving. In other successful schools, data teams analyze, summarize, and present student achievement information to staff to promote data-driven evaluation, monitoring, and planning.

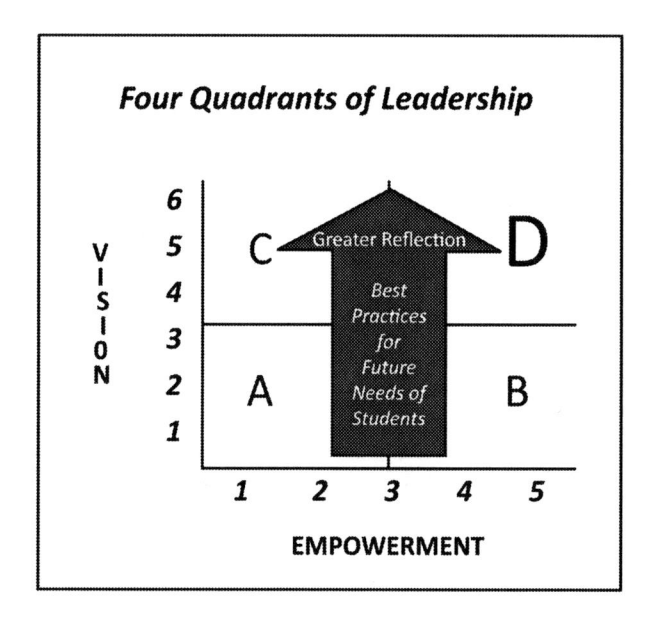

Four Quadrants of Leadership

VISION (vertical axis, 1–6) vs. EMPOWERMENT (horizontal axis, 1–5)

- A: lower-left quadrant
- B: lower-right quadrant
- C: upper-left quadrant
- D: upper-right quadrant

Arrow labeled "Greater Reflection" / "Best Practices for Future Needs of Students"

A Systemwide Approach to Leadership

These types of team initiatives are very important for increasing leadership density throughout a school community. Simply creating teams is not enough, however. Team-building activities are important, too: They give staff and students a chance to get to know one another, develop a level of trust, and facilitate a team's ability to tackle problems and develop creative solutions.

When a school leader is open to new possibilities, others are empowered to take leadership roles. Even with extensive knowledge and experience of his or her own, a leader will be most effective when he or she consistently and publicly encourages new ideas, listens to them carefully, and evaluates their potential effectiveness. Good leaders reflect on their own behavior to be certain that their language or actions do not discourage new suggestions and possibilities from being shared. When a change is successful, they are quick to credit others for the success and avoid taking credit for themselves. As they work to increase empowerment of leadership, they look for opportunities to involve students and listen to their input regarding school practices.

The shift from Quadrants A and B to Quadrants C and D on the Transformational Leadership Framework — movement vertically along the vision continuum — is characterized by the shift in thinking that guides leadership action. Leadership is not guided simply by past practices and traditions; rather, decisions and actions are based on reflective thought, which includes paying attention to students' future education needs so that they can succeed in a complex and rapidly changing world.

When schools defend the status quo or are complacent about current results, organizational leadership is operating in Quadrants A and B. When organizations are dissatisfied with current student achievement, passionately pursue higher expectations for all students, and implement creative solutions, they are more likely functioning in Quadrants C and D.

Supporting Decision Making with Data Systems

Raising student expectations and communicating those expectations to all students raises the level of leadership. When a school commits to a focus on rigor and relevance for all students and uses the Rigor/Relevance Framework extensively, expectations rise. Leaders can also raise staff expectations by becoming more data-driven in their decision making. This focus on using data to drive change that increases student achievement is a component of the DSEI. Sharing student achievement results, creating and collecting more and other types of data about student progress, and analyzing and sharing data raises the knowledge level of school leaders and the quality of leadership.

Successful schools rely on more than just test scores for their decision making. The International Center's Learning Criteria encourages schools to broaden their definitions of what can and should be measured when evaluating the quality of the student learning experiences. The Learning Criteria's four dimensions — Foundation Learning, Stretch Learning, Learner Engagement, and Personal Skill Development — help schools collect and consider more comprehensive data. When multiple measures of student success are considered, staff members develop a broader perspective, and expectations rise.

A Future-Focused Approach

A focus on nurturing the whole student — including the factors of nutrition, health, and emotional well-being that help create a strong foundation for lifelong learning and healthy living — also increases expectations. While they are not the primary purposes of public education, these factors must be woven into the fabric of academic success for every student. The added sense of responsibility raises the level of leadership for students and staff alike. It also contributes to a future-focused approach to education.

Concentrating on students' future needs is a way to raise the level of leadership. Rather than concentrating instructional improvement efforts on fixing things that are not working or that do not meet expectations, leaders across the organization can focus on setting actions that the school community can take to poise students for success in all aspects of their lives, not just academics.

Leading in Different Quadrants

There will always be situations that are handled most appropriately and effectively in one quadrant or another. For sustained, long-term improvements to take hold, however, leadership must aspire to be transformational, functioning in Quadrant D. Over time, the more leadership moves toward transformational leadership practices, the more a school can adapt to changing conditions and achieve and sustain improvement.

When leadership is based in one quadrant area, it creates certain characteristics in a school. Leadership in each quadrant exhibits its own unique attributes, although there are similarities and some overlap among the styles. Transformational Leadership draws from elements of each of the other quadrants. The most startling contrast in leadership styles is between Quadrant A and Quadrant D, as shown in the following table. Leadership in Quadrants B and C fall along a continuum between these two styles.

Comparing Authoritative School Leaders (Quadrant A) and Adaptive School Leaders (Quadrant D)

Quadrant A	Quadrant D
Manage the current system	Change the system, as appropriate
Use past experience to solve problems	Learn new ways to adapt and change
Promote standards and procedures	Adapt to unique situations
Replicate practices with fidelity	Create new practices to meet needs
Maintain traditional leadership structure	Cultivate leadership density
Look to superiors for answers	Look to staff to take actions
Rely on expertise	Rely on each other
Tie change to an individual leader	Create sustainable change because of leadership density

Quadrant A Leaders

Quadrant A leaders tend to focus on implementing and ensuring compliance with established routines and procedures rather than on changing or modifying existing structures. Under this managerial style, there is a traditional chain of command, and the leader is the primary decision maker in the school. While following standard procedures may work well for a safety issue, such as a fire drill, such an approach may be less effective in increasing student engagement and encouraging students to enroll in advanced courses.

Traditional leaders tend to use past experiences when solving problems. Confronted with an issue, they draw on their past experience, usually with great confidence about their problem-solving expertise. Whenever a new program is implemented, these leaders focus on ensuring that staff members replicate practices with fidelity. As issues or problems that appear too difficult, complex, or risky to solve on their own arise, traditional leaders tend to look to superiors for answers and guidance. While there may be some success associated with this leadership style, it usually is not associated with the highest-quality education experience for students, and it is rarely sustainable.

A good example of Quadrant A leadership was evident in a large suburban high school that, based on quantitative data, was perceived to be successful. Students met state test requirements; most students went on to college. There were few discipline problems, and the community was proud of the school. However, there was more to the story. Students did the minimum they needed to do and could not wait to graduate. Most students who went on to college needed remediation, and many students dropped out because they showed little commitment to the importance of lifelong learning. Likewise, teachers did only the minimum required of them, left at the contractual end of the day, and frequently complained about problems that the administration needed to fix.

Leadership in this school was based on a single individual, who focused on keeping things running smoothly within the rules. The principal confused rule compliance with a culture of engagement and passion for learning. While student achievement was perceived of as good, it was barely meeting minimums. There was little capacity for the school to improve. The school was fortunate to have a primarily wealthy student population. If confronted with the demographic diversity that exists in most schools, it is unlikely that this school would have been able to coast along on the marginal results, and it would not have had the ability to respond to the changing environment to achieve true success.

Quadrant C Leaders

Leaders who operate in Quadrant C are similar to Quadrant A leaders in that both styles generally are based upon the single-leader model. Unlike a Quadrant A leader, however, a Quadrant C leader tends to understand the contemporary challenges facing education and seeks to make significant changes. Quadrant C leaders might be labeled "visionaries." They seek to innovate, primarily through the power of their personalities.

An example of this type of leadership was observed in an urban high school that was struggling with discipline problems, poor attendance, high dropout rates, and isolated instruction. The principal embraced the model of Small Learning Communities (SLCs) and introduced the structure to the school. The SLCs consisted of six themed academies. Teachers from each discipline were grouped together and assigned to different areas of the building to create the academies. The academies were supported by community and business partners, as well as university partners who provided instructional improvement coaching. The creative principal often was hard at work outside the school, nurturing these partnerships.

The change yielded some success, but not throughout the school. Only some of the staff bought into the SLC philosophy. Those who did worked together and created islands of innovation in the school. Others continued to follow traditional approaches, functioning as SLCs in name only. Eventually, the leader left the school. The momentum for school improvement slipped because the creative leader was no longer there. This is the characteristic of schools that have leadership primarily in Quadrant C. Success is partial and varied, for it is tied to the presence of the individual leader.

Quadrant B Leaders

A Quadrant B leader cultivates leadership capacity throughout the school community. The result is an environment that is described as "collaborative" because of the leadership density. In this model, the "top" individual leader serves to empower the leadership of many others.

One large rural comprehensive high school exhibited the characteristics typical of Quadrant B leadership. Many students in this school lived in poverty, and their parents' education level was generally low. The school benefited from state redistribution of funds and had a higher level of funding than the local community could provide. There was a focus on high expectations for students, which was manifest in several areas of the school. The career and technical programs were exceptional, with nearly all students completing programs. Students were extensively involved in internships in a nearby resort community. There was an excellent music program in a brand-new facility. There were many Advanced Placement and dual-credit courses. An outstanding guidance department used volunteers to assist students with college applications and financial aid.

The school's apparent success largely was due to good leadership density, especially compared to what is found in many rural schools. Several departments had very strong leaders. However, there were not schoolwide improvement efforts. The school community was not united with a common vision. Despite many examples of success, the school had not attained a path to significant, sustained school improvement. The current leader was predominately operating in Quadrant B. Typical of this style, the leadership focus in the school was mainly internal. The principal did not reach outside of the school for new ideas and best practices to improve instruction. There was a general satisfaction with the status quo — each department functioned well independently — so there were few attempts to create a cohesive vision for which all staff and students could take responsibility.

Chapter 3: Setting High Expectations and a Vision as a Transformational Leader

Transformational Leaders

Transformational leaders, who operate in Quadrant D, always seek ways to change and improve the system. They are quicker to recognize areas in which the current system limits the potential for student success, and they are open to considering ways to revise the system to meet student needs more effectively. Constantly looking for new ways to adapt and change, transformational leaders are able to break away from established procedures and routines.

Transformational leaders promote a highly collaborative culture that places a greater premium on teamwork than on individual expertise or past experience. When transformational leaders are confronted with a significant challenge or issue, they look primarily to staff to develop effective solutions. The school culture is focused on meeting individual students' needs and on celebrating the unique characteristics of the school community. Staff members are encouraged to adapt to unique situations and to be flexible in supporting the personal and academic growth of each and every student. A school under transformational leadership is adaptive. It is either on a clear path toward rapid improvement or is positioned to sustain improvement.

Examples of Transformational Leadership in Action

A.J. Moore Academy, in Waco, Texas, is one model school that showcases transformational leadership. In the late 1990s, the school was a struggling alternative/career center in the Waco Independent School District. Under the leadership of the principal, leadership team, and business partners, the school has transformed itself into a nationally recognized model career academy high school. A culture of high expectations and high levels of support is clearly evident the moment one enters the school. A.J. Moore appears to be more of an adult work environment than a typical school. The school has accomplished this with a socioeconomically disadvantaged and racially diverse student population.

The school kicked off its transition by adopting a clear vision for preparing students for careers and continuing education. Staff members were recruited into ambitious and hardworking teams, which created an innovative curriculum and accomplished the instructional planning necessary to achieve the vision. A.J. Moore demonstrates that there is no shortcut to success. Success takes hard work, but teamwork makes the work feel less burdensome. The school embraces the idea that success is not a destination, but a journey. Staff and students give a great deal of credit to their very dynamic principal, but leadership in this school does not reside in her solely. Every day, teachers and students act in ways that support the school's mission and vision.

One specific example of Transformational Leadership at A.J. Moore occurred a few years ago, when several communities around the nation were staging demonstrations about immigration issues. Rumors emerged that there would be a sizeable demonstration in Waco. A couple of staff members recognized this as a learning opportunity and crafted a lesson that addressed immigration, civil disobedience, and ways to influence government leaders. The staff did not go to the principal and say, "Here is a problem, do something!" Instead, they identified the issue, saw its potential, and forged a solution. They taught the lesson the day before the local event. On the day of the demonstration, no A.J. Moore students skipped school, but other schools in the district were scrambling to decide how to punish the large number of students who had cut classes to attend the rally. In this incident, A.J. Moore staff and students exhibited the characteristics of Transformational Leadership. They worked together toward the common vision of connecting learning to the real world in a manner that made sense for the school community.

A.B. Combs Leadership Magnet Elementary School in Raleigh, North Carolina, is another good example of a school shaped by Transformational Leadership. In 1999, this highly diverse school was one of the lowest performing schools in the Wake County Schools district. The staff did not feel good about their teaching, and student performance was not satisfactory. School staff felt that the district leadership had no understanding of the challenges of working with a very diverse student population. Then the school was issued an ultimatum by the district: Improve, or close. The school responded to the challenge by inventing and implementing a learning model that was different from that of any other school in the nation. This successful learning model was designed to require no additional money or staff. The process that unfolded is an elegant study in Transformational Leadership.

Under the outstanding leadership of the principal, the school adopted a vision based on the leadership principles of Stephen Covey, whose model for personal responsibility as a means of achieving success was the focus of the bestselling book *The 7 Habits of Highly Effective People*. Using a collaborative style, the principal empowered staff to create rigorous and relevant learning experiences to engage students and make learning meaningful. With no script to follow, staff members created innovative, effective instructional strategies. Although they did not ignore test scores, they did not make high performance on state tests the goal; rather, the school leadership team kept a diligent focus on student data to measure the school's progress.

Transformational leadership nurtures the connection between student leadership and staff leadership. Schools that aspire to function at the highest level of leadership need to involve students in taking active responsibility for their own behaviors and learning. A.B. Combs has accomplished that with its elementary students, who show outstanding confidence and maturity as a result of the school's culture and practices. The school continues to be highly collaborative and high-performing. A visitor needs only to be greeted by one of the confident, smiling 2nd-graders upon entering the school or to sit in the pep-rally type morning staff meeting to affirm the unique leadership environment. In addition to being a regular at the International Center's annual Model Schools Conference, A.B. Combs is featured prominently in Covey's book *The Leader in Me*.

Situational Leadership

Transformational leadership is the aspiration; but in reality, leaders frequently shift among the skills characteristic of each. It is the balance among the four quadrants that collectively leads to transformational leadership. Aspiring transformational leaders should constantly reflect on practice and ask themselves if there are opportunities to raise the level of leadership toward Quadrant D when working in the other quadrants.

Quadrant A Leadership Situations

As discussed, there are many school situations in which the managerial style typical of Quadrant A leadership is warranted, such as:

- addressing student safety and security issues
- ensuring that staff members follow standard procedures consistently
- ensuring compliance with ethical and legal requirements
- dealing with significant student behavior disruptions
- introducing new state mandates
- maintaining fiscal controls
- handling school maintenance issues
- dismissing a staff member

Quadrant B Leadership Situations

In Quadrant B, the emphasis is on building a collaborative school community. One critical circumstance that requires the application of Quadrant B skills is low staff morale as a result of layoffs or fiscal cuts. At such times, staff members need strong collaborative support. Many other key situations require building collaborative leadership — the hallmark of a Quadrant B approach — among them:

- hiring staff and establishing mentoring responsibilities for experienced staff to work with new staff
- developing strategies for addressing significant demographic changes within the school community
- considering the implementation of a new program, such as a different reading series or other curriculum item
- easing transitions in the school community when there are many new staff in leadership positions, such as principals or assistant principals

Quadrant C Leadership Situations

A school must establish a vision in which all students are supported to achieve their highest potential. The time is ripe for the more visionary approach of Quadrant C leadership when:

- student achievement is poor overall
- gaps in achievement among different groups of students call for a deep focus on data and lofty goal setting
- staff must be encouraged to move beyond the status quo of traditional instruction
- expectations for students are too low or are not clearly articulated and supported

Transformational Leadership Situations

Any time is the right time for transformational leadership. If a school is working very well but wishes to move to an even higher level of student performance, one that is based on a broader range of measures, then a transformational leadership approach is critical. For a school that is mired in routine but looking for an innovative approach to address recommendations from the leadership team or district, transformational leadership may inspire a breakthrough. When a district is creating a new school or planning to take a large school and break it into small learning communities, striving toward transformational leadership is appropriate.

In any situation, there are steps along the way that require the leadership approaches that are characteristic of the other quadrants. A transformational approach demands creation of a clear vision, consensus building around the vision, and development of the structures to support collaborative leadership across all levels. Transformational leadership is especially important when:

- a *good* school is striving to become a *great* school
- an innovative approach is required to move beyond the status quo
- there are "islands" of innovation and excellence — that is, particularly strong individual teachers or groups of teachers at a grade level or in a department or program — that must be united to create a cohesive culture
- a school wants to sustain successful school improvement efforts
- there is evidence of low student engagement
- there is a shortage of prospective transformational leaders within existing leadership or staff
- a school is experiencing a transition, or a series of transitions, to new leadership
- a district is planning for a new school or for a reorganization of existing schools into smaller learning communities

Superficial Versus Genuine Transformational Leaders

A genuine transformational leader understands that different situations will call for different strategies, including authoritarian ones, and is able to move among the leadership strategies easily. For this leader, however, an authoritarian style is a temporary detour.

Sometimes a leader may seem to embrace transformational leadership, but his or her actions are consistently in Quadrant A, betraying the belief that authoritarian management is the best strategy for running a school. Because he or she may talk a great deal about the ideals that true transformational leaders exhibit, spotting a "covert" Quadrant A leader may be difficult. Certain behaviors, however, are common among these types of leaders. A clandestine Quadrant A leader:

- **Speaks first, speaks loudly, and speaks long.** When it is time to discuss issues, share perspectives, or brainstorm solutions, the covert Quadrant A leader quickly voices his or her perspective and the rationale for supporting it. The leader's intention is to squelch other perspectives. The danger to the organization is clear: Valuable insights and potential solutions may never surface.

- **Assumes that all staff members know what they need to know.** Staff members may be invited to assist in key decision making, planning, and problem solving even if they do not possess the expertise necessary to participate meaningfully in these practices. This can result in poor decision making and frustration on the part of participants, which is then used to justify the authoritarian leader's suppositions that collaborative decisions are inferior.

- **Behaves as though empowerment is primarily about making his or her own life easier.** In this case, the work that the administrator "shares" is really intended to reduce the "administrivia" — essential but often tedious tasks — with which he or she must contend. There is nothing wrong with such assignments unless these are the only tasks that the administrator shares. If the knotty problems and the global issues confronting the district remain the exclusive purview of the nominal leaders, the group's creative energy and ideas are not engaged.

- **Provides inadequate time and resources.** The covert Quadrant A leader can make a show of inclusiveness by identifying stakeholders as part of strategic decision making and planning. However, if the plans are not supported with the time and resources to accomplish such tasks, it is unlikely that meaningful, high-quality solutions will result.

- **Conducts bad meetings.** Few things do more to diminish the drive and willingness of teachers and community members to solve difficult problems than poorly run meetings. The covert Quadrant A leader knows this and can avoid the messy interference of outside contributions by not providing adequate materials, sufficient documentation, or needed data and literature. Other autocratic maneuvers include the failure to use proven approaches such as timed agenda items, best practices for decision making, and strategies for defining next steps effectively.

- **Changes the rules late in the game.** When an administrator engages his or her colleagues without clarifying the task or revealing constraints on the group's decision-making authority, trouble ensues. When participants are not informed about parameters that will undo hard work already completed or negate decisions already made, they will be wary the next time they are approached to engage in problem solving.

- **Uses policies, rules, and laws as camouflage.** The leader who unnecessarily raises the specter of regulatory constraints to maintain exclusive decision making or other authority may be masking a Quadrant A disposition. Consider a superintendent who justifies excluding teachers and parents from having a role in selecting new principals by citing a legal requirement for recommendations for principal hires to come to the board from the superintendent. While rules about a final recommendation may be specific, they do not prevent others from participating in activities leading up to the recommendation. This type of action is more about a leader's unwillingness to relinquish power than it is about a leader's prudent adherence to the law.

- **Keeps it in "the club."** In this situation, a leader seems to support leadership across many levels of the organization but actually gives key assignments to those who hold traditional leadership titles and roles, such as the principal, assistant principal, superintendent, and board members. There are good reasons to choose capable individuals consistently; but for some leaders, this is a strategy intended to stifle consent and to create comfortable pathways for traditional managerial action.

- **Says, "I told you so!"** The covert Quadrant A leader may give lip service to inclusive leadership but is frequently searching for vindication to show how such governance is flawed. Failures, or just missteps, by a group to whom a decision has been delegated are used as proof of this. It is normal for groups who are working on solutions to big challenges and novel problems to experience some setbacks, but a covert authoritarian will use early stumbling blocks as evidence rather than as opportunities. He or she may lay the blame on participants or democratic leadership practices — and self-righteously pull back authority.

- **Takes credit for others' hard work and success.** School victories are often hard-won, especially when there are monumental challenges to conquer. Few things send a more resounding message of covert Quadrant A leadership than a leader's taking credit for successes without acknowledging the hard work and contributions others have made. (Ward, Mike and MacPhail-Wilcox, Betty, "About the Covert Autocrat")

Using the Transformational Leadership Framework

Leaders can use the Transformational Leadership Framework to shape their leadership actions. For example, consider a leader who is confronted by the release of test data that reveal that an unacceptable number of students are not meeting state benchmarks in reading comprehension. There are several ways this leader could handle this information to begin influencing school improvement.

One way would be to act as a Quadrant A leader and take action unilaterally. A Quadrant A leader would present the results to staff and announce that the required amount of instructional time devoted to reading will be increased, effective immediately. Teachers might be required to participate in a workshop focused on incorporating reading in the content areas. A Quadrant B leader would not make a unilateral decision but would involve a staff committee, perhaps including students at the high school level, to explore options for increasing reading instruction and support. In a school led by a Quadrant C leader, staff would feel empowered to seek out research-based best practices for improving literacy and to bring them forth as new ways to tackle the reading comprehension problem.

While the actions of the Quadrants A, B, and C leaders would have some impact on increasing reading scores, actions at higher levels of leadership would be more likely to create innovative solutions, to result in practices that could be sustained over time, and to elicit fewer negative emotions among staff. In a transformational leadership setting, however, the leader already would have established collaborative structures to support staff in creative problem solving. Staff would be empowered to connect the need to increase reading comprehension to other initiatives and to establish an expectation for improved reading comprehension. These broader efforts would focus on more than just an increase in state test scores and would support an overall set of expectations to prepare students for the future.

Understanding the Transformational Leadership Framework gives school leaders a mental model for attacking the adaptive challenges of instructional leadership. Instructional leadership involves developing a common vision of good instruction; of building relationships; and of empowering staff to innovate in instruction, give one another feedback, and share best practices. Context, target, and practices are three elements of instructional leadership, and they will be examined in detail in Chapter 4. Here, however, is a brief overview of each element and how it relates to the quadrants of leadership.

Context

Context describes the work to build the elements of a strong collaborative school community that is eager to innovate and share. These practices are similar to the strategies to move to the Quadrants B and D side of the Transformational Leadership Framework.

Context skills involve:

- analyzing data about student achievement and school culture
- reflecting about school practices that influence school culture and relationships
- applying strategies that promote innovation and change in the school culture
- developing the perseverance to overcome obstacles and challenges
- identifying supportive behaviors that build positive relationships
- becoming familiar with a broad range of effective strategies and organizing them into a pyramid of intervention for addressing the needs of every student
- understanding the need to develop a positive school culture so that learning opportunities, both within and outside of the school, are available to all students
- developing data systems to monitor student reading progress
- reviewing curriculum and research data to identify high-priority standards and benchmarks for the state

Target

Target is about setting the strong vision of instructional leadership and building agreement among school community members about the specific aim and purpose of instructional improvement efforts. Focusing on "increasing student achievement" is a measurement of results but not an appropriate target for instructional leadership, because it does not inform teachers how to adjust their instructional practices. Target focuses on:

- identifying a specific objective for instructional improvement initiatives rather than simply embracing a broad objective to improve instruction
- aligning all instructional practices with the agreed-upon target
- recognizing that having a target is more important than what the target is
- realizing that is it easier to "get all staff on board" when you introduce the target before introducing a practice, such as professional learning communities or classroom walk-throughs
- creating multiple professional learning activities aligned with the target
- selecting among several optional targets that have been successful in rapidly improving schools in increasing student achievement

Practices

Practices are the total of programs, activities, and strategies that leaders use to influence instruction. Practices are effective only if leaders address the context and have a clear target. Good practices help leaders:

- get the right teachers in the right places
- foster development of teacher leadership
- ensure that leaders across all levels are focusing on instructional leadership
- develop and use effective classroom walk-through procedures and select questions and activities that stimulate teacher reflection on instructional practice
- make difficult decisions about staff
- develop teachers into effective instructors through ongoing professional learning

A Systemwide Approach to Leadership

- reflect about current conditions and practices of professional learning
- create and implement coaching and mentoring practices
- evaluate the effectiveness of professional learning

The 25 Major Practices

There is no single approach to improving instruction, but the following 25 major practices are identified as contributing to instructional leadership:

1. Academic intervention
2. Balanced assessments
3. Celebrations
4. Classroom walk-throughs
5. Co-teaching/team teaching
6. Grading
7. Individualized professional learning
8. Instructional coaching
9. Instructional technology
10. Leadership teams
11. Mentoring
12. Needs assessment/strategic planning
13. Peer review of student work
14. Personnel and budgets
15. Policies and procedures
16. Professional development workshops
17. Professional learning community
18. Rigor/Relevance Framework
19. Master schedule/teacher assignments
20. Staff meetings
21. Staff reviews and evaluations

Chapter 3: Setting High Expectations and a Vision as a Transformational Leader

22. Student achievement data analysis
23. Teacher incentives and rewards
24. Teacher observations/study tours
25. Vision/mission/goals

These practices can be grouped into four areas: (1) management, (2) empowerment, (3) vision, and (4) culture. Leaders will use many of the 25 practices, depending on particular circumstances. All of the practices are aligned with the mental model of the Transformational Leadership Framework, which guides leadership in deciding which processes will work best in a given situation.

The graphic that follows shows how the 25 practices are organized along the continuums of the Transformational Leadership Framework. Some of these practices are connected to the lower levels of leadership described as Quadrant A; others are connected to the characteristics of Quadrant D Leaders must balance multiple initiatives to improve instruction.

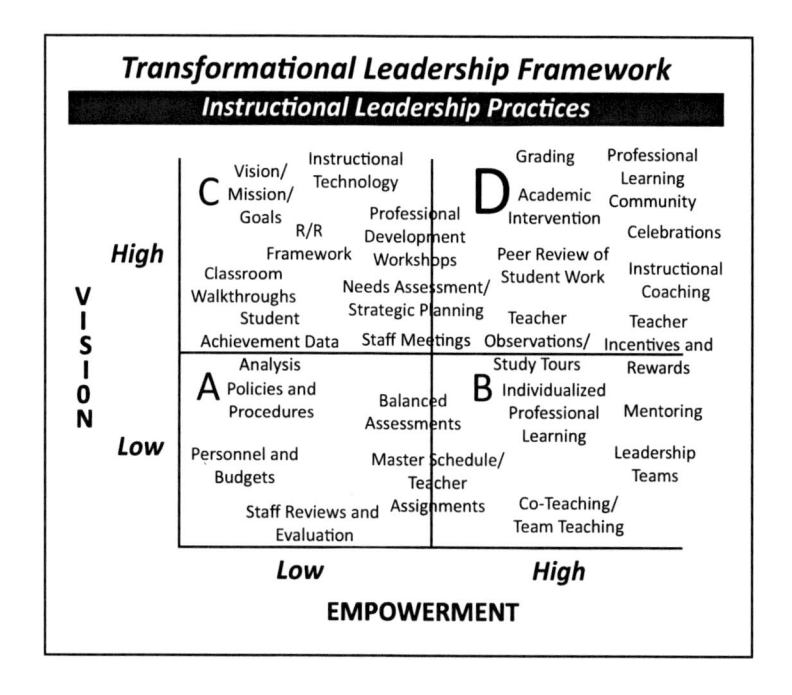

Transformational Leadership Framework
Instructional Leadership Practices

VISION: High / Low
EMPOWERMENT: Low / High

Quadrant C (High Vision, Low Empowerment):
- Vision/Mission/Goals
- Instructional Technology
- R/R Framework
- Professional Development Workshops
- Classroom Walkthroughs
- Needs Assessment/Strategic Planning
- Student Achievement Data Analysis
- Staff Meetings

Quadrant D (High Vision, High Empowerment):
- Grading
- Professional Learning Community
- Academic Intervention
- Celebrations
- Peer Review of Student Work
- Instructional Coaching
- Teacher Observations/Study Tours
- Teacher Incentives and Rewards

Quadrant A (Low Vision, Low Empowerment):
- Policies and Procedures
- Personnel and Budgets
- Staff Reviews and Evaluation

Quadrant B (Low Vision, High Empowerment):
- Balanced Assessments
- Master Schedule/Teacher Assignments
- Individualized Professional Learning
- Mentoring
- Leadership Teams
- Co-Teaching/Team Teaching

© International Center for Leadership in Education

A Systemwide Approach to Leadership

Management practices are essential for addressing necessary tasks, but they demand lower levels of leadership. When leaders are using these practices, they generally are operating in Quadrant A, as shown:

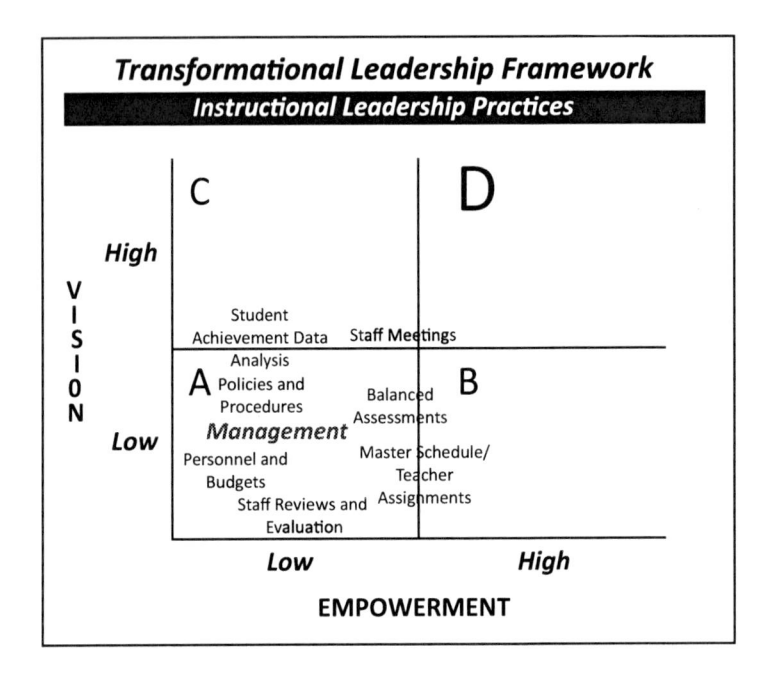

```
Transformational Leadership Framework
      Instructional Leadership Practices

                  C                    D
        High
  V
  I
  S                Student
  I           Achievement Data    Staff Meetings
  O              Analysis
  N          A  Policies and
                 Procedures      Balanced      B
                Management       Assessments
        Low
               Personnel and     Master Schedule/
                 Budgets         Teacher
                Staff Reviews and Assignments
                  Evaluation
                 Low                   High
                      EMPOWERMENT
```

Management practices include:

- **Policies and procedures.** Schools, as systems, must have common, clear, and practical ways of operating to ensure consistency of instruction while taking care not to stifle innovation. The DSEI emphasizes that a school functions as system and that coherence and alignment must occur at the system level to be effective.
- **Personnel and budgets.** Hiring decisions and the allocation of limited resources are at the administrative core of high-quality learning. According to the DSEI, organizational leaders need to adopt a "talent management system" for the selection of teachers.
- **Master schedule/teacher assignments.** It is essential for leaders to create school master calendars that ensure that time is being used wisely and that instructional assignments enable teachers to apply their talents toward greater school success.

Chapter 3: Setting High Expectations and a Vision as a Transformational Leader

- **Staff meetings.** Staff meetings are more productive and have a greater impact on school success when agendas focus on instructional issues rather than on administrative ones.
- **Staff reviews and evaluations.** Staff improvement results from periodic, high-quality staff reviews, evaluation, and feedback.
- **Balanced assessments.** Students and teachers benefit from a cohesive system of formative and summative assessments to measure progress toward learning goals.
- **Student achievement data analysis.** High-stakes, standardized tests provide valuable data to inform areas of instruction in need of improvement. The DSEI identifies supporting decision making with data systems and facilitating data-driven decision making to inform instruction as key functions of leadership.

Empowerment practices reflect high levels of leadership application and empowerment but suffer from the lack of a fully defined common school vision. They appear as part of Quadrant B in the Transformational Leadership Framework.

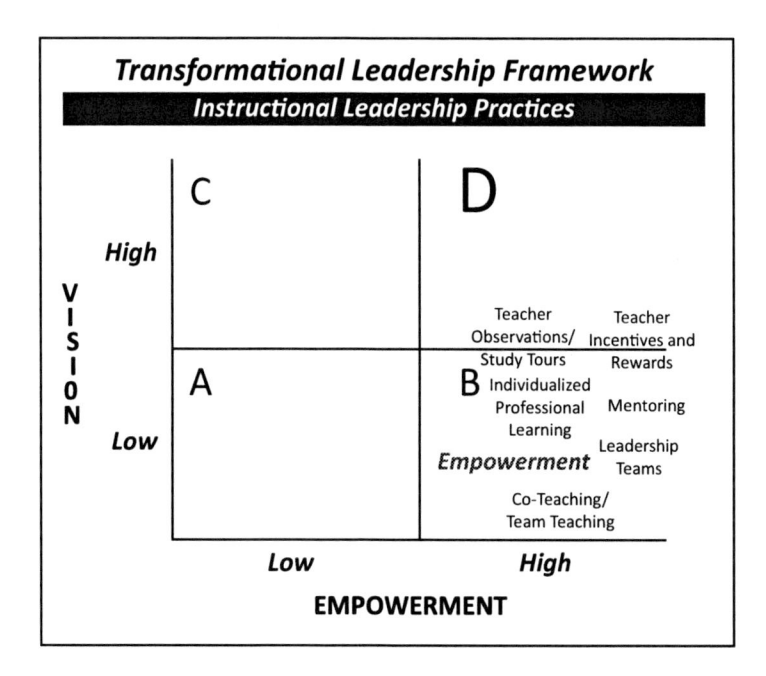

Transformational Leadership Framework
Instructional Leadership Practices

	Low Empowerment	High Empowerment
High Vision	C	D
Low Vision	A	B — Teacher Observations/Study Tours, Teacher Incentives and Rewards, Individualized Professional Learning, Mentoring, Empowerment, Leadership Teams, Co-Teaching/Team Teaching

© International Center for Leadership in Education

Empowerment practices include:

- **Leadership teams.** Collaborative teams build a common focus, enhance schoolwide problem solving, embrace data-based decision making, and share best practices.
- **Mentoring.** Beginning teachers or those who are new to a school learn from master teachers through ongoing personal conversations.
- **Co-teaching/team teaching.** Teachers working collaboratively build on strengths and share best practices to benefit students.
- **Teacher incentives and rewards.** Individual recognition and other incentives encourage teachers to take the steps necessary to improve.
- **Teacher observations/study tours.** Actually observing good instructional practice in action is an extremely powerful tool for teachers to improve their own instruction.
- **Individualized professional learning.** Self-directed learning offers professionals learning opportunities that relate directly to their needs.

Vision practices, which are associated with Quadrant C leadership, may reflect high levels of knowledge of leadership and creativity, but they also indicate a less fully developed approach to empowerment.

Chapter 3: Setting High Expectations and a Vision as a Transformational Leader

```
Transformational Leadership Framework
         Instructional Leadership Practices

                      Instructional
           Vision/    Technology
         C Mission/                    D
           Goals      Professional
              R/R     Development
  High    Framework   Workshops
         Vision
                      Needs Assessment/
         Classroom    Strategic Planning
         Walkthroughs


           A              B
  Low

         Low              High
              EMPOWERMENT
```

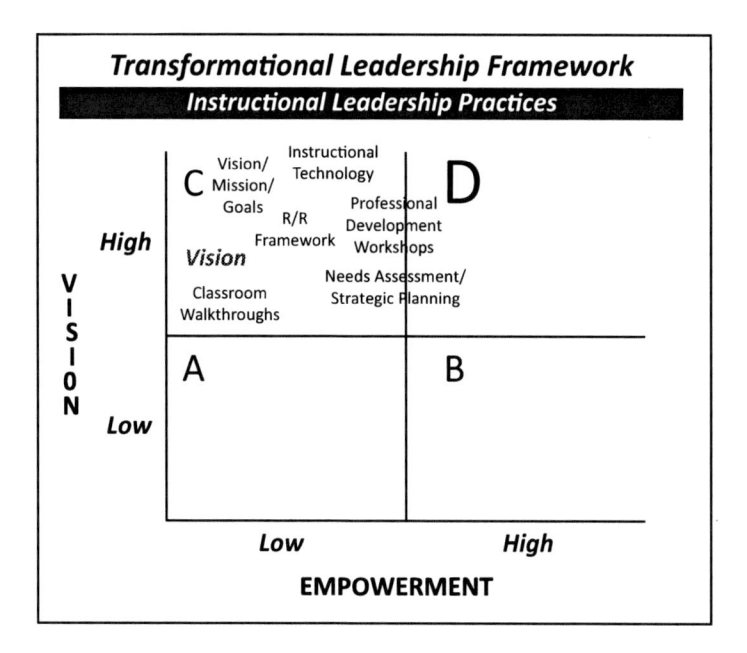

Vision practices include:

- **Vision/mission/goals.** When a leader establishes a vision for change that is based on new or revised goals, the school community begins to see the possibility of improvement.
- **Instructional technology.** Using current instructional technology in the classroom helps to introduce 21st century learning as well as to engage students. Instructional technology conveys a vision that schools are up to date with contemporary society and relevant in preparing students for their future.
- **Rigor/Relevance Framework.** This is the most powerful tool for quantifying aspirations for rigorous and relevant instruction and assessment.
- **Needs assessment/strategic planning.** To achieve success and provide targeted improvement, leaders must help staff carefully craft strategic actions based on observed needs.

- **Classroom walk-throughs.** Short, frequent classroom observations reinforce expectations, create opportunities to engage and support staff, and build a rich culture that supports quality instruction.
- **Professional development workshops.** High-quality group learning from experts is a key strategy for improving instruction.

Culture practices help establish an environment that supports improvement. These transformational leadership practices reflect high levels of knowledge and an application of leadership that will sustain significant instructional improvement.

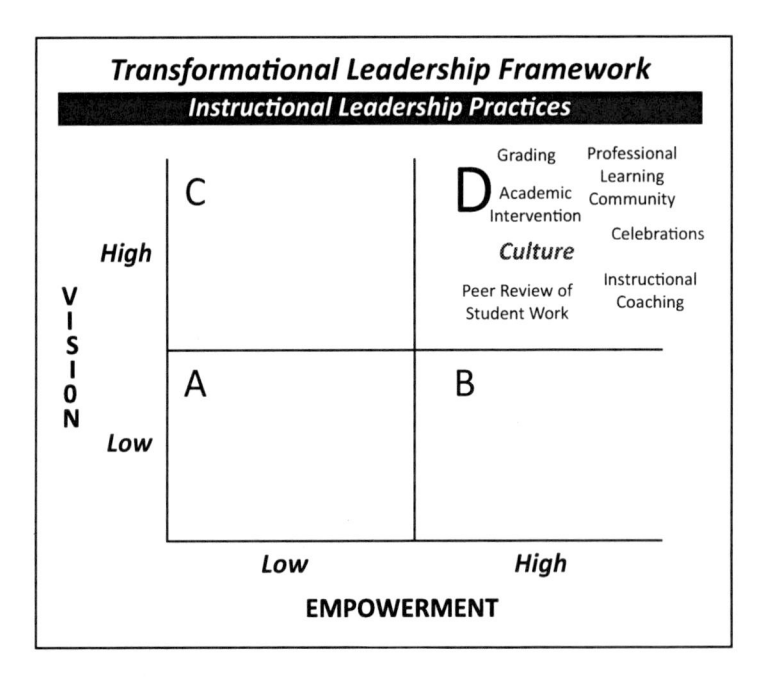

Transformational Leadership Framework
Instructional Leadership Practices

	Low EMPOWERMENT	High EMPOWERMENT
High VISION	C	D — Grading, Academic Intervention, Professional Learning Community, Celebrations, *Culture*, Peer Review of Student Work, Instructional Coaching
Low VISION	A	B

Culture practices include:

- **Academic intervention.** Ensuring that every student succeeds frequently requires timely intervention to provide personalized, alternative instruction.
- **Instructional coaching.** Onsite peers stimulate teacher reflection and change through regular observation, frequent support, and personal advice in implementing proven instructional practices.

- **Peer review of student work.** When teachers share high-quality student work with one another, they support the development of high-quality instruction.
- **Grading.** School policies and teacher practices relating to grading have a significant impact on the school culture in terms of instruction and student achievement.
- **Celebrations.** Public recognition, rituals, and social events are means of renewing staff enthusiasm and the commitment to school success.
- **Professional learning community.** Transformational leaders cultivate an environment in which teachers share values, vision, and leadership and support one another in collective, ongoing learning.

Effective leadership does not reside in a single position; it encompasses the diversified skills of many. It is this distributed leadership that defines successful schools. The Transformational Leadership Framework guides leaders in their daily actions and encourages them to reflect on the role of school leadership in sustaining school improvement and student achievement.

Transformational leadership is characterized by a leader's understanding of and ability to use varying strategies to create the structures, systems, and collaborative and supportive culture necessary for sustained change. True transformational leaders will move among the skill sets of each of the framework's quadrants in order to meet the demands of running a school, but they do so with an eye toward cultivating leadership density and empowering staff and students to play significant roles in decision making and problem solving.

Creating a Shared Vision

Quadrant C is home to vision practices. These practices may reflect high levels of knowledge of leadership and creativity, but they are weaker in their focus on empowerment. A leader who is operating in Quadrant C may be a strong visionary and may create helpful professional opportunities for staff development to support instruction, but this leader has a harder time letting others develop leadership skills to create solidity across the organization. When a Quadrant C leader leaves an organization, it may be difficult for his or her good work to continue, even if that work is well defined, because so much of the progress was tied to the individual strengths of the outgoing leader.

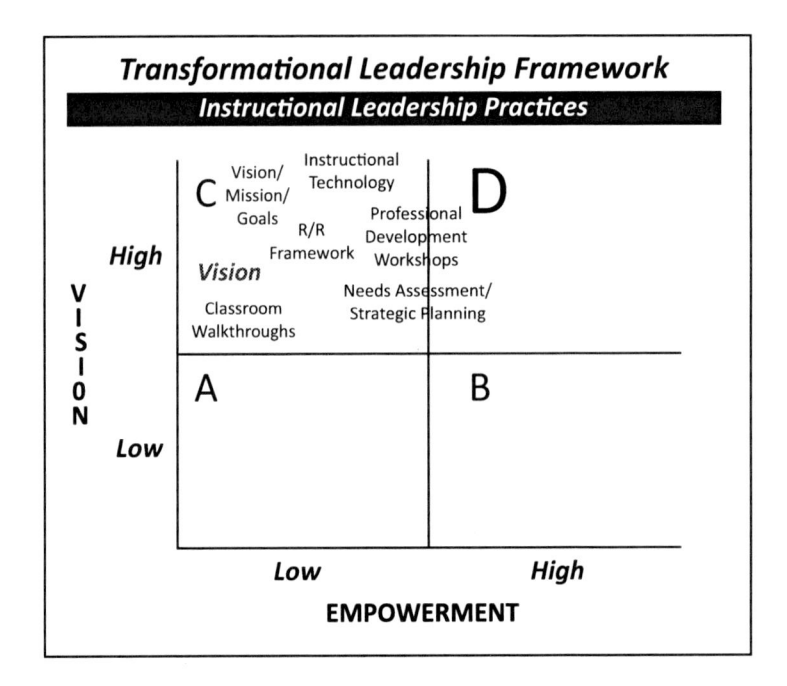

Transformational Leadership Framework
Instructional Leadership Practices

```
                    Instructional
          Vision/   Technology
       C  Mission/              D
          Goals   R/R   Professional
 High            Framework Development
      Vision              Workshops
                    Needs Assessment/
         Classroom  Strategic Planning
         Walkthroughs

       A                    B
 Low

         Low              High
              EMPOWERMENT
```

(Y-axis: VISION; X-axis: EMPOWERMENT)

Vision, Mission, and Goals

Sometimes a school has fallen into an apathetic routine. Staff members do their jobs, but with little enthusiasm and commitment. This may be a time for the individual leader to initiate a new vision, mission, or goals. Envisioning encourages others to believe that things can be different in the school. Through the vision of a leadership team or leader, a school staff can imagine what it would be like to have problems solved, processes run more smoothly, and/or outcomes be more successful.

Leadership Strategies

The strategy of vision may be referred to as "vision," "mission," "goals," or "core values." When working on vision, leaders may also be focusing on one or more of the other three components. Is there a need for all four components? Not necessarily. Leaders should reflect on the needs of the organization. If there is considerable confusion or if the school is new, it is essential to spend time on all four components; in other situations, it may be more efficient to address only one or two aspects of the vision.

Chapter 3: Setting High Expectations and a Vision as a Transformational Leader

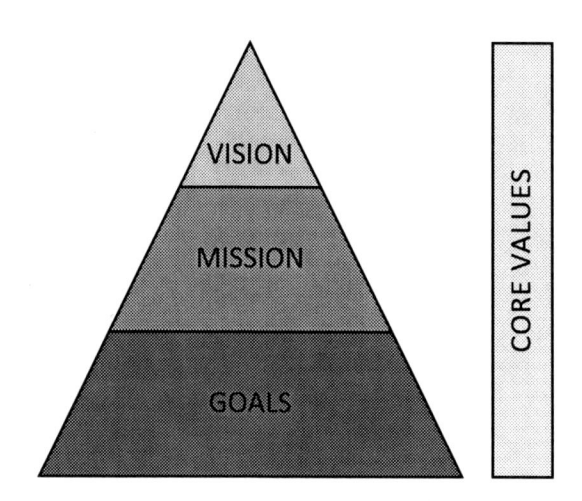

```
         VISION
        MISSION          CORE VALUES
         GOALS
```

This diagram shows the relationship among the four components. Vision, mission, and goals set the direction for an organization; all relate to one another and build on one another. Vision, the highest level, takes the broadest view of the organization. Mission, the next level, becomes more specific and focused on the organization. Goals are the lowest level because they are more closely linked to the operation of the organization.

Core values are the fundamental principles that everyone in the organization believes in. They stand alone and influence the entire process. They are embodied in statements such as these:

- Value self, others, property, and diversity.
- Treat people equally and make decisions without favoritism or prejudice.
- Be accountable for your actions toward yourself, others, and the community.
- Involve parents as essential partners in effective student learning.

By having a set of core values — and stating them — leadership groups and organizations create a common set of assumptions and beliefs that guide the development of the vision, mission, and goals.

Vision and *mission* are frequently confused. *Vision* defines the where the organization is going; *mission* defines how to get there. What is the difference between a vision statement and a mission statement? A vision statement describes *a desired state* whereas a mission

© International Center for Leadership in Education

statement describes *the action and purpose* of the vision. Vision should determine a school's mission. The vision is a bigger picture and future-oriented; the mission is more focused on the immediate present. The vision defines the end game; the mission provides the roadmap that will take one there. Vision statements are most often written about students and student learning; mission statements are most often written about school staff and work that the school will do. Are both vision and mission necessary? No, but it is helpful to have both.

A vision statement, as implied in the construction of the term itself, puts forth a statement of the envisioned future. A nonexistent, ambiguous, or weak school vision is a recipe for ambivalence and poor student achievement. It would be akin to the proverbial ship without a rudder, adrift without any direction or control.

Sample Vision Statements

A vision statement is what the organization wants to become. It describes how the future will look if the school achieves its mission. A vision statement describes a picture of the "preferred future," as in the following examples:

- We will provide a stimulating learning environment with a technological orientation across the whole curriculum, maximizing individual potential and ensuring that students of all ability levels are well equipped to meet the challenges of education, work, and life. Students will:
  - develop the skills, knowledge, and attitudes to be productive and responsible citizens
  - become proficient in academic core areas in accordance with district and state standards, emphasizing literacy, numeracy, technology, and civility
  - develop essential life skills to become self-directed and lifelong learners
  - conduct themselves in a way that contributes to a safe and orderly atmosphere and that ensures the rights of others
  - broaden perspectives in order to respect and appreciate diverse cultures within their school as well as within their community
- We will have a welcoming environment, in which students can experience academic success and prepare for postsecondary education, the world of work, and life's challenges. Students will receive the message "You are important. You can do it. I will not give up on you."

- X Elementary School strives for excellence in academic achievement through a quality education by providing a positive, safe, challenging environment, with opportunities for all leading to high expectations, accountability, and responsibility.
- At X High School, students, staff, parents, and our community partners understand what it takes to foster successful lifelong learning. All school community members have a voice and work together toward the development of the whole child, preserving his or her uniqueness while preparing him or her to be a productive, contributing member of our diverse society.

Sample Mission Statements

A mission statement concerns what an organization is all about and gives the overall purpose of an organization. A mission statement explains what the organization does, for whom, and the benefit to others, as in the following examples:

- We promote active learning, self-worth, and a shared sense of responsibility.
- We provide a caring, stable environment and academic excellence while preparing its pupils for lifelong learning.
- The X Middle School exists to serve the unique academic, physical, social, and emotional needs of students who are in a special and critical period of their lives as they move from childhood to adolescence. The staff of X Middle School is committed to creating and maintaining an orderly, trusting, and caring environment, where teaching and learning are exciting and students are assisted as they develop responsibility. All aspects of the school's organization, curricular, and cocurricular activities are child centered and designed to accommodate individual learning styles so that all may experience success.
- The mission of X Middle School is to provide each student with a diverse education in a safe, supportive environment that promotes self-discipline, motivation, and excellence in learning. The X team joins the parents and community to assist students in developing skills to become independent, self-sufficient adults who will succeed and contribute responsibly in a global community.
- To provide our students with success in learning, we are dedicated to individual development of the attitudes, skills, knowledge, and responsibilities that are essential to successful achievement in school and society. We actively involve parents and the community in supporting student learning and development.

- The mission of X Elementary School is to provide opportunities for students to achieve their personal best, to become responsible and productive citizens, and to embrace lifelong learning in a safe and positive environment.
- X High School will provide a safe, supportive learning environment with opportunities for each student to develop the skills and knowledge to become a responsible, successful citizen.

Goals

A mission describes what the school intends to do, but only in a broad statement. Goals statements offer quantifiable measures that can be examined at a later time to see if the organization is making progress.

The acronym SMART has been used to identify effective goal statements for planning. SMART has slightly different variations, depending on the author. Regardless of how the acronym is labeled, it can be used to provide a more comprehensive definition for goal setting:

S: specific, significant, stretching

M: measurable, meaningful, motivational

A: agreed-upon, attainable, achievable, acceptable, action-oriented

R: realistic, relevant, reasonable, rewarding, results-oriented

T: time-based, timely, tangible, trackable

The following broader definition of SMART can be helpful in achieving success in both business and personal life. When managing a project the next time, take a moment to consider whether the goals are SMART goals:

- **Specific**
    - well-defined
    - clear to anyone that has a basic knowledge of the project
- **Measurable**
    - knowledge of whether the goals are obtainable and how far away from completion
    - knowledge of when the goals have been achieved

- **Agreed-Upon**
  - a unified view among all stakeholders about what the goals should be
- **Realistic**
  - within the availability of resources, knowledge, and time
- **Time-Based**
  - enough time to achieve the goal
  - not too much time, which can affect project performance

As good as SMART goals are, individual leaders should be cautious about getting bogged down with goals that represent only incremental achievement. Sometimes it is the ambitious goal that captures people's attention, interest, and passion. Schools frequently set goals that describe what they hope to accomplish over the coming year. These goals help align staff to working together more effectively. Often these goals are very tactical, such as, "Achieve 10% of students meeting the state reading standard." These are specific measures, but they do not capture passion and generate enthusiasm.

The phrase *big hairy audacious goal* (BHAG, pronounced BEE-hag) was proposed by James Collins and Jerry Porras in their 1996 article entitled "Building Your Company's Vision." A BHAG encourages companies to define visionary goals that are more strategic. In the article, the authors define a BHAG as a form of vision statement — " . . . an audacious 10-to-30-year goal to progress toward an envisioned future."

A true BHAG is clear and compelling, serves as a unifying focal point of effort, and acts as a clear catalyst for team spirit. It has a clear finish line, so the organization can know when it has achieved the goal; people like to aim for finish lines. *No Child Left Behind* set such a BHAG goal when it called for 100% of students to be proficient by 2012. Has every student and school met that? No, but certainly such an ambitious goal captured attention, and many schools have made significant progress.

Case Study of A.B. Combs Leadership Magnet Elementary School

A.B. Combs Leadership Magnet Elementary School, discussed earlier in this chapter as an example of transformational leadership in action, is an example of an elementary school that redefined its vision and mission to initiate school change. It serves as a valuable model for the role of visions, mission, and goals. When one walks into Combs, which is tucked into a diverse neighborhood between North Carolina State University and Research Triangle Park, one is awash in a sea of diversity, with approximately 800 students from 68 countries speaking 28 languages. Combs has the largest elementary international population in this Wake County district. It provides ESL instruction; it also is one of the few public schools offering instruction for the deaf and hard of hearing. Eleven years ago, Combs was faced with the mandate to reinvent itself, or cease and desist. Dwindling magnet enrollment and mediocre test scores threatened the loss of the school's magnet status. Today, Combs is considered a national leader in the creation of a new learning-centered paradigm that focuses on leadership development in young children. It has implemented many exemplary practices, but its overarching instructional focus is on leadership. Combs created and implemented a new learning-centered, leadership-focused paradigm in the throes of burgeoning enrollment (a 35% increase since 1999) and equally daunting increases in the number of ESL, free/reduced lunch, and special needs students. During the past 10 years, the percent of students performing at or above grade level has risen to levels never dreamed about. Evidence of the success of the Combs model is reflected in the sustained rise of end-of-grade test scores.

Leadership Through the Use of Instructional Practices

Many instructional practices were woven into the Transformational Leadership Framework, including Edwards Deming's work in quality management, Stephen Covey's *The 7 Habits of Highly Effective People* and *Principle-Centered Leadership*, the International Center's Rigor/Relevance Framework, Larry Lezotte's *Correlates of Effective Schools*, Howard Gardner's multiple intelligences, LEGO SERIOUS PLAY and LEGO robotics programs, Robert Cooper's *Executive EQ: Emotional Intelligence*, Ron Clark's *The Essential 55*, and Rick DuFour's professional learning communities. Because of the school's success and popularity, Combs is featured in Dr. Covey's *The Leader in Me*. Dr. Covey has stated many times, "A.B. Combs is a model that should be replicated around the world." To date, the school has hosted more than 3,000 visitors from every corner of the world.

The Covey and Baldrige philosophies, along with the Rigor/Relevance Framework, create a culture that supports Combs's mission, "To develop global leaders one child at a time," which guides the school in bringing to fruition the vision "By dwelling in possibilities, we will create pathways of excellence that will inspire hope and promise for a better tomorrow." All staff members receive training in the application of these philosophies.

Chapter 3: Setting High Expectations and a Vision as a Transformational Leader

The Combs program is grounded in the belief that building cooperative relationships and nurturing responsibility, kindness, and good judgment form the basis for creating a successful community of learners. By developing the whole child — socially, emotionally, academically, and ethically — the program fosters a climate of principle-centered personal leadership. Empowering students to be leaders of their own learning has resulted in more engaged and happy students.

As a result of infusing the Baldrige practices and using quality tools, data collection and analysis, problem-based learning, and rubric development in the classroom, students are empowered as decision makers and leaders of their own learning. At Combs, assessment drives instruction. Formative assessments are used to measure learning early in the learning process, allowing teachers to fine-tune their instructional strategies to respond most effectively to students' individual needs. Quarterly benchmark assessments allow individual and grade-level analysis.

The goals for the Combs school community are to develop a collective vision of student success, to serve as strong role models, and to use data to track progress and drive instruction. The four roles of leadership taught by Dr. Covey have guided many of the changes that the school has undertaken. One of the four crucial roles of leadership is to model, or "walk the talk of leadership." Leadership is modeled at Combs in the following initiatives:

- **Spotlight on Leadership.** Through this program, the school invites local, state, and national leaders to be interviewed by its students, underscoring the guests' leadership qualities and accomplishments as well as the contributions they have made to the community.
- **Student Greeters.** In this practice, students who model social etiquette and strong communication skills meet each visitor at the entrance to the school.
- **Laboratory for Learning.** Combs has provided more than 200 hours of staff development training in a four-year period. It has been recognized as a model elementary school for leadership development in young children, with teams of teachers serving as consultants and trainers for elementary schools across the United States and Canada.
- **Leadership Day Programs.** In that same four-year period, more than 3,200 educators from around the world have visited the school to learn more about the school's leadership development model through its Leadership Day programs. The school has recently hosted international guests from 26 countries.

Alignment

Another of the four roles of leadership, alignment, assures that processes, systems, and human resources are reflected in the school's mission. To align classroom instruction with student achievement, many different assessment techniques are used to reflect student progress, including the following:

- **Elimination of random acts of improvement.** To ensure that everything that Combs does is aligned with its vision and mission, each initiative is examined to validate its place in student achievement. Baldrige Criteria and the application of quality tools enhance classroom instruction and promote continuous academic improvement. The staff and students developed criteria for excellence and then designed and adopted rubrics that resulted in significant increases in the caliber and quality of project-based work.
- **Data notebooks, electronic portfolios, and student-led conferences.** At the beginning of each nine-week period, students, in collaboration with their parents and teacher, set their own personal and academic goals. Progress toward these goals is charted daily in students' data notebooks or electronic portfolios, which serve as the basis for quarterly student-led parent-teacher conferences.
- **Victory folders and self-assessment.** Each week, students are given the opportunity to reflect on their work and select samples of their finest efforts for insertion in their Victory Folders. These samples create a portfolio of student work that charts progress over the course of the year.
- **Achievement as measured by standardized tests.** According to the North Carolina state standards, schools with more than 90% of end-of-grade test scores at or above grade level are designated Schools of Excellence by the State Board of Education.

Mission Statement

Staff members know that they are making a difference in the lives of their students. Evidence can be found in classroom grades and scores on standardized tests, but even more so in students' perspective of what is possible in their lives. This change was most evident in the student-led creation of the program's mission statement. The children, led by a master Baldrige/Covey teacher, created the following mission statement through a process of asking *Why?* five times:

Chapter 3: Setting High Expectations and a Vision as a Transformational Leader

Q: Why are you at Kids Club?
A: To get help with homework.

Q: Why do you need help with homework?
A: So we can pass to the next grade.

Q: Why do you want to pass to the next grade?
A: So we are not in the same grade next year.

Q: Why don't you want to be in the same grade?
A: So we can go to college.

Q: Why do you want to go to college?
A: To make our dreams come true.

The mission statement motivates students and inspires everyone involved with the program. As a Combs ESL teacher remarked, "This is the first time I have ever heard the children express an awareness of college, let alone a desire to attend."

Combs students understand that true leaders give back to their community. Each grade-level team of students undertakes a community service project, such as collecting toys for needy children, conducting a winter coat drive, or raising funds for the Duke University Cancer Ward. Students also give back through schoolwide efforts, such as collecting canned goods for the North Carolina Food Bank. Combs has collected more food than any other school in eastern North Carolina. However, student generosity is most evident in gestures of the heart, such as raising more than $1,400 to help a classmate's fight against leukemia, collecting a mountain of goods and donations for an immigrant family that unexpectedly lost its father, and raising more than $1,400 for Oprah's Leadership Academy for Girls.

Leadership is also a focus for parent and community involvement. A Leadership Advisory Council, composed of parents and community leaders, provides feedback on leadership initiatives. Effective integration of technology is about increasing student engagement and learning; it is not just about changing the way that education happens. It is also about changing the way that everyone thinks about teaching and learning. More information, ideas, and professional development activities related to parent involvement are found in the International Center's handbooks *Engaging Parents in Student Learning — Grades K6* and *Engaging Parents in Student Learning — Grades 7–12*.

A Systemwide Approach to Leadership

Summary

Leadership in schools is essential to the improvement of student achievement. The Transformational Leadership Framework provides a mental model to guide leaders as they move toward transformational leadership practices. Transformational leadership builds a culture of high expectations with a shared vision, mission, and goals.

Reflection Activity

1. Consider the following statement:

    "School leadership is not a position; it is a *disposition* for taking action."

    What attitudes and actions of school leaders would demonstrate the truth of this statement? Share and discuss your responses with others.

2. Think about the characteristics of a transformational leader. Which specific characteristics do you feel would most impact student achievement at your school or in your district? Why? Write a short summary of your response.

3. Creating a shared vision and mission is an essential part of school leadership. Consider the following questions:

    - Does your school have a vision statement? Does it clearly describe a picture of the "preferred future" of the school? Does it emphasize high expectations? How could the vision statement be improved?

    - Does the school's mission statement clearly identify the school's purpose? What changes would you propose for the mission statement?

    - Does the school have a set of defined goals? Are they current? Is there a BHAG (Big Hairy Audacious Goal) that inspires your school community?

Chapter 4

Instructional Leadership

Instructional leadership is a key component of the DSEI. In Chapter 3, the concepts of context, target, and management practices as they relate to school leadership were introduced. Here, we will examine each of these concepts in an in-depth way. The role of data in leadership and decision making is also explored in this chapter.

Using Instructional Leadership to Address Challenges

Instructional leadership is one of a school leader's most important responsibilities, and its positive impact on student achievement is documented by Hattie. (Hattie, John, *Visible Learning*) Unfortunately, it is often neglected. Addressing instruction requires action over a long period of time, but leaders frequently are called upon to attend to more urgent problems. Challenges that require sustained vigilance are considered "adaptive challenges" while issues that are resolved through quicker, more definitive action are called "technical challenges." By better understanding how to address instructional leadership as a unique adaptive problem, school leaders can become more effective in supporting staff to deliver the highest-quality instruction.

Because technical challenges and adaptive challenges differ fundamentally, addressing them requires two very different approaches. In their work around leadership, Ronald Heifetz and Martin Linsky of the John F. Kennedy School of Government at Harvard University describe these types of challenges (Heifetz, R., and Linsky, M., "When Leadership Spells Danger"):

> Problems that we can solve through the knowledge of experts are technical challenges. Problems that the experts cannot solve are called adaptive challenges. Solutions to technical problems lie in the head and solving them requires intellect and logic. Solutions to adaptive problems lie in the stomach and the heart and rely on changing people's beliefs, habits, ways of working, or ways of life.

School leaders constantly are called upon to solve technical challenges such as school facility issues, transportation issues, and student behavioral issues. School leaders must address these challenges, but doing so can be time consuming. If not addressed, however, technical challenges can have significant impacts on teaching and learning within the school.

One good thing about technical challenges is that they often can be dispatched through set procedures and with limited involvement by others. Generally, success is easy to measure through follow-up observation. In the case of a facilities issue such as a boiler problem, for example, the principal makes a call or two to have the problem addressed and follows up to make sure that the matter has been resolved. Handling a chronically late school bus might be more involved, but a conversation with the bus driver or transportation director may identify the cause of the problem and enable a solution. The complexity of student behavioral issues varies according to the circumstances, but schools have specific guidelines and procedures for handling these situations. Usually, an administrator selects the appropriate actions and carries them out with the involvement of the student and and/or parents.

Over time, a leader can use proven procedures, norms, and methods to build expertise in handling technical challenges. A Quadrant A authoritative leadership style is appropriate for addressing these types of issues efficiently. No teams need to be consulted, no meetings are necessary, no consultation is needed, and no additional learning is required. Resolution requires identifying a solution and taking action.

Adaptive challenges are much more complex than technical challenges. There are no specific scripts or steps to follow that result in a quick and easy resolution. Leaders who see instructional leadership only as a series of technical challenges are likely to fail in addressing the larger challenge of persuading people within the system to adopt a change. Heifetz asserts that "the biggest source of failure in leadership is treating adaptive challenges as technical problems." Clearly, improving instructional leadership is a far more complicated undertaking than ensuring that a school bus arrives on time. As described by Heifetz and Linsky (Heifetz, R., and Linsky, M., *Leadership on the Line: Staying Alive Through the Dangers of Leading*):

Adaptive challenges require experiments, discoveries, and adjustments from many places in the organization or community. To make the adaptive leap to survive in the new environment requires people to learn new ways of behaving and adopt new values and attitudes. Sustaining change requires the people with the problem to internalize the change itself.

Adaptive challenges require a more systemic approach, along with the collaborative leadership style characteristic of transformational leadership. Addressing an adaptive challenge — such as instructional improvement — requires significant intervention over a longer period of time, using more complex strategies that are intended to change other people's attitudes and behaviors. To find a solution, a leader must empower leadership throughout the organization and cultivate a common vision. The leader must be prepared to consult with others, to research, and to learn.

In order for an adaptive challenge to be addressed successfully, people within the system must change over time. An adaptive challenge is influenced greatly by the varied beliefs and emotions of the people involved, so addressing the challenge fully requires flexibility. Proposed solutions may have unexpected consequences. Just as a stone thrown into a pond creates ripples that radiate in all directions, so, too, can a leader's efforts to move toward resolution. When a leader attempts to solve an adaptive challenge, he or she should be prepared for a ripple effect to spread throughout the organization.

Since adaptive change involves bringing together people who have different viewpoints, attempts to solve challenges on a schoolwide level may produce a wide range of reactions. Even when they are committed to seeking solutions, various factions of people will worry about the impacts on their own responsibilities. They may lobby for changes in the solution to diminish the effect on their comfort zone of day-to-day work. Even if the leader has the best solution for an adaptive problem, that solution may not be achieved or may be perceived as ineffective because of the opposition that evolves through attempts at implementation. Consequently, even good solutions often are judged as failures, which is an added burden for leaders attempting to address the adaptive challenge.

Adaptive challenges must be approached in a more systematic manner than is done for technical challenges. Too often, leaders try to implement an instructional practice, such as a professional learning community, in the same manner in which they might address a technical problem, such as a late school bus. Simply giving directions and laying out expectations will not make it happen. Approaching an adaptive challenge requires a leader to take a wider view of the organization. While successful schools offer lessons about which best practices work and how to implement them, each school is unique. Nonetheless, there are three questions that instructional leaders should consider as they attempt to address an adaptive problem:

1. Which parts of the "organizational DNA" must be altered or discarded in order to achieve the school's instruction vision?
2. Which parts of the school's DNA must be preserved?
3. How will creativity and innovation be stimulated to create a new, more adaptive DNA and school culture?

The reflection activity at the end of this chapter will give you an opportunity to apply these questions to an adaptive challenge your school is facing.

Of course, not all problems fall neatly into the categories of technical challenge or adaptive challenge. Some aspects of instructional leadership are technical. For example, the process used to select textbooks, the methods used to prepare students for specific exams, or the steps used to create a new course all pose technical challenges. Each of these elements contributes to instructional change; however, the bigger issue of modifying instruction is more adaptive in nature.

To bring about instructional change, instructional leaders must understand the leadership role. This is where the Transformational Leadership Framework, described in Chapter 3, is essential, for it offers leaders a mental model to guide their daily actions and to think about situational interventions. The next part of the process involves three steps: (1) creating a context for instructional change, (2) defining a specific target for instructional change, and (3) developing an array of instructional leadership practices. This three-part process will yield instructional changes that have lasting impacts.

Creating a Context for Instructional Leadership

The first of the three big approaches to instructional leadership is to address context. *Context* involves looking at the school environment, particularly the staff — the way staff members work together and what they think about teaching and learning. If context is not addressed, even the most effective instructional practices will fail.

Creating a context for leadership utilizes three main areas of strategy: (1) staff relationships, (2) collaboration, and (3) sense of purpose and urgency.

Staff Relationships

Relationships are the foundation of the context for instructional leadership. A school leader cannot move very far or very fast until strong positive relationships are established and there is a high level of trust. For teachers to make changes in instruction, they must take risks and try new techniques so that school change can develop over time. Teachers are reluctant to take risks unless they have supportive relationships with peers who can encourage them when they try new approaches or are unsuccessful in initial attempts. This is why context is so important: It sets a foundation within a school community in which instructional innovation can flourish. School leaders must nurture relationships in order to create a positive climate for instructional improvement.

The Relationship Model

Relationships are an essential element in school success. In working with model schools across the nation, the International Center has endeavored to help schools recognize relationships as a viable aspect of school improvement. This work has led to the development of a Relationship Model. A clear taxonomy for relationships enables schools to quantify relationships in a manner similar to the way in which the Knowledge Taxonomy and the Application Model have helped define *knowledge* and *application* on the Rigor/Relevance Framework.

The Relationship Model can drive improvement by helping schools connect people to learning. The model can be used to describe relationships between and among students, between adults and students, and between and among adults. In this setting, the model is used to describe staff relationships. It describes seven levels of relationships within a collaborative learning community:

> **Level 0 — Isolated:** Staff members perform their work but feel significant isolation from other staff or a lack of frequent feedback from school leaders and others.
>
> **Level 1 — Known:** Staff members know each other personally, including one another's interests, aspirations, and challenges.
>
> **Level 2 — Receptive:** Teachers, support staff, and leaders have frequent contact and respect each other's contributions to the school environment. All exhibit behaviors of interest in others.
>
> **Level 3 — Reactive:** There are many examples of teachers or support staff working together, and staff members consistently and eagerly help when requested.
>
> **Level 4 — Proactive:** Strong levels of collaboration exist, and there is obvious ongoing commitment to team teaching, mentoring new teachers, and professional development.

Level 5 — Sustained: There is demonstrated, ongoing collaboration from all staff over a significant period of time. New staff members are incorporated into the school culture of collaboration.

Level 6 — Mutually Beneficial: Staff members work as a total community, committed to each other and to school goals.

Quantifying Relationships: The We Survey Suite

Asking students and staff for feedback about their experiences in school can initiate innovative, meaningful school change. The *We Survey* suite is a straightforward tool to help school leaders gather essential insight about the people who make up their school. The suite includes five surveys, which can be used together or independently. Each survey takes about 10 minutes to administer. Items are rated on a Likert scale from "strongly agree" to "strongly disagree."

The *We Learn — Student Survey*, designed for grades 6–12 or grades 3–5, asks students to respond to statements related to rigor, relevance, relationships, and leadership. Among other goals, it seeks to determine whether students feel challenged or see the connections between school and the real world. Sample statements include:

- This school has high expectations for all students.
- My teachers present lessons in different ways.
- My teachers know my academic interests and goals.
- Students are involved in important decisions at school.

The *We Teach — Instructional Staff Survey* is for the adults who have a role in teaching and learning in the classroom. This survey is a companion to the *We Learn* surveys so that perceptions of staff and students can be compared. Items also relate to rigor, relevance, relationships, and leadership and include such statements as:

- In my class, students discuss and solve open-ended questions and problems.
- There is strong communication between school administration and staff.
- I make learning exciting for my students.
- I am a source of encouragement for my students.

The *We Lead — Whole Staff Survey* assesses staff perceptions of the school administration. Items are based on three key elements, which have been identified by the Successful Practices Network in partnership with the International Center as essential aspects of leadership in successful schools. In order for students to reach their full potential, a school must have (1) a coherent vision, (2) empowerment, (3) school management, (4) culture of learning, and (5) community partnerships. *We Lead* survey statements include:

- I am supported to grow professionally.
- School administrators see me as a leader.
- The school administration creates a climate of trust.
- I am proud of this school.

The *We Support — Parent/Community Survey* is intended for all community members. This survey assesses community perceptions of the school experience as well as the community's expectations of the school system. Sample items include:

- The school system helps students develop healthy attitudes for success in life.
- The school system helps students make informed decisions about post-high school plans.
- Students of all abilities are encouraged equally in the district.

Collaboration

Schools focused on continuous school improvement engage in specific practices to improve the quality of the connections that influence staff collaboration, such as collecting feedback from the We Surveys. Practices like this are divided into two types: (1) *collaborative behaviors* — ways that leaders and staff behave to form good relationships, and (2) *collaborative initiatives* — strategies schools implement to support staff in working together. Data collected from the We Surveys can help inform perceptions of the collaborative nature of the school.

Successful collaboration results when values and attitudes are shared among staff, opportunities for collaborative behaviors are nurtured, and collaborative initiatives that encourage cooperative efforts are put into place. Strong leadership is at the foundation of strong collaboration, so school leaders should start by reflecting on their own behaviors and requesting constructive feedback from staff. There are specific initiatives that help to create high levels of staff cooperation, but these are effective only if the school leader has cultivated a collaborative culture.

Following is a discussion of seven types of collaborative behaviors.

Showing Respect

Respect is one of the most frequently cited essential behaviors. All teachers should be respected equally, whether they are providing AP French instruction or basic mathematics skills to struggling learners. School leaders must pay close attention to how they treat each teacher and every staff person in the school. Likewise, it is important to call attention to any disrespectful staff behaviors. Disagreements are natural — in fact, they are integral to the improvement process — but in successful schools, staff are able to disagree and still respect one another.

"Being There," Frequent Contact, Active Listening

It is difficult, if not impossible, to collaborate with colleagues effectively if one is not present, both physically and mentally. "Being there" means focusing fully on each and every person during personal contact, regardless of other pressures or how trivial a question or concern may seem. School leaders are always busy and have incredible demands on their time. Despite this, they must strive to give each person full attention. Strong leaders encourage this behavior in others, supporting the foundation for improved staff relationships.

Frequent contact, verbal or written, is essential to collaboration. How staff members communicate is established through the administration. Consider how memoranda, meetings, and e-mails can enhance relationships within the school walls. Leaders who are absent or who are perceived to be absent or uninterested are not effective.

Finally, active listening — rephrasing what is heard as a question or opinion to ensure understanding of another's point of view — shows respect and interest, which fosters ongoing, open communication.

Building Trust

Trust is a fundamental element in effective organizational change. Think of trust as a lubricant: With a liberal amount of trust, even the biggest changes glide toward implementation more easily. Without it, friction dominates; every little movement becomes a struggle, and progress is slow.

Steven Covey, noted leadership and personal skill speaker and author, points out that to build trust among others, you must first trust yourself. He describes self-trust as credibility. Increasing one's credibility means renewing a focus on integrity, intent, capabilities, and results. Integrity is more than being honest; it is "walking the talk" and acting in a manner that is consistent with the delivered message. Self-trust also is about building competence and getting results. Covey has identified 13 behaviors that are characteristic of highly trusted leaders (Covey, Stephen. *The Speed of Trust: The One Thing That Changes Everything*):

1. **Talk straight.** Trusted leaders are honest and straightforward in all conversations, avoid false flattery, do not talk behind others' backs, and do not hold back information or attempt to spin communication to manipulate others' thoughts or actions.

2. **Demonstrate respect.** Effective leaders behave in ways that show genuine care for others and show them that they are valued regardless of their position in the organization.

3. **Create transparency.** When a leader is genuine and honest in all dealings and avoids secrets, hidden agendas, and false impressions, he or she earns trust.

4. **Right wrongs.** These leaders take actions to correct mistakes or make restitutions. They apologize when they are wrong.

5. **Show loyalty.** Trusted leaders give credit to others and always speak about them as if they are in the room.

6. **Deliver results.** A trusted leader defines the desired results of any action well in advance and ensures that they are within his or her capabilities. Then he or she devotes the energy to making those results occur.

7. **Get better.** Continuous improvement — both personal and for others — should be a leader's goal. Stagnating at a particular level of expertise does not inspire trust.

8. **Confront reality.** Leaders who take on real issues earn others' respect and trust. They do not avoid tough issues hoping they will disappear, and they do not take the easy or popular approach if they do not feel it is the best course.

9. **Clarify expectations.** To prevent mistrust, an effective leader makes sure everyone understands and agrees to the expectations. This instills trust that people can meet expectations and prevents misunderstandings, disappointments, or a sense of false promises.

10. **Practice accountability.** Trusted leaders hold themselves and others accountable for responsibilities.

11. **Listen first.** Trust in a leader is strengthened when he or she seeks to understand another's thoughts, feelings, and viewpoint before trying to influence or prescribe a solution.

12. **Keep commitments.** When leaders follow through on commitments, they build hope and trust among staff.
13. **Extend trust.** The most trusted leaders understand that trust is reciprocal. When trust is extended, trust is earned.

Enthusiasm, Positive Humor, Avoiding Put-Downs

Enthusiasm and positive humor make the hard work of school less burdensome. Enthusiasm is contagious; and when staff members observe their leader being excited, energetic, and smiling, it helps to diminish feelings of frustration and fatigue. Leaders should be passionate and should look for opportunities to exhibit positive humor. They must take their work seriously, but they must not take themselves too seriously. Staff members often respond well when a leader looks for opportunities to poke fun at his or her own personality and role as school leader. However, when seeking humor, leaders must be sure to avoid put-downs when it comes to others.

Identifying and Encouraging Talents and Strengths

Leaders need to make a special effort to encourage staff members by identifying and celebrating their unique talents or strengths. Asking someone to take on new responsibilities, try new things, or attempt to accomplish something again in hopes of greater success shows a leader's interest and supportiveness. A leader can convey a sense of value through encouraging notes or comments, assignments related to a staff member's distinctive skills, and other forms of recognition.

Celebrating Accomplishments, Praising Peers, Being a Role Model

Instructional leaders should look for ways to celebrate staff members' accomplishments, such as putting extra effort into making significant progress toward specific goals. Finding ways to show appreciation personally — for example, direct praise, a handwritten a note, or a shared compliment with a teacher's spouse, partner, mentor, or other significant person in his or her life — conveys warmth and appreciation.

Praise from peers is even more important. Peer recognition helps to foster good working relationships and supports collaborative approaches. Leaders should encourage peers to compliment one another on good work, especially through modeling the behaviors.

One-to-One Communication, Encouraging Idea Sharing

Being an effective leader requires more than the ability to lead, serve as a spokesperson, stand up in front of a group and talk, or manage a meeting. While these all are important roles, some of the most important, but least visible, work of a leader occurs through one-to-one communication. Large meetings may be a venue for reinforcing the vision, but individual conversations are essential for building staff relationships. Such communication provides opportunities for personalized encouragement, coaching, or feedback about negative behaviors. When trying to get volunteers to take on a new challenge, staff may be reluctant to volunteer in a group meeting; a one-to-one conversation, however, can create a more comfortable setting for a staff member to take on something new. These conversations are also important in encouraging staff to express ideas and opinions.

Collaborative Initiatives

Providing opportunities for focused professional collaboration and growth is one of the five overarching elements of the instructional leadership segment of the DSEI. A series of 10 collaborative initiatives is described below.

Social Activities

Developing shared visions and goals for the school community and encouraging collaboration are enhanced by opportunities for teachers to meet, socialize, and get to know each other not only as colleagues but also as people. This is particularly important at the start of a school year. Unlike most jobs, teachers have up to eight weeks of separation from their fellow employees during summer vacation. At the beginning of a new school year, there is some trepidation and uncertainty as the staff reconvenes to begin another year. Welcome luncheons, picnics, and breakfasts sponsored by the administrative leadership or the parent organization are ways of developing and rekindling friendly, supportive relationships.

New teachers, especially, benefit from social activities. Start-of-school events provide a setting for introductions and help new faculty, staff members, and student teachers begin to integrate into the school culture. New staff feel supported when they are invited to lunch, introduced to others by veteran staff members, offered assistance in locating classrooms or supplies, and so forth. These small but significant activities send a welcoming message and lay a foundation for trust and collaboration.

A Systemwide Approach to Leadership

Team Building

Authentic relationships are fostered through shared work and shared responsibilities. Providing opportunities for staff to work together and participate in team-building strategies and training sessions support collaboration. Creating student groups that are taught by interdisciplinary teams of teachers or organizing a school into small learning communities are two strategies for integrating team building into a school's culture.

Interdisciplinary teaching teams usually share the same physical space and have common planning time. Because teaching teams share the same students, there are more opportunities to personalize learning. Together, the team can focus on student needs more easily. Before individuals can be expected to contribute well in team teaching, however, they must develop friendly relationships and trust with their fellow team members. Instructional leaders can help foster trust among staff by arranging for team-building strategies, such as trust walks and ropes courses. Activities such as these create a sense of interdependence, as team members must work together to succeed. The cooperative-action-for-success mindset developed through these types of activities is intended to carry over into the teaching team's collaborative capacity and creativity.

Instructional leaders need to cultivate an awareness of unity for all team members. Each team member must recognize that there are opportunities to contribute to the team, learn from others, and work together to achieve common goals. Leadership empowers the team to act together to reach a joint objective, thus enabling the team to function effectively in a participative leadership manner. Every team member feels responsibility for the team's success, all team members share a common purpose and a sense of ownership in the work, and communications within the team create a climate of trust and openness.

Rewards, Recognition, and Incentives

Everyone likes to be recognized for work well done, and educators are no exception. Rewards, recognition, and incentives motivate teachers to participate in the school community. Recognition affirms for teachers the value of their profession and their contributions to it. It is important to recognize publicly professional achievements and milestones, such as an instructional success, the attainment of a degree, the completion of a professional development activity, or the development of a curriculum, curricular map, or Gold Seal Lesson. Announcing teacher accomplishments at schoolwide meetings, in parent newsletters, or in the school newspaper are common ways to provide teachers with recognition.

As with learners, teachers respond positively to recognition and are motivated to continue to develop activities and initiatives that improve teaching and learning. Rewards must be known, and the criteria for receiving them need to be defined clearly. Typical incentives for educators include financial honorariums, time allotted during the school day to engage in planning for various initiatives, and opportunities to assume leadership roles. Just as schools have monthly student awards, some schools hand out teacher- or employee-of-the-month awards. A teacher might be awarded a temporary, special parking place near the building or other special privilege for a school contribution. Summer scholarships for additional study in a teacher's discipline or area of expertise are an excellent incentive for some educators. Candidates for this type of an award may have to apply and indicate why they feel they deserve the honor. Summer internships at local businesses or organizations also may be motivators.

Character Education

Character education programs are usually associated with students, but well-designed programs for staff have the same benefits as those for students. As with character education for students, programs for staff result in teachers who perform more effectively, show greater self-control, demonstrate better control of their anger and frustration levels, and are more willing to share with others. When an effective program is in place, staff recognize that character education can strengthen positive personal relationships.

Character education refers to activities and behaviors that focus on the development of personal characteristics that promote:

- high levels of personal and academic functioning
- positive interpersonal relationships
- a school environment conducive to teaching, learning, and academic achievement
- successful adult roles and contributions to society

Most character education programs are based on a series of guiding principles. The International Center has identified 12 guiding principles to consider when building a character education program: (1) adaptability, (2) compassion, (3) contemplation, (4) courage, (5) honesty, (6) initiative, (7) loyalty, (8) optimism, (9) perseverance, (10) respect, (11) responsibility, and (12) trustworthiness. In a well-organized character education program, these principles become part of everyday experiences, activities, and interactions in the school. Faculty and staff promote and model these guiding principles; and functioning by them supports a more sensitive, caring, friendly, cooperative, and helpful atmosphere for staff and students alike.

A Systemwide Approach to Leadership

Conflict Resolution

Conflict occurs when there is disagreement about ideas or actions. Poor communication among groups or individuals, differences in the sense of mission, a lack of openness and honesty, individual needs or egos, or an individual's pursuit of power at the expense of others may contribute to conflict in an organization. Dissatisfaction with the current leadership (because it is weak or, perhaps, because there has been a recent change in leadership) may also lead to clashes throughout the organization.

Though conflict is inevitable, it may be minimized, solved, or even harnessed to create positive change. Recognizing the cause of conflict is a first step in resolving the problem. Causes of conflict include:

- needs or wants not being met
- limited knowledge
- differing values
- unrealistic expectations
- assumptions translated into fact
- perceptions and values being questioned
- differences in personality, values, race, or gender

Conflict can be either destructive or constructive. It is destructive when it polarizes people and decreases collaboration and cooperation. Sometimes, conflict may divert attention to areas that are not significant. In some instances, it may lead to irresponsible decisions or behaviors. Conflict is constructive when it helps to relieve anxiety and stress. When instructional leaders support a culture of strong relationships, then cooperation, support, and understanding become more natural responses. Sometimes, conflict may lead to solutions to problems facing the group.

Groups experiencing conflict must collaborate to reach some sort of consensus or general agreement. When group members collaborate, each individual is respected and supported. All members are permitted to provide their opinions, whether they agree or disagree. Holding differing points of view is commonplace and healthy for a group. Eventually, the group reaches a point of acceptance and forms some kind of consensus.

In highly successful schools, instructional leaders ensure that staff members experience and demonstrate respect for one another throughout the conflict resolution process. Consensus is not reached until everyone has an opportunity to share ideas and willingly agrees to the compromise.

Travel

Travel can be an effective element in a district's professional development plans. Travel of all types — extended release time, exchange programs, internships, and professional conferences — has the potential to support professional growth, increase an educator's personal and professional self-esteem, expand knowledge, improve instructional technique, and more. Ultimately, students profit from their teachers' adventures.

Some school districts offer teachers extended release time or sabbaticals. Many teachers use sabbaticals to travel and enrich their knowledge of the subjects they teach. International experiential education opportunities allow teachers to learn unique pedagogical approaches found in different parts of the world. Other study abroad programs may focus on countries in which students face daily challenges unlike those that students in this country face. In these situations, the teacher usually meets with members of the business community and other leaders to gain a deeper understanding of the culture and its impact on education. Teacher travel exchanges also can be worthwhile. There are a number of options for teachers to explore. A teacher might exchange positions with someone in his or her own discipline, for example. For a language teacher, exchanging with a colleague from a native-speaking country of their language of expertise may be exciting. Using an exchange to immerse himself or herself in a culture about which he or she teaches benefits a teacher personally and professionally.

When teachers travel together to attend professional conferences and workshops or to chaperone students on field trips closer to home, the travel experience can serve as an opportunity for relationships to form and grow. When staff members attend a conference together, for instance, they may discuss the value and relevance of the ideas learned. From these conversations, the group may initiate dialogue about a new program, curriculum, assessment instrument, or other activity within the school community.

Sharing Life Stories

Everyone has a story to tell, and effective instructional leaders understand the value of encouraging staff to share life stories. Uncovering life stories involves two basic but essential tasks: asking questions, and truly listening to the responses. Even the most basic questions — Why did you become a teacher? What were your first teaching responsibilities? What is your most enjoyable teaching experience? Who is your education hero and why? — can create valuable opportunities to build and strengthen relationships.

Storytelling is one of the most effective methods for engaging, teaching, increasing group participation, and establishing trust. As the pace continues to quicken in our high-speed society, it is increasingly important to find ways to build interpersonal connections and a sense of community. Storytelling is an effective and timeless communication skill. Telling relevant personal stories can be a fun, informative, and interesting way for a leader to help group members develop a sense of humanness, realness, and trust about him or her. This supports a sense of cohesiveness within the group, which supports the group in progressing toward its goals. Small-group settings allow staff to share and listen to stories while building relationships and trust.

When sharing personal stories:

- **Do** talk about personal experiences; they are best for engendering trust.
- **Do** keep stories succinct and interesting.
- **Do** tell stories that offer a deeper message or meaning.
- **Do** tell stories well and with appropriate emotional engagement.
- **Do** be certain that stories relate to the group's mission and ideally help move the group forward.
- **Don't** tell stories to avoid or dance around what is happening in the group.
- **Don't** tell a story that may be offensive or involves someone who might not want it told.

Family Partnerships

Teachers and instructional leaders need to reach out to parents and engage them in their student's program. Making connections with a student's family usually strengthens the support a student receives for learning. When parents understand the school's programs and vision as well as the learning goals for their children, they tend to be more supportive of instructional activities, classroom rules and policies, grading systems, and so forth.

Schools may use methods such as these to involve parents:

- social events, such as a family days, school picnics, "get to know your school" nights, and the like
- volunteer opportunities for activities, such as tutoring or chaperoning student trips

Chapter 4: Instructional Leadership

- dinner events that include a brief program focusing on a priority issue
- information sessions and/or printed materials describing instructional approaches or explaining a new assessment program
- presentations about college admissions, scholarship opportunities, and financial assistance programs
- meetings to explain specific programs
- student-led conferences
- parent-teacher organizations
- school visits

Community and Business Partnerships

Having a community or business partner can bring many benefits to a school, classroom, and teacher. Business partners may donate up-to-date equipment to the school or allow students and teachers to access their equipment. They may offer internships or summer jobs for teachers and/or students. They may provide awards for exceptional teacher performance or student achievement. Some community partners create and manage collaborative programs to support learning while building relationships among a range of organizations.

In support of instruction, a business partner may be able to advise teachers about curriculum. This is especially helpful in career and technical education programs or career academies, where members of the business community serve as advisors. The International Center's handbook *Convergence of Academics and Career and Technical Education* is an in-depth resource that can be used to explore the advantages of CTE. Because the global marketplace changes so quickly, it can be difficult for an educator to stay current in the practices within some fields. Through internships or summer work, teachers gain insight into the expectations and requirements of a particular workplace or field. This helps them to create engaging and relevant lessons for their students.

Community and business representatives may support instruction through mentoring programs for students, student internships, or student work study opportunities. Some businesses encourage employees to serve as tutors for students who need academic assistance.

Individuals from the community and businesses may also become a part of a school's character education program. At Kennesaw Mountain High School in Kennesaw, Georgia, business and community representatives co-teach the character education program. A senior student presents a guiding principle or character trait, and the business or community representative provides real-world examples of how it is applied.

Businesses benefit from partnerships with schools, too. A vibrant public education system is part of a healthy community. When they engage in partnerships with schools, businesses support the health of the communities where their employees and customers live and work. Businesses also benefit by having the chance to get to know students whose talents and interests might make them excellent employees in the future.

Community Service

A number of schools require students to complete a specified number of hours in community service programs. When a teacher is asked to identify service opportunities for students, he or she has a chance to meet or speak with many community members, including representatives from various community and governmental agencies, churches and synagogues, and civic and service organizations. In this way, these programs offer important life experience for students; they also result in positive public relations for the school, students, and staff.

Just as students participate in community service programs, many educators participate as well. Among other benefits, community service provides opportunities for teachers to feel personal satisfaction, create a better school image, and gain a deeper understanding of the community and its relationship to the school's mission and goals. Networking that may occur through these connections also may lead to additional beneficial partnerships with the school.

Finding Time for Collaboration

One of the most frequently cited reasons for lack of collaboration is lack of time. With a priority on instruction and the obligation of keeping students fully supervised during school hours, teachers may find collaborative time difficult to come by. This situation must be rectified if schools sincerely expect to have an impact on instruction. To accomplish lasting changes in instruction, teachers need to observe, discuss, and reflect about instruction with their colleagues. It is essential to ensure that teachers are given time to collaborate.

Once planning time has been created, teachers can maximize its value by avoiding loose agendas. The practical value of collaboration time is enhanced when the team focuses on specific instructional needs, such as improving student writing or implementing differentiated instruction practices. Successful schools have found creative ways to fulfill state requirements, negotiate employment contracts, and properly supervise students — and still make time for teachers to collaborate. Following are some ways that schools can carve out time for teacher collaboration.

Use master schedules. The best, but perhaps hardest, way to create time for collaboration is to build it into the school day as part of the master schedule. A master schedule that allows teachers to have time to work together in both interdisciplinary teams (small learning communities) and content teams is best. It is important to decide up front what the priority is and to start with that to build the master schedule. For example, many schools have found that teachers will naturally find discretionary time to meet with colleagues in the same discipline but that teachers on interdisciplinary teams who work with a common group of students may be less likely to meet on their own. In these instances, schools may have greater impact on student achievement by creating collaborative time for interdisciplinary teacher teams formed around a group of students.

Daily and weekly team time within the school day must be given the highest priority in the master schedule. Class schedules should be planned after group planning times are placed on the schedule. Some schools find that in order to accommodate essential planning time for groups of teachers, they must adjust the number of special offerings for students.

Schedule late arrival or early dismissal days. Periodic 90-minute late arrival or early dismissal days will not reduce instructional time significantly, but such time blocks can provide precious collaboration opportunities for teachers. Some schools use late arrival or early dismissal days on a monthly basis to ensure that regular team planning time is available.

Some middle schools and high schools schedule these blocks on a weekly basis to nurture staff collaboration. The International School of the Americas in San Antonio, Texas, for example, uses a four-week rotation, with one week for full staff meetings, one for grade-level meetings, one for department or subject meetings, and one for professional learning sessions.

Hire additional staff. Hiring floating substitute teachers to cover classrooms allows regular teachers to plan or learn together. Floating substitutes move through the school, class period by class period, to free up time for teachers to collaborate. Also, support staff and assistants can help to reduce the supervision duties that teachers frequently have so they can use that time for collaboration.

Use contractual staff development days. Most teacher contracts build in noninstructional days for professional development. Instead of scheduling general workshops for these days, schools can create multiple collaboration and staff development activities that meet individual needs. Instead of day-long, stand-alone activities, schools can try scheduling blocks of time across the calendar to provide shorter and more frequent school-based learning opportunities.

Modify staff meetings. Some schools find success in replacing some of their traditional full staff meeting times with collaboration sessions. Administrative business traditionally covered in staff meetings is accomplished through e-mails or other forms of communication so that professional collaboration can occur.

Create alternative learning days. Day-long, offsite field experiences for students can be organized in order to create collaboration blocks for teachers. Another way to free up time for teachers while creating meaningful experiences for students is to develop a series of student workshops led by parents, community members, or administrators.

Plan beyond the instructional calendar. Teachers may find great value in multi-day summer learning institutes that allow them to focus in-depth on areas of strategic importance for the district. Multi-day breaks for students during the school year can be used to support teacher learning.

School Leadership Teams

Leadership is one of the keys to school success, but it need not be vested in a single individual, such as a traditional school principal. Recall that the DSEI identifies building the leadership capacity of the school as a primary function of organizational leaders. Successful schools abound with models of distributed and shared leadership, which occurs when many are empowered to lead. In nearly all schools, it takes many leaders in various roles to make a successful school. This does not mean that a school has many independent decision makers working toward their own unique visions of learning. Shared leadership is successful only when there is a common vision. A shared understanding allows individual teachers and groups of teachers to make incremental decisions consistent with the overarching vision.

Chapter 4: Instructional Leadership

There are many different structures for staff involvement in building leadership teams. For example, there might be a traditional team that is composed of an elementary teacher from each grade level or a secondary school teacher from each department. In a school with multiple magnet programs or career academies, there might be a leadership team representing each sector of the school community. Multiple teams also may be formed around school functions, priorities, or goals, such as safety, instruction, partnerships, literacy, or technology.

For building-level leadership teams to be empowered to function effectively, they need to:

- have clearly defined responsibilities that align with the overall school vision
- meet frequently
- be held accountable by recording and communicating decisions and actions
- possess skills in communication and consensus decision making

Establish Critical Friends Groups. A Critical Friends Group (CFG) is a special structure of teacher collaboration that was created over the past decade by the Coalition of Essential Schools (CES), the National School Reform Faculty, and The Annenberg Institute. A CFG brings together small groups of teachers within a school for at least two years so that staff members can help each other look seriously at their classroom practices and make adjustments. The three key components of a critical friends group are (1) collegial support, (2) substantive conversation, and (3) collaborative inquiry.

After developing a solid grounding in group process skills, CFG members focus on setting learning goals for students and instructional strategies for themselves. The goals are stated specifically enough so that others can observe them in operation. CFGs devise strategies to move students toward the specified goals and collect evidence in a variety of ways. In a setting of mutual support and honest critical feedback from trusted peers, teachers strive to affirm their goals and revise their strategies.

CFG members share their students' work, lesson plans, case studies, classroom problems, peer observation evidence, and prospective texts and materials. Using specific protocols to guide the discussions, CFG members help each other fine-tune their teaching by analyzing and critiquing artifacts, observations, and issues pertaining to instructional practice. There are unique strategies for looking at student work, classroom observations, classroom dilemmas, or text-based conversations. The highly structured protocols are designed to produce high quality conversation and reflection to maximize the use of teacher collaboration time.

Successful CFGs usually meet with a trained coach or facilitator for at least two hours once or twice a month. Over the course of a school year, this can add up to 18–30 hours of teacher development. Many schools have multiple CFGs, and typically, the groups broaden their perspectives and connections with others through partnerships and regional meetings with CFGs from other schools.

Establish professional learning communities. A staff that functions as a professional learning community comes together for learning as a supportive group. Participants interact, test their ideas, challenge one another's ideas and interpretations, and process new information gleaned from one another. Typically, teachers meet to discuss topics of their own choosing related to instruction, student achievement, and assessment.

Authors and education researchers Shirley Hord and William Sommers assert there are five components of professional learning communities (Hord, Shirley M. and Sommers, William A. *Leading Professional Learning Communities: Voices from Research and Practice*):

1. shared beliefs, values, and vision
2. shared and supportive leadership
3. collective learning and its application
4. supportive condition
5. shared personal practice

When the five components are in place, a group is able to meet regularly to solve problems and make decisions. Doing so benefits teachers by:

- decreasing a sense of isolation
- increasing commitment to the school's mission and goals
- encouraging collaborative responsibility toward student achievement and school success
- renewing the motivation to teach
- lowering rates of absenteeism
- increasing knowledge about students' needs and successful teaching practices

Hold teams accountable for learning. Establishing teams is a positive step toward creating a context for empowered instructional leadership, but there must also be actions to hold teams accountable. Accountability is a combination of expectations and follow-

Chapter 4: Instructional Leadership

up, and it is an essential part of empowerment. Holding teachers accountable for student learning begins with building a belief system that reflects the premise that all students can and should learn. Observable teacher behaviors, actions, and words must communicate to each individual student, "I know you can learn what I am going to teach." High expectations are observable. It is the responsibility of school leaders to help teachers create a culture of high expectations.

Have the principal participate in team meetings. An instructional leader should participate occasionally in team meetings to have conversations with the teachers about expected student performance goals. It is very valuable for teachers to have opportunities to share issues, ideas, and teaching results not only with peers but also with the principal in a supportive atmosphere. Instructional leaders can help keep the team focused on achievement goals while offering support and help when needed. Their presence has a positive impact on productivity and performance by ensuring that everyone understands the learning expectations.

Focus on learning. Improvement comes when teachers change instructional practices in the classroom. Teams need to be reminded of this. Change is best accomplished using deliberate analysis and discussion in team meetings. Formative and summative student achievement data must be an incessant focus in team meetings. Who successfully taught an objective to students who had been struggling? Whose students made the most gains on an objective, and what strategies were used?

Teams can use district benchmarks or can develop their own to assess progress, but they must be timely and be incorporated as part of the process. Each teacher's results are examined so that the teacher can receive guidance for implementing better instructional strategies. The team should provide a forum for instructional practices and improvement to be discussed with an overall focus on results — namely, student learning.

Invite feedback. Successful instructional leaders invite students to bring to them directly any performance issues that teachers do not seem to be addressing. If teachers understand that their performance might be reflected in direct student feedback to the school's leader, they will act more responsibly in following up on team recommendations and working toward stated learning goals. Students play a role in instructional change. When students understand teachers' expectations of themselves and of the students, they become partners in the process.

Express expectations and recognize performance. Every interaction between a teacher and a student is an opportunity for learning. Instructional leaders should recognize performance and reinforce expectations at every opportunity. It is essential to acknowledge when teachers teach a rigorous lesson with depth and complexity. Doing so validates the importance of the time it takes to plan, teach, and grade in order to bring each student to a higher level of learning. One of the most effective ways to recognize teacher accomplishment is to spend time with teachers and students in the classroom and to applaud their work.

Share successes. Sharing successful strategies during team time is vital. Master teachers whose students learned the required content are able to address factors that interfere with learning and help develop solutions to overcome obstacles. They can model the concepts, guide practice problems, or share strategies for assessing understanding. The process follows these steps: (1) instruction occurs, (2) student learning is assessed, and (3) student scores are reviewed in a team meeting. If the students do not score well, the teacher group can discuss approaches to help the teacher develop new strategies.

Nurture teacher leadership. As a result of planned team collaboration time, collegial relationships become supportive and positive. As problems arise, the team finds solutions. Teachers in need of help are coached to achieve increments of success. As teams become more confident, they become more willing to be held accountable. Members feel empowered to assume leadership roles in school improvement efforts. As team members, teachers may feel less threatened about expected performance. Each has the opportunity to ask for help; and if more intense training is needed, onsite or off-campus staff development sessions can be arranged.

Terminate ineffective teachers. There are instances when teachers do not improve and must be counseled into endeavors outside of education. Team efforts make it easier to make hard decisions about terminating ineffective teachers. When repeated opportunities for professional growth and support are offered but are unsuccessful, documentation exists to recommend termination. Termination should be a last resort, but teams that have been actively involved in improvement will support termination of poorly performing teachers if that becomes necessary. Collegial efforts should be considered part of each teacher's annual evaluation. This expectation should be communicated to the staff during every staff meeting.

Develop a sense of purpose and urgency. One of the key components for building a context for instructional leadership is to build a sense of purpose and urgency. Little will change in instruction if teachers do not feel a need to improve. Teacher teams must have a clear purpose and a sense of urgency to use their time wisely and productively. According to the DSEI, instructional leaders must offer proof statements, such as research or authoritative testimony, that helps establish a sense of urgency to change.

Become future-focused. Efforts to improve instruction through instructional leadership may leave teachers on the defensive. When teachers hear that their instruction must change and improve, they may focus their time on protecting the status quo rather than listening to new ideas and taking risks to try new approaches.

The vast majority of teachers are responsible, devote considerable effort to their work, and perform as well as their knowledge allows. Creating a sense of purpose and urgency for these teachers may require a delicate approach that includes recognition of what they have done well in the past while reflecting about what can be improved in the future. This approach will not work for the minority of teachers who choose not to work hard or whose efforts reflect minimal contributions to student learning. Teachers who knowingly perform at a low level require strong and direct supervision that requires them to put forth greater effort in improving instruction.

Focusing on the future is a positive and effective approach to improving instruction and changing practices. It is not useful to dwell on past behavior or current performance; doing so may lead teachers to become defensive, rather than motivated, about change. Instructional leaders should avoid presenting initiatives as efforts to fix something that is broken. Although there may be evidence of poor instructional practices, leaders are more successful if they avoid being overly critical of those practices and shift attention to the potential for success using new practices.

Successful change leaders enlist teachers' support for the implementation of instructional practices that will result in improvements of student achievement in the future. They encourage teachers to take risks, try new practices, evaluate effectiveness, and reinforce those practices that improve student achievement. A future focus is an important component of creating a context in which instructional leadership can take place in the school.

Commitment to 21st Century Learning

The term *21st century learning* has inspired many teachers, school leaders, and community leaders to raise expectations for education. While much of the discussion of 21st century skills has focused on preparing students for the future, it is time to face the fact that the future is now. The changing nature of work, technology, and competition in the global job market has far outpaced what the U.S. education system provides for students, despite ongoing efforts by educators and communities to improve their schools. Priorities and goals set by educators at all levels of academia are not closing the gap.

A Systemwide Approach to Leadership

Globalization and rapid technological advancements are having dramatic effects on the ways we communicate and conduct business in our professional and personal lives. Education should increase students' understanding of the world around them. Unfortunately, there is little or no connectivity or integration between subjects and grades in most American schools. As students move from class to class and progress through the grades, they are exposed to isolated bits of content-specific knowledge, but they are not taught how content across classes interconnects or how it can be applied in the world outside of school.

The failure to prepare students is not merely an academic conundrum: Employers are not satisfied with the degree to which students are being prepared for their chosen careers. In 2006, The Conference Board, Corporate Voices for Working Families, the Partnership for 21st Century Skills, and the Society for Human Resource Management produced the report *Are They Really Ready To Work? Employer's Perspectives on the Basic Knowledge and Applied Skills of New Entrants to the 21st Century U.S. Workforce.* Based on an extensive survey and interviews with human resource professionals, the report examines whether the skills of graduates of high school and two- and four-year colleges are adequate for success in today's workplace.

The results were overwhelmingly negative. The skills that most schools focus on are out of sync with what most employers want and need, which means that most students are not receiving an education that will help them to be successful outside of school. For example, the level of literacy required for entry-level jobs is higher than that of many graduates.

According to The Conference Board: "The education and business communities must agree that applied skills integrated with core academic subjects are the 'design specs' for creating an educational system that will prepare our high school and college graduates to succeed in the modern workplace and community life. These skills are in demand for all students, regardless of their future plans, and will have an enormous impact on our students' ability to compete."

The disconnection between what students are learning in classrooms and the learning that they need to succeed in the real world should not come as a surprise. Reports such as 1983's *A Nation at Risk* and others identified this troublesome trend long ago. So why are our students still so ill prepared? Workforce expert C. Michael Ferraro asserts that the basic problem is that "schools don't believe they are in the workforce readiness business." Instead, schools focus on academic excellence. (National Commission on Excellence in Education, *A Nation at Risk: The Imperative for Educational Reform*)

Chapter 4: Instructional Leadership

The need for change is clear, and Americans have been attempting to shift our nation's education focus to preparing students with the skills necessary to thrive in the 21st century. Some early obstacles to this movement were a lack of definition for 21st century skills, no sense of which methods for teaching them would be most effective, and no efficient and effective system for assessing that the skills were being learned.

In an attempt to define 21st century education needs, the U.S. Department of Education, in cooperation with several other organizations, founded the Partnership for 21st Century Skills (P21). P21's mission is "to serve as a catalyst to position 21st century skills at the center of U.S. K–12 education by building collaborative partnerships among education, business, community, and government leaders." The partnership maintains that in order "to successfully face rigorous higher education coursework, career challenges and a globally competitive workforce, U.S. schools must align classroom environments with real world environments by infusing 21st century skills."

P21 has identified the knowledge and skills that students need to master for success. These elements go beyond the traditional core subjects. The skill sets are organized into four categories, each with its own subset (Partnership for 21st Century Skills: www.21stcenturyskills.org):

1. Core Subjects and 21st Century Themes
   - Global Awareness
   - Financial, Economic, Business, and Entrepreneurial Literacy
   - Civic Literacy
   - Health Literacy
2. Learning and Innovation Skills
   - Creativity and Innovation
   - Critical Thinking and Problem Solving
   - Communication and Collaboration
3. Information, Media, and Technology Skills
   - Information Literacy
   - Media Literacy
   - Information, Communications, and Technology (ICT) Literacy

4. Life and Career Skills
   - Flexibility and Adaptability
   - Initiative and Self-direction
   - Social and Cross-cultural Skills
   - Productivity and Accountability
   - Leadership and Responsibility

The P21 framework is invaluable, but putting it into practice requires schools to shift from a traditional approach to one that incorporates the demands of a 21st century learning experience. Cisco Systems, Inc., a leading international communications technology company, has been an integral partner in the 21st century skills movement. Cisco describes the needed shift in education as moving from Education 1.0 to Education 3.0. Education 1.0 refers to the traditional education systems. Education 2.0 is the next phase, which focuses on curriculum, teachers, accountability, and leadership. The final phase, in which 21st century learning will occur, is called Education 3.0. Education 3.0 requires what Cisco calls a "holistic transformation" of education that incorporates these core areas:

- 21st century skills that complement a core curriculum
- 21st century pedagogy to teach these skills effectively
- technology to enable and support the pedagogy
- an agenda for integrated, systemic reform

The International Center agrees with most educators that the efforts of P21 and Cisco capture the essence of the 21st century skills necessary for students to achieve success beyond the classroom. Student learning must go beyond the foundational academic knowledge of core subjects, and students must be taught how to apply this knowledge to the real world. There is a clear progression that education can follow to make this happen if educators identify clear goals and embrace a systemic approach to achieve them. (Cisco Systems, Inc. *Equipping Every Learner for the 21st Century*)

Chapter 4: Instructional Leadership

Target for Instructional Leadership

The target for instructional leadership refers to the agenda for making improvements in instruction. Agenda is not about the practices of instructional leadership, such as classroom walk-throughs or common assessment, but rather about the basic list of items on which instructional leadership is focused.

There is universal agreement that instructional leadership is important. There is less agreement as to what the agenda for instructional leadership should be. Principals and assistant principals are regularly encouraged to adjust their daily activities to spend less time on administrative tasks or disciplining students and more time in classrooms as an instructional leader. However, it is less clear what the agenda should be for principals and assistant principals in the classroom. Do they look for daily objectives written on the whiteboard? Do they look at classroom configuration, seating arrangements, or bulletin board displays? Do they look at the level of participation of students to observe their interest or lack thereof? Do they look for the many aspects of instruction that influence learning or only a few? Do they look for strengths about which to compliment teachers and for weaknesses to provide suggestions for improvement?

Before principals and assistant principals spend precious time in instructional walk-throughs, they need to be clear about what they are looking for, so that they can spend time on the most important aspects of instruction. It is important to decide on the agenda for instructional leadership before creating processes for instructional leadership.

The target of instructional leadership, then, is making a clear selection of the aspects of instruction that leaders will look for in walk-throughs and other activities, encouraging staff to address these aspects in teaching and learning, and providing ongoing professional learning and collaboration around this target, or instructional leadership agenda.

One of the challenges for instructional leadership, particularly at the secondary level, is that leaders may lack a depth of content knowledge in the classroom being observed. This is less of a problem at the elementary level, because most elementary principals have been elementary teachers and therefore have acquired deep knowledge of the instructional content. However, elementary principals may experience this lack of content knowledge when observing special subject teachers, special education teachers, or English for Speakers of Other Languages (ESOL) teachers.

A Systemwide Approach to Leadership

Lack of deep knowledge can be a significant problem for secondary principals. For example, if their teaching background is in social studies, they will be less comfortable when observing math or science classes and reluctant to give advice to the teacher. Consequently, one of the best ways of preparing for instructional leadership is to focus on those characteristics of good instruction in which all principals and assistant principals should have skills and knowledge, without requiring deep content knowledge.

Instructional leadership should also focus on big issues of instruction. When instructional leadership focuses on compliance activities, such as submitting lesson plans to the office, or on classroom management routines, it misplaces the emphasis on the bigger vision of instruction. An objective classroom walk-through that gives equal weight to routine instructional tasks, such as posting objectives and giving daily homework assignments, and to powerful indicators, such as student engagement or high rigor and relevance, sends the wrong message to teachers. Routine tasks may be necessary, but they are not sufficient to elevate the effectiveness of instruction. This is the message of transformational leadership. Routine compliance instructional tasks fall in Quadrant A leadership. School leaders need to strive for the leadership tasks that are consistent with the higher expectations of the Transformational Leadership Framework in Quadrant D.

There are six agenda suggestions on which instructional leaders should focus. These areas encompass broad and powerful aspects of teaching and learning. They apply equally across all grade levels and every subject area: core academics, special subjects, and electives. School leaders who focus on these aspects of instructional leadership can have profound impacts on teaching and learning. Leaders can develop deep knowledge in these instructional areas and use them to improve instruction in all subjects in all grades without having great content knowledge in the subject being taught. These six areas are as follows:

1. Align with priority standards.
2. Strive for rigor, relevance, and relationships.
3. Use "begin-with-the-end-in-mind" planning.
4. Focus on literacy.
5. Personalize instruction.
6. Engage students.

Align With Priority Standards

The first and most important aspect of instructional leadership is making sure that teachers focus on the "right" student learning. Schools have become standards-driven over the last two decades, using external standards developed nationally by subject areas (as with the CCSS) or internally within their state. Standards provide educators with a comprehensive list of student learning upon which to base classroom instruction. Aligning curriculum to standards is an overarching element of instructional leadership in the DSEI.

Therefore, the first aspect of instructional leadership is making sure that instruction is aligned with the appropriate standards. This may be partially observed in classroom instruction, but it also requires documentation through cross-reference of instructional units to various standards via curriculum maps. Many school districts also create detailed pacing guides built upon a curriculum map, placing standards to be taught at each grade level on a timeline in which they should be covered. Suggested instructional experiences are often provided to help students learn the standards.

Curriculum maps and pacing guides are excellent tools for ensuring that the standards are covered. They offer the advantage of providing teachers comprehensive information on standards, and they help to ensure that all teachers in the same grade level or subject move at a common pace. If a student transfers between classes or district schools, fewer gaps will occur in that student's learning. The limitation of pacing guides is that they often reduce the flexibility of teachers to incorporate creative instructional ideas or to tailor instruction to meet the needs of individual students. A better practice is to use curriculum maps and/or pacing guides as a reference on standards to be covered but to encourage teachers to apply their own initiative to modify instruction to meet student needs. For classroom walk-throughs, principals can use curriculum maps and pacing guides as references to inquire of teachers which standards they are teaching toward. Teachers should always be able to connect the experiences in the classroom with learning standards.

One limitation of the standards movement is that it gives the impression that all standards are created equal. States put together comprehensive standards documents with the implication that all standards must be covered and that all should be given equal importance when translated into instruction. This often creates a school culture in which coverage of the topics takes precedence over learning experiences that result in a deepening of student knowledge and understanding.

Teachers should understand this and give greater emphasis to priority standards in their teaching activities. In reality, some standards that are less important might merely be covered, while more important standards would be extensively reinforced through greater application of learning and more challenging learning experiences.

In this era of state testing and accountability requirements, teachers place considerable emphasis on teaching to standards that are directly tested. In many cases, this results in the poor practice of teaching through test rehearsal and practice on released test items. Standardized tests are meant to be a sample measure of student learning in the standards. The assumption of these state tests is that if instruction is based on standards, sampling through standardized test items should indicate the degree to which students are meeting the standards.

Too often, teachers jump to test rehearsal, thus spending less time ensuring that students develop a deep understanding of the important standards. Tests are important in providing a minimum measure of accountability; however, they should not be the sole measure of student success, nor the endpoint of expected learning for the students. Teachers should focus on standards, make sure that they understand the types of questions on the state test, and prepare students through similar learning experiences to elevate their confidence at test-taking time.

Some essential standards are not tested because they do not translate easily into a test format that can be administered on a large scale and scored efficiently and reliably. Learning experiences in which students are expected to write extensively or give verbal presentations that reflect higher-level thinking are difficult to translate into multiple-choice questions. In focusing instruction mainly on state tests, teachers overlook opportunities to develop important standards that may not be tested. The large volume of state standards in every state makes it difficult for teachers to determine what to emphasize and what to minimize.

Research by the International Center in its National Essential Skills Study (NESS) collected public opinion as to which standards (curriculum topics) are deemed most essential by a wide audience. These essential topics are correlated to each state's standards through the International Center and Successful Practices Network's Next Navigator's alignment search tool, which provides a valuable resource for schools on which standards are the highest priority. Decisions about what to emphasize in curriculum should be made schoolwide and not left to individual teachers.

Instructional leaders are responsible for ensuring that instruction is related to the highest-priority standards as determined by the district and the school. The International Center and Successful Practice's Next Navigator provides a powerful resource in helping teachers focus on those standards that are most frequently tested and deemed by the public to be essential skills for students to learn. Teachers in many states will be challenged by the introduction of the Common Core State Standards. The International Center's Next Navigator is a tool that can be used to ease this transition. Also, the International Center's handbook *Shifting Instruction to Meet Fewer, Clearer and Higher Expectations: Common Core State Standards* can be used to learn more about these standards.

Strive for Rigor, Relevance, and Relationships

Recall that creating a culture of high expectations is emphasized in the DSEI. Education research emphasizes that to improve performance, teachers should have high expectations for students. But translating high expectations into daily teacher actions or instructional practices is difficult. What should principals look for as evidence of high expectations when they walk into a classroom? Is it the teacher with great discipline and control of students? Is it the teacher who is asking difficult questions? Is it a teacher with highly engaged students who show great energy and enthusiasm for what they are learning? One of the powerful ways that teachers can exhibit high expectations in their teaching is using the vision of rigor and relevance. The notion of greater rigor and relevance has broad-based public support as a desirable goal of student learning. The International Center's handbook *Supporting Instructional Excellence Through Rigor, Relevance, and Relationships* provides professional development activities that provide insight into this aspect of leadership.

The public recognizes the importance of education in our constantly changing world. Technological advances, social changes, and economic cycles demand that students be able to solve complex problems and reflect on the impact of their decisions. The public translates this into the necessity that all students learn at higher levels. The concept of academic rigor for every student appropriately describes moving from an education system that requires only memorizing content for short periods of time to one that is rigorous for everyone.

When employers charge that many high school graduates do not possess the skills needed to function in the workplace, they point out that recent graduates are unable to apply knowledge that they once had. Schools typically require students only to recall information on an objective test and then hope that they can apply that learning in the real world. Hope is not sufficient for preparing students for the technological workplace and our global economy. Educators must facilitate learning experiences in which students apply their learning in relevant situations that will deepen their knowledge and give greater assurance that in the future, students can apply what they have learned. The public expects that learning will be relevant beyond school and that students will have the ability to use their learning in all aspects of their everyday lives.

A Systemwide Approach to Leadership

By studying high-performing schools, the International Center has observed that relevance makes rigor possible. Many students will not become actively engaged in learning unless they see the connection between a learning experience and their lives. It is only when they understand the relevance of a learning experience that they will invest significant emotional and cognitive energy in mastering the content.

"Rigor, relevance, and relationships" is a nice alliteration, but it also makes the important connection between relationships and high levels of student learning. Relationships are not an end goal of education, but they deserve to be a target for student learning connected with rigor and relevance. If teachers do not focus on building relationships with students, they may never get an opportunity to take students to higher levels of rigorous and relevant learning. We need only to listen to students to see how important it is to recognize this connection between relationships and the investment and effort that they make in their own learning, as shown by feedback gathered through the *We Learn — Student Survey*, conversations with students, and other means.

The International Center has created a tool for quantifying rigor and relevance and moving rigor and relevance from a fuzzy concept into an objective practice. Using the Knowledge Taxonomy from Benjamin Bloom, which many teachers already understand, is an effective way to identify and move instruction to higher levels of rigor. However, the Knowledge Taxonomy only measures rigor; it fails to address levels of relevance. Moving to higher levels of relevance is defined by the Application Model, which describes the continuum from just acquiring knowledge in a discipline to complex applications in the real world. These two scales combine to define the four quadrants of learning.

Quadrant A is low rigor and low relevance, but not low importance. It defines the fundamental learning that exists in all disciplines: basic vocabulary, basic concepts, and fundamental skills. Quadrant B learning moves to higher degrees of application of learning, in which students get a chance to use their knowledge and skills. Programs such as CTE and subjects such as art and music naturally teach through application. Academic subjects such as English language arts, math, and science can likewise provide more instruction at higher degrees of application, not only to ensure that students retain their learning but also to increase the level of student engagement. When students experience and recognize the relevance of what they are learning, they naturally become more engaged.

Quadrant C learning is defined by high levels of the Knowledge Taxonomy, in which students are expected to think creatively and critically and to analyze, reflect on, and evaluate their work. Quadrant D is defined by the combination of the high rigor of Quadrant C and the relevance of Quadrant B. In this quadrant, students are expected to tackle challenging real-world problems and to think critically and creatively to solve those problems.

Rigor/Relevance Framework®

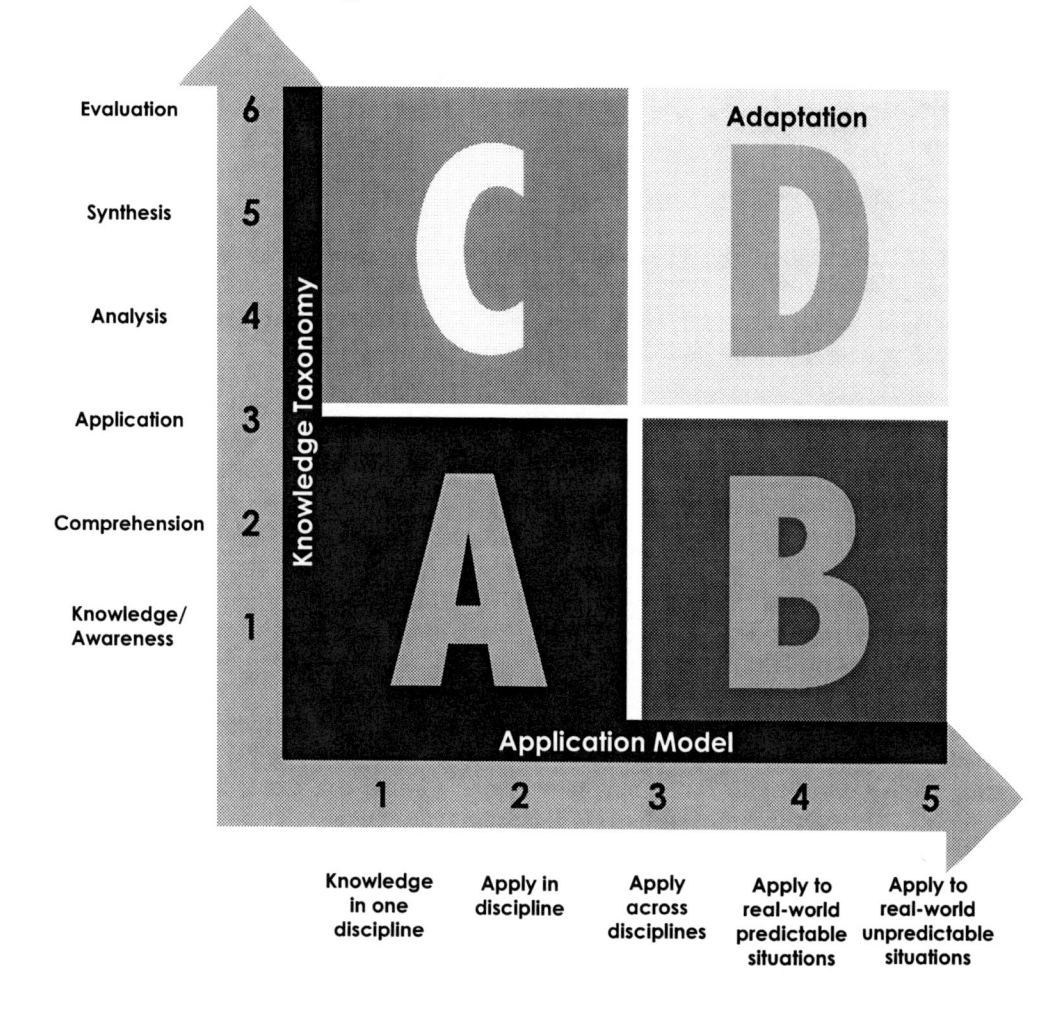

Knowledge Taxonomy (vertical axis):
- 6 Evaluation
- 5 Synthesis
- 4 Analysis
- 3 Application
- 2 Comprehension
- 1 Knowledge/Awareness

Application Model (horizontal axis):
1. Knowledge in one discipline
2. Apply in discipline
3. Apply across disciplines
4. Apply to real-world predictable situations
5. Apply to real-world unpredictable situations

Quadrants: A (low rigor, low relevance), B (low rigor, high relevance), C (high rigor, low relevance), D — Adaptation (high rigor, high relevance).

Learning in this quadrant is highly engaging; it also ensures that students have learned their skills thoroughly and have a chance to apply them in real-world problems.

If we expect students to be able to apply their learning once they leave school, which is what the public expects of us, we must provide more students with experiences in Quadrant D learning. In addition, the rapidly changing world elevates the importance of education if students are to be successful in the workplace and in their community; students require a higher level of skills than any previous generation. This is the challenge to schools: to develop high-rigor, highly relevant learning.

Instructional leaders can ensure that teachers have high expectations for students when they design instruction for Quadrant D of the Rigor/Relevance Framework.

Use "Begin-With-the-End-in-Mind" Planning

Instructional leadership often focuses on a teacher's preparation for instruction. There are many good practices for planning instruction, such as anchoring instruction in learning standards, defining learning objectives, using advanced organizers to connect students to the learning, and selecting powerful learning strategies.

From an instructional leadership perspective, the most important task related to planning is to encourage teachers to plan instruction backward from the "end" of a particular unit of instruction. Once teachers have defined a set of standards and clarified student learning for a unit, they need to identify the end goal of a lesson and how students will demonstrate their learning. They then specify the assessment: how they will evaluate the quality of student work that demonstrates learning. A quiz or test can be the culminating evidence for a unit of instruction, but more valuable would be a performance, an extended piece of writing, or a presentation in which students demonstrate the skills and knowledge they have acquired.

Too many teachers begin planning instruction with the content and then deliver that content to students, give them practice time, and finally quiz them on the knowledge they have acquired. According to Hattie's meta-research, a better practice is for teachers to be clear from the start about how students will demonstrate learning at the end. This is particularly true when teachers are striving for higher levels of rigor and relevance, when identification of how students will demonstrate the learning becomes even more important. (Hattie, John, *Visible Learning*)

Planning instruction in this manner helps teachers to commit to "learning facilitation" activities in order to get students to higher levels of learning. Teachers are challenged to define the steps needed to get students to that final demonstration. They are further challenged to look at any gap between where students are — with all of their diverse backgrounds, prior experiences, and abilities — and where they need to be. Doing so encourages teachers to focus on the students instead of themselves and the content that they are teaching. The teacher begins to recognize that the task is to take students from where they are to where he or she wants them to be at the end of the unit. This may seem like a subtle difference, but it is a very powerful one for changing the paradigm of planning instruction.

As principals engage in instructional leadership, their conversations with teachers should reveal whether teachers identify clearly the end goal for the lesson in their planning process and how that drives the decisions about the instructional strategies and assessments selected to take students through to the culminating performance. Thus, one of the important aspects of instructional leadership is for leaders to ask questions about the end goal of a lesson and how students will demonstrate their learning. This will help ensure that teachers approach their instructional planning with "the end in mind."

Instructional planning is often divided into three components: curriculum, instruction, and assessment. Curriculum is what students will learn, instruction is how students will learn, and assessment is in what way and how well students are expected to demonstrate what they have learned as a result of the instruction.

Traditionally, these three elements have been approached as three separate steps, one following the other, as shown in the following figure. Many teachers learned to plan their lessons using this linear model: Decide what to teach, design how to teach it, and then decide how to measure student achievement.

Teaching also proceeds in a linear manner. Topics are introduced one after the other, pausing only long enough for a chapter or unit test. Particularly at the secondary level, instructional planning focuses on covering the topics at a uniform rate of speed.

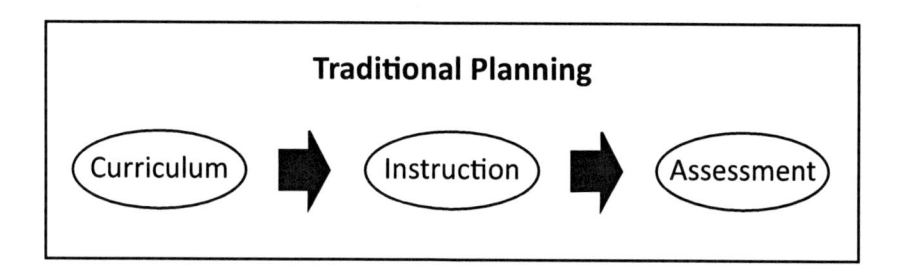

Traditional Planning

Curriculum ➡ Instruction ➡ Assessment

Recent research and innovations in teaching and learning have concluded that curriculum, instruction, and assessment are not separate and linear but interrelated. Good learning takes place when there is a dynamic linkage of instruction and assessment. In a rigorous and relevant learning model, instruction and assessment, in particular, should have significant overlap, as shown in the following figure.

Student learning is the result of a combination of facilitated instructional experiences and assessments, as shown in the Rigor/Relevance Learning Model. Rigorous and relevant student learning starts with a specific expected student performance using the Rigor/Relevance Framework. After completing a unit, the teacher can reflect on the actual level of student performance and decide whether it is necessary to modify and attempt to improve the instruction and assessment to attain higher levels of performance.

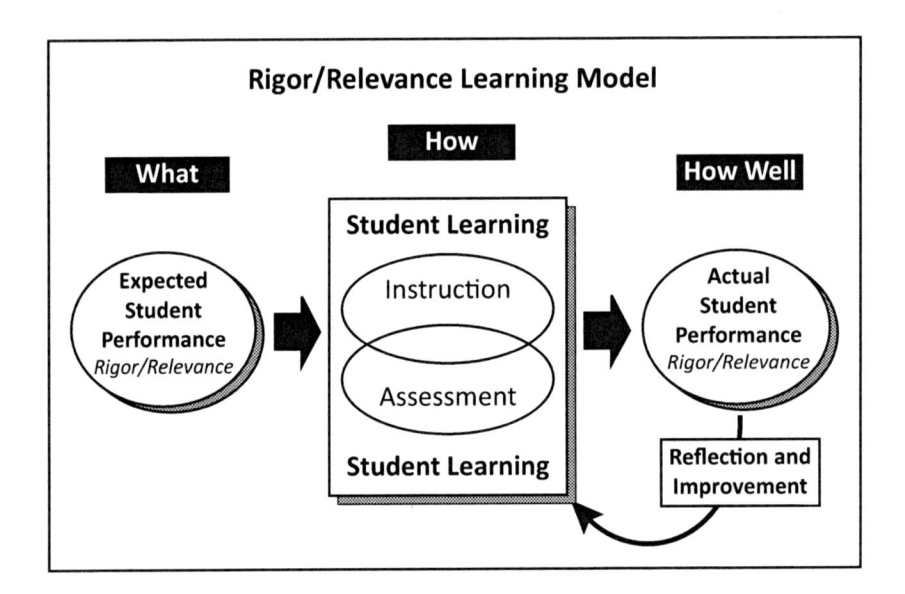

Rigor/Relevance Learning Model

What → Expected Student Performance (Rigor/Relevance)

How → Student Learning: Instruction / Assessment — Student Learning

How Well → Actual Student Performance (Rigor/Relevance)

Reflection and Improvement

Curriculum planning does occur prior to instruction and assessment. Without effective planning, there is very little likelihood that students will achieve the expected rigor and relevance. Curriculum planning is a complex process. It is much more than simply picking out a work of literature or a textbook chapter and deciding that it would make a good instructional topic. Teacher experience and data should be considered in order to make thoughtful decisions about instruction and assessment.

When teachers hear the word *curriculum*, they generally think of unit or lesson plans that describe teacher procedures and/or student activities that would take place in a classroom. It is natural for teachers to think about these plans and immediately jump to imagine what they would look like in their classrooms. Teachers are under constant pressure to present activities that engage students, and there is precious little time to do much planning — such is the structure of the U.S. education system.

Chapter 4: Instructional Leadership

Although curriculum must lead to unit plans and lesson plans, curriculum planning does not begin with them. Teachers who begin and end their curriculum planning by writing a lesson plan miss important curriculum decisions.

The curriculum is a means to an end: a performance by the student. Teachers typically focus on a particular topic (for example, volume of three-dimensional figures), use a particular resource (such as the Periodic Table of Elements), and choose specific instructional methods (for example, problem-based learning) to cause learning that meets a given standard. However, each of these decisions is actually a step in a learning process that should end in a performance by the student. Student activity without an end performance in mind is busywork. Instruction, no matter how engaging or intellectual, is only beneficial if it ends by having students demonstrate their knowledge and skills resulting from the learning experience. A performance approach to curriculum planning starts with the specific student performance.

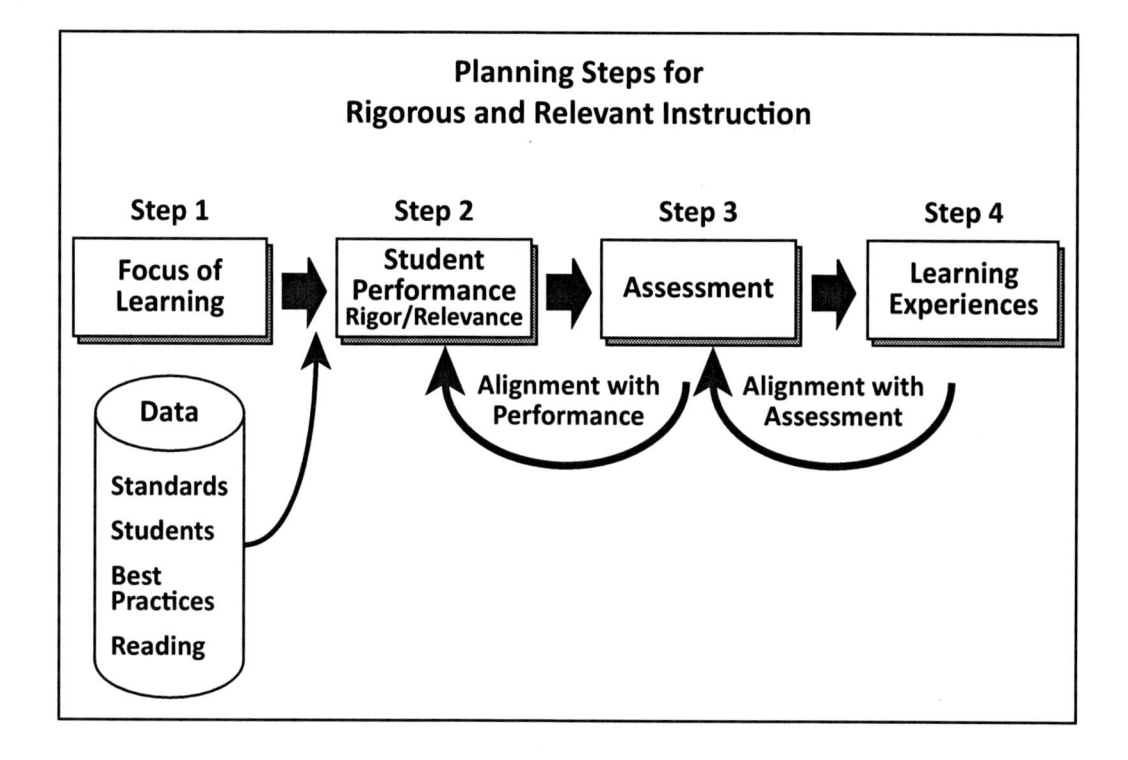

Planning Steps for Rigorous and Relevant Instruction

- **Step 1** — Focus of Learning
- **Step 2** — Student Performance (Rigor/Relevance)
- **Step 3** — Assessment
- **Step 4** — Learning Experiences

Alignment with Performance (between Step 2 and Step 3)
Alignment with Assessment (between Step 3 and Step 4)

Data (feeding into Step 2):
- Standards
- Students
- Best Practices
- Reading

A curriculum process that begins with the end in mind is referred to by Wiggins and McTighe in *Understanding by Design* as "backward design." It may seem backward to many teachers who move "forward" with textbooks, favored lessons, and time-honored activities rather than deriving those tools from targeted goals or standards. The *Understanding by Design* model is one of a number of excellent approaches to designing curriculum with the clear goal of student learning as the first step. Regardless of the model selected, teachers should start with the end — the desired results (goals or standards) — and then derive the curriculum from the evidence of learning (performances) called for by the standard and from the teaching needed to equip students to perform.

Backward design may be thought of as purposeful task analysis: Given a task to be accomplished, how do we get there? What kinds of lessons and practices are needed to master key performances? This approach to curriculum design is a logical systems approach, but it runs contrary to conventional habits, whereby teachers think in terms of a series of activities or how best to cover a topic.

This backward approach to curricular design also departs from another common practice: thinking about assessment as something to plan at the end, after teaching is completed. Rather than creating assessments near the conclusion of a unit of study (or relying on the tests provided by textbook publishers, which may not assess state standards completely or appropriately), backward design calls for teachers to think about the work that the student will produce and how it might be assessed as they begin to plan a unit or course.

Curriculum planning is a complex process that occurs prior to instruction and assessment. Without effective planning, there is little likelihood that students will achieve the expected rigor and relevance.

Focus on Literacy

The connection between academic success and reading skills may be obvious. The connection between lifelong success and reading skills may be equally obvious. Yet, an increasing number of students are ill equipped to read and comprehend the textbooks designed for proficient secondary readers. This reality is recognized by teachers everywhere.

What may not be so widely accepted, however, is the idea that content-area teachers can assist the struggling readers in their classes. Does this mean that content teachers should become reading teachers? No — but it does mean that content teachers can structure lessons to assist students to improve their proficiency when they read. Having a reading focus across an entire school is an extremely effective approach to improving learning and student achievement. The integration of literacy across content areas is an overarching element of leadership in the DSEI.

In most school districts, formal reading instruction on a regular and systematic basis ends in grade 6, as the focus on "learning to read" shifts to literary appreciation and "reading to learn." Reading content material becomes an everyday activity, but no consistent effort is made to teach students how to improve their reading comprehension. The integration of literacy across the curriculum is supported by the Common Core State Standards, which include standards that link literacy to other subjects, such as science and history.

While content-area teachers are often the first to recognize students with inadequate reading skills, most feel unprepared to address the issue because they have little training in the teaching of reading skills or strategies. Moreover, with the pressures of proficiency testing, they are concerned that teaching reading strategies will take time away from their primary emphasis: the teaching of course content standards.

All teachers can and should focus on literacy. Literacy can be a powerful target in improving instruction. Following a "before, during, and after reading" approach, for example, can help teachers to plan purposefully and give students a clear idea of what they need to accomplish in order to become successful lifelong readers.

Personalize Instruction

When teachers are seen as facilitators of learning rather than dispensers of knowledge, the focus shifts from teaching to learning. Teachers naturally become more student-focused when they analyze how to take students from where they are to where the teacher wants them to be in their learning.

Most people remember significant teachers in their lives — teachers who demonstrated sincere caring and encouraged students to strive to be more than they thought they were capable of being. This is the responsibility of teachers: to get to know their students, develop relationships with those students, and inspire them to higher levels of learning. This is what personalization of learning means: making each student feel important, empowered, and able to achieve great things.

Personalization also relies on a number of instructional practices, such as differentiation of learning and modifying instruction to take advantage of individual learning styles and multiple intelligences. These practices break down large-group instruction into different types of small-group and individual instruction, which are much more effective in getting all students to meet high standards.

Instructional leadership efforts should closely examine the degree to which teachers are getting to know their students, building instruction around individual student needs, and differentiating instruction to provide multiple pathways for all students to be successful.

Engage Students

To some, instructional leadership implies examining teachers to evaluate the quality of their work. One of the best indications of teacher quality is observing the students, especially their level of engagement. In classroom walk-throughs, principals and assistant principals should focus on the students. What are they doing? Are they engaged? Are they being stretched to think at high levels? Do they appear excited about what they are doing and committed to being successful and to rising to the challenge of high-level learning experiences?

Instructional leadership should focus on student engagement, not on teacher behavior. Disengaged students will not move toward high levels of achievement. Leaders can quantify the level of student engagement by looking at aspects of body language, the way in which students conduct themselves in the classroom, the absence of classroom distractions, and the presence or absence of a common focus. They can also focus on student responses, noting how frequently students have opportunities to speak and to answer questions that require complex thought rather than simple facts. Another measure of engagement is the degree to which students demonstrate confidence and show enthusiasm for their work.

Principals seeking to identify the level of student engagement should not only observe behavior in the classroom but should also talk to students about their learning to determine the degree to which they are cognitively and emotionally engaged. Some questions that instructional leaders might ask include:

- Are you committed to the work that you are doing?
- Do you want to be successful?
- Do you find the work meaningful?
- Do you feel that you can get additional assistance if needed?

The answers to these questions reveal a deeper level of student engagement that reflects the quality of instruction in the classroom.

Many practices can increase student engagement, but an initial responsibility of the instructional leader is to determine the level of student engagement and to use that as a basis for determining whether additional work needs to be done on changing teaching practice and the school culture.

Management Practices

Running an organization requires a leader to address some basic managerial and administrative tasks. These are called management practices. Make no mistake: Management practices are essential, but they demand lower levels of leadership. When a leader operates only at this level or takes an authoritarian approach to management, he or she is considered a Quadrant A leader.

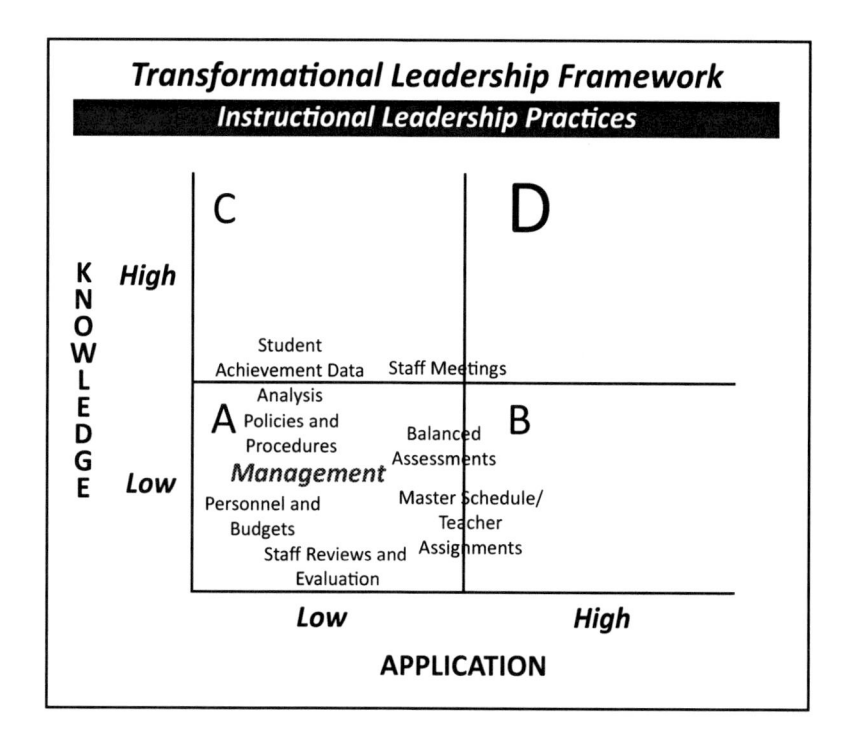

Transformational Leadership Framework
Instructional Leadership Practices

KNOWLEDGE: High / Low
APPLICATION: Low / High

- **C** (High Knowledge, Low Application)
- **D** (High Knowledge, High Application)
- **A — Management** (Low Knowledge, Low Application): Student Achievement Data Analysis, Policies and Procedures, Personnel and Budgets, Staff Reviews and Evaluation
- **B** (Low Knowledge, High Application): Staff Meetings, Balanced Assessments, Master Schedule/Teacher Assignments

Management practices include the following:

- policies and procedures
- personnel and budgets
- master schedule/teacher assignments
- staff meetings
- staff reviews and evaluations
- balanced assessments
- student achievement data analyses

The foundation of the DSEI is the concept that it takes a system, not just a teacher, to improve instructional effectiveness and student achievement. Schools, as systems, must have common, clear, and practical ways of operating that ensure consistency of instruction in meeting student needs but that do not stifle innovation or creativity. Teachers need to be aware of school practices and follow established procedures. Leaders need to evaluate their policies on a regular basis.

Leadership Strategies

Policies establish minimum expectations for instruction, and they are essential to the efficient operation of a school, but they rarely foster excellence. Effective policies help to reduce staff time spent in supervision and problem solving; hence, more time can be devoted to improvement. However, not everything should be put into a policy. Reducing good instruction to a set of detailed policies can result in too much attention devoted to "doing the right thing" in teaching and too little attention paid to facilitating learning. Try to create and maintain a minimum set of policies, but do not let policies be the main strategy for improving instruction.

The benefits of creating instructional policies are as follows:

- Policies ensure uniformity and consistency in decisions and actions related to teaching and learning.
- Policies help to create a stable system in which people know their roles and responsibilities.

Chapter 4: Instructional Leadership

- Policies that are consistent with legal and ethical requirements help to ensure that staff members operate within those legal and ethical boundaries.
- Policies add strength to the position of staff when possible legal actions arise.
- Policies save time when a problem can be handled quickly and effectively because of its relationship to an existing policy.
- Policies foster stability and continuity; they maintain the direction of the school even during changes in the positions of administrators and/or teachers.
- Policies provide the framework for building high-quality instruction.
- Policies provide a basis for performance evaluation and accountability.
- Policies clarify functions and responsibilities.

The following discussion relates to instruction about policies that schools frequently establish and maintain, rather than the provision of an exhaustive list of all school policies.

Minimum teaching day. Usually there are specific school policies regarding the length of the instructional day, including specific arrival and departure times for teachers. These policies may also identify the minimum and maximum teaching loads for individual teachers. Some policies may address how much time should be devoted to certain subjects or specific instructional practices that should be included each day.

Curriculum guide/course of study. Many schools and districts have established curriculum maps and pacing guides in order to ensure that instruction is aligned with state standards. Policies may be established regarding the use of these maps and guides; teachers may be required to seek approval for variation from these curriculum requirements.

Policies may also be established for the creation of new courses. Secondary schools, in particular, may establish a submission process for approving new courses. Requirements would include necessary information about seeking approval, a timeline, and the criteria for approval.

Duties of school leaders. Policies and procedures may include descriptions of duties and the responsibilities of various school leadership positions and teams. As schools create new positions and teams to support instructional change, written descriptions of these positions and teams can be very helpful for everyone.

Classroom observations. Schools may establish policies on classroom observations, including the frequency, timing, and notification of observations. These policies may also clarify the purposes of observations and identify who would be involved in observations.

Lesson plans. Schools may establish policies for teachers about the requirements for creating, obtaining approval of, and storing lesson plans. The school may establish a specific format for lesson plans or elements that may be included in a lesson plan. The school may also have policies regarding the submission of lesson plans for approval, storage, and public access. Schools frequently require the preparation and maintenance of emergency lesson plans in a public file that can be used when necessary.

Substitute preparation. In order to maintain continuity of instruction, schools often have specific policies or procedures regarding the current classroom instructional content that substitutes would need in case of a teacher's absence.

Homework. Schools may establish policies on homework that define what homework is and the expectations for minimum and maximum amounts of required homework in specific grades. Policies may also define criteria for consistently high-quality homework and the appropriateness of assigning homework over vacation periods. They may specify student responsibilities in completing homework, how to handle absences, and grading homework. Establishing minimum definitions of homework is a long-standing tradition in many schools; however, recent research questions the educational value of homework in many teaching situations. Schools should be cautious about mandating homework that merely becomes busywork and is not tied to effective instruction.

Grading. Schools may establish policies on grading practices. Teachers may be required to meet standards for timeliness in grading student work and in maintaining records. These policies may also address parent communication and consequent records of the communication.

If the school maintains a website with grade information, specific policies regarding grade information may be posted. Schools may also have specific policies for at-risk students and for retesting and makeup exams.

Field trips. Schools frequently have policies regarding the scheduling of field trips, including obtaining parent permission. Activity request forms require approval. Policies usually include guidelines for keeping field trips curriculum-based. Similar policies also relate to approvals necessary for bringing in resource people for instructional purposes.

Discipline referrals and student code of conduct. In order to make classroom environments free of distractions, schools usually develop schoolwide polices and procedures for student discipline, along with a student code of conduct. These policies describe examples of behaviors that invoke disciplinary action and provide a hierarchy of disciplines for repeat or more serious infractions. Having set procedures makes communicating disciplinary action to students easier. Achieving a consistent enforcement of policies helps build a positive school climate.

Technology. With the extensive use of technology in schools, policies regarding the use of technology are necessary. Polices may exist on the scheduling and use of shared technology equipment or computer rooms, the appropriate use of technology, and the protection of student privacy.

Parent communication. Parent communication is essential to supporting high expectations in the classroom, increasing student engagement, and supporting students in undertaking challenging work. Schools may have specific policies on communicating with parents about grades or students who are at risk of failure.

An important practice in parent communication is the establishment of frequent communication. Such communication builds a relationship that can then address problems when they arise. Parents should not expect to hear from teachers solely when there is bad news; policies may require frequent communication with parents about any update in the progress of their children. Teachers should also be encouraged to share good news and to compliment students on a regular basis when talking with parents.

An Overview of Personnel and Budgets

Decisions about whom to hire and where to allocate limited resources will set the foundation for high-quality learning. Perhaps the most important decision regarding a school is whom to hire (or, sometimes, fire). School leaders also struggle with limited budgets to provide the resources necessary for good instruction; the largest portion of the budget is allocated to staff salaries and benefits. The effective use of staff time is the most important aspect of resource management in a school.

Leadership Strategies Applied to Hiring Procedures

One of the most critical decisions in school leadership is deciding whom to hire. Successful transformational leaders consistently emphasize the importance of hiring people who have a passion for teaching and a genuine concern for students. Teachers today also need to be prepared to be continuous learners who work effectively with colleagues. Hiring procedures should seek to identify potential teaching candidates who have these characteristics.

Before hiring staff, a review of laws and regulations is necessary to be aware of hiring practices that might result in discrimination. In order to avoid problems, these requirements need to be understood thoroughly. A dedicated human resources staff in the district is valuable in helping to clarify applicable laws and appropriate interview procedures. For example, certain questions should never be asked. A good practice is to have a set group of interview questions prepared in advance and then to ask all candidates the same questions.

Methods of screening and selecting candidates differ widely, and no single system is better than another. Hiring procedures will depend upon the size of the school district, the role of other administrators, and the traditions for hiring candidates in the district. Increasingly, school leaders are seeing the value in soliciting many different opinions in interviewing prospective candidates. Valuable opinions can come from teachers with whom the teacher will work, from students, and from parents. Although a hiring decision is not one that should be delegated to others, leaders should solicit extensive input from many individuals in the process of collecting data about a potential candidate.

Leaders are recognizing that they need more information than what is obtained from an interview, a resumé, or recommendations. Prospective teachers may be observed interacting with students, teaching a lesson, or engaging in professional problem solving with other teachers. These rich and varied experiences provide more authentic information in making the important decision on whom to hire.

In an ideal world, whenever a new position is available within a school, the leadership team should have an opportunity to scan a wide range of possible candidates and select the most qualified person for the position. In reality, in larger schools teachers are often reassigned among schools as a result of budget cuts or seniority. In some situations, a principal or leadership team will have little say over who becomes a new hire within a particular school district. In these situations, it is critical to determine the strengths and weaknesses of a new candidate, for the best placement of that individual can help to maximize his or her potential for success and for making a positive contribution to student achievement.

An additional area of consideration in hiring procedures is school assignments. In elementary grades, teachers may choose to switch grade levels due to personal or professional interest. In high schools, teachers who develop more seniority may desire to teach more advanced courses, which are frequently smaller and include more highly motivated students. Regardless of the type of school, the leadership team needs to recognize that the decisions about assignments and responsibilities of staff need to be based upon how to maximize student achievement and contribute to overall school success.

Budgets. Schools use a variety of budgeting practices. Frequently, schools in large districts are allocated a budgeted amount per student, and financial decisions are delegated to the school. In these situations, the leadership team has substantial leeway in how to use funds. While there are advantages to this system, there are also greater risks, and the leadership team has to take greater responsibility in managing these funds effectively. There is no pool of district resources to dip into if funding mistakes are made. In smaller districts, money is allocated in budget categories. The district office usually maintains greater responsibility and decision making on the use of those funds. In these instances, the leadership team is frequently negotiating the amounts of money in each budget category.

When seeking to focus on instructional improvement and related professional development, school leaders often find it a challenge to allocate funds within annual school budgets. The best available resource is federal title money, but that must be used for additional improvement efforts rather than for basic support of school staff and expenses. In these cases, leadership teams need to follow federal guidelines on the appropriate uses of funds. Another important resource is discretionary grant money, which often carries more leeway in how funds can be used. The leadership team should encourage all staff departments to seek grant funding on a continual basis, for these funds can have a substantial impact on instructional improvement efforts. Even local small businesses may have grants that support individual teacher or school efforts.

Many schools have found that foundations are an effective strategy for supporting school improvement efforts. School foundations are not-for-profit entities that can receive donations from outside sources. School leaders need to remember that any not-for-profit foundation functions independently of the school and that school leaders do not have complete discretion over the use of those funds. Relationships between foundation leaders and school leaders are critical to ensuring that these foundations support the appropriate needs of the school. Many schools have used local foundations effectively to support significant school efforts. In some cases, foundations might give small grants to teachers for the unrestricted use of professional development materials or for recognition to teachers.

A related funding stream is the booster clubs that frequently function to support high school sports or music programs. Booster clubs can provide significant volunteer support to assist in these programs. They often raise money through fundraising activities or concessions. Leadership teams should be careful to establish clear guidelines and expectations on the use of these funds and their correlation to overall school improvement efforts.

Data-Driven Instructional Leadership

School leaders cannot make much progress in instructional improvement without the effective use of data. The use of data-driven decision making to inform instruction is a key aspect of leadership, as described by the DSEI.

Data standardize experiences. Data enable us to standardize our experiences. For example, we all react differently to weather and may use subjective terms to describe weather that is warm, cool, rainy, or cloudy. By using data, we have standardized weather experiences by identifying specific temperatures and predictions for temperatures. We have refined our ability to describe weather further by adding quantifiable values for phenomena such as wind chills and the severity of tornadoes and hurricanes.

Data standardize transactions. The use of data is so commonplace in our transactions that we often take it for granted. Our monetary system is based upon standard quantities, which make it easier to place values on goods and services and to negotiate transactions when buying and selling. Think about how difficult it would be to select a job with only vague notions of what the salary might be. Clothing sizing is another example of how data have helped us standardize; we are able to select clothes by size, which makes shopping more efficient.

Data facilitate fast and accurate communication. Perhaps the greatest advantage of data is to speed communication. Over the years, the development of ZIP Codes, telephone numbers, GPS coordinates, and IP addresses has enabled us to locate where we are and where we want to go. The instant communication of the Internet is possible because of data systems.

Data enable evaluation. We are constantly making subjective evaluations about others and about ourselves and our lives. Everything from whether one is having a good day to how strong a friendship is to how attractive one finds a potential new partner is open to a subjective evaluation. Data enable us to quantify evaluative judgments and improve the decision-making process.

Of course, data are most useful for evaluation when interpreted and presented in a straightforward manner. The real estate market bust in recent years is an excellent example of what happens when data are obscured. Through their practices, many finance companies and banks made interpreting data an extremely complex process for prospective homeowners, making it difficult for buyers to determine the actual cost of a new home. As a result, many homebuyers made decisions to purchase homes beyond their means.

Chapter 4: Instructional Leadership

Educators' Need for Data

It is difficult, if not impossible, for a school to move toward sustainable change if school leaders do not have a good idea of what is actually happening in their classrooms and with their students. For educators, data are essential for:

- **Planning.** Data make planning processes more efficient and effective. Imagine trying to open a school without knowing how many students might attend. A school must know the numbers of students as well as the characteristics those students bring to learning. Successful education leaders use data effectively to plan school development and programming to meet student needs.
- **Goal setting.** Effective organizations have specific goals. In the case of schools, it is essential to establish quantitative measures for what a school expects to accomplish for its students.
- **Progress measurement.** A school can and should periodically measure results to determine where it has been successful and where it needs to strive for greater improvement. Graduation rates and standardized test results are useful, but these data reflect only the outcome of the education process. They do not help schools evaluate the education process and make adjustments to improve upon it before a student's education is completed. It is essential for schools to collect data throughout the education process to better inform the daily decisions that lead to positive outcomes.
- **Evaluation.** Data are used to evaluate various practices and the effectiveness of instruction. When a new initiative is introduced, educators must determine whether it is effective by using data to evaluate results.
- **Communication.** Education serves many constituencies in addition to school staff and students. Schools must communicate with parents, taxpayers, community leaders, state agencies, and the federal government. Having data as part of that communication process is not only efficient but also effective in reaching the various stakeholder groups.

Data Types

All data are not the same. Several years ago, Victoria Bernhardt, Ph.D., executive director of Education for the Future, professor, and author of numerous books about data analysis, identified four major types of data. Bernhardt's system is now one of the standard

A Systemwide Approach to Leadership

categorizations used in education and communications. Effective use of data involves a balance among the four types, and schools will make little progress in improving instruction without achieving this balance. (Bernhardt, V., *Data Analysis for Continuous School Improvement*)

- **Demographics** includes data that describe the characteristics of students, such as ethnicity, gender, grade level, language proficiency, and socioeconomic groupings.
- **Perceptions** includes the results of surveys that quantify the opinions of staff, students, and parents regarding program effectiveness. These surveys might collect feedback about the quality of the school, quantify values and beliefs, or enable observations about the quality of student learning.
- **School processes** includes data relating to the description of school programs and processes, such as the suspension rate, enrollment in career and technical education, or the percentage of students completing service learning requirements.
- **Student learning** includes data that demonstrate the levels of student learning. Data might include results from large national assessments such as the ACT or SAT, state assessments, commercial assessments, teacher tests, or industry certification exams.

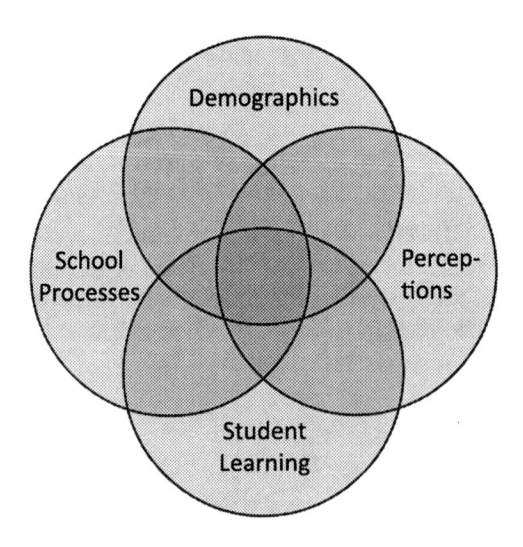

Student learning is the measurement of results. If the amount of data used to measure results is very small or uses limited measures, leaders will have an unrealistic measurement of student learning. It is similar to the old story of the blind men and the elephant, in which the blind person who feels only the elephant's leg, trunk, tail, or body has a very different perception of the subject than his fellows do.

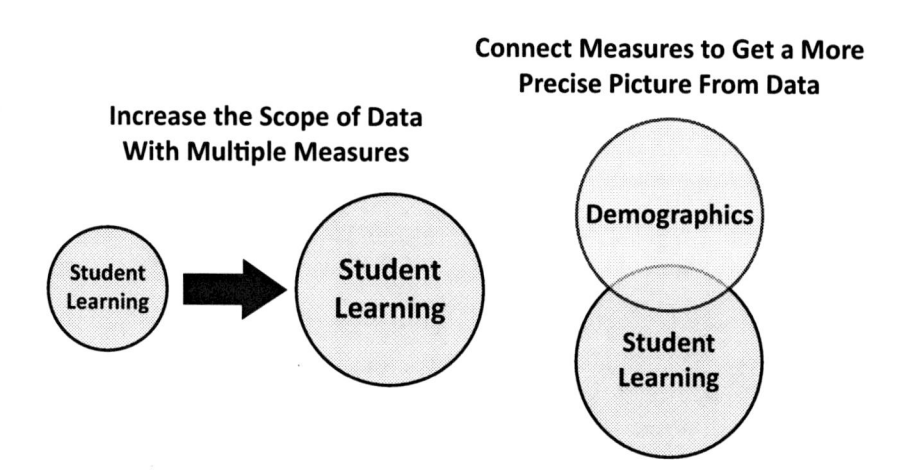

Increase the Scope of Data With Multiple Measures

Connect Measures to Get a More Precise Picture From Data

Student Learning → Student Learning

Demographics ∩ Student Learning

To fully judge the effectiveness of student learning, leaders need to use multiple types of data. The first aspect of effective data use is to expand the scope of data measures used to assess student learning.

The second aspect of using data effectively is to connect demographics and student learning. The disaggregation of student learning by sub-populations of students is a requirement of *No Child Left Behind*. In doing this, leaders get a more precise picture of learning by all students rather than describing learning results by totals that might obscure the fact that many students are not meeting targets.

Looking at student learning and demographics alone does not inform school staff about what or how to measure to determine whether initiatives are making a positive change. By collecting and analyzing data about school processes and perceptions, leaders have a more complete picture of learning results and the progress that has been made toward achieving those results.

Data Strategies

The following are important strategies that educators should use in data-driven instructional improvement.

Analyze forces of change. An important context for instructional leadership is establishing a sense of purpose and urgency to address instructional issues. Data regarding the environment, including demographic changes, social changes, economic changes, and technology, is useful in quantifying the driving forces to which educators must respond. For example, the percentage of minority students in K–12 schools in 2007 was 40%. By 2023, it is estimated that the rate will exceed 50%. With the knowledge these data provide, schools can begin long-range planning to address the needs of this increasing population of students.

Identify student learning needs. To better understand the students who attend the school, educators can use various assessments and surveys to quantify student learning needs. The processes for identifying learning disabilities and the needs of English language learners have become very sophisticated. Knowing as much as possible about incoming students ensures that schools are better able to support unique learning needs. For example, the number of English language learners has doubled in the last 15 years. Schools whose students increasingly have these needs must have strategies in place for supporting their success. The International Center's handbook *Supporting English Language Learners Systemwide* provides more information on serving ELL students.

Set student learning goals. Education is more effective when schools identify specific goals for students. These goals can be quantified in terms of state assessments, reading levels, or graduation requirements. Schools should communicate learning expectations to students and parents. Data tracking will enable the school to adjust instruction to help achieve that goal.

Set school goals. Once a school has set learning goals for individual students, it can aggregate the goals that it has as an entire school community. This creates ambitious expectations about the number of students who will meet benchmarks in reading or the requirements for graduation. Schools might also set goals for achievement in individual programs, such as for students completing career and technical education programs or for students taking advanced courses in math, science, and technology. A good example of a school goal is for the graduation rate for a cohort's entering the high school to be 95%.

Set individual goals. After a school has established overall school goals, individual teachers can see their role in working toward those goals and can set personal goals. They might set goals for student achievement within their individual courses or goals that are part of efforts to help a grade-level group of students to achieve. For example, a teacher may set a goal that 95% of his or her 9th-grade Algebra 1 class will pass and be prepared for Algebra 2. Collecting data through tests and other evaluations allows the teacher to address obstacles to achieving that goal.

Analyze school practices. As schools seek to improve instructional practices, they can use data to analyze patterns in achievement. They might ask:

- Where are students having the greatest successes or the greatest challenges?
- Are individual teachers achieving greater results with specific students?
- Which students are having difficulty?
- Are there differences in student performance over time or within individual subjects?

By comparing data and looking at trends, educators can begin to identify strengths and areas in need of improvement. Data may allow a school to make a correlation — for example, 80% of students who miss five or more days of school are failing at least one class — and then develop strategies to address the problem.

Test hypotheses. School leaders continuously need to seek solutions that will meet the unique learning needs within their school. Practices that are highly successful in one school may not be successful in another. Every innovation that is put into place with an expectation for improvement should have a hypothesis as to how it will improve learning results. Data collection around the results of an intervention or change can highlight whether to expand, modify, or abandon a particular innovation. For example, school leaders may wish to consider the hypothesis "Do students taking honors English and regular English have an equal chance of achieving a score of 18 on the ACT?" Data will help them answer this question.

Quantify perceptions. Not every aspect of evaluating the quality of schools can be measured by a student assessment. There are nuances of success in learning that do not show up in standardized tests. Data quantifying these perceptions are equally important in making judgments about what is working and what needs to be changed. Educators can quantify these perceptions with well-constructed surveys that examine the perceptions about what is or is not working effectively in schools. For example, the *We Learn — Student Survey* shows that only 62% of students have a teacher with whom they feel they can confide or share problems. Knowing this, how can a school leader work with staff to strengthen relationships between students and teachers?

Opinion-Based Versus Data-Driven Decision Making

The following chart compares opinion-based, or subjective, decision making with more objective data-driven decision making. Using data consistently leads to improved decision making.

Opinion-Based Versus Data-Driven Decision Making

Opinion- and Tradition-Based Decision Making	Data-Driven Decision Making
The top priority is maintaining the status quo.	The top priority is achieving goals and results.
Budgetary decisions are based on prior practice, priority programs.	Budget allocations to programs are based on data-informed needs.
Staff assignments are based on interest and availability.	Staff assignments are based on student needs as indicated by data.
Reports to the community focus on school events and individual stories.	Organized reports to the community focus on student learning progress.
Goal setting is based on favorite initiatives or fads.	Goal setting is based on data about student needs.
Staff meetings focus on operations and the dissemination of information.	Staff meetings focus on strategies and issues raised by the local school's data.
Staff development programs are scattered.	School uses focused staff development programs as an improvement strategy to address documented problems and needs.
Parent communication is limited to open houses and occasional newsletters.	Parent communication regarding student progress is frequent and often online.
The grading system is based on each teacher's criteria of acceptable work.	The grading system is based on common student-performance criteria that are keyed to progress on the standards.
Periodic administrative team meetings focus solely on operations.	Administrative team meetings focus on measured progress toward data-based improvement goals.

Collecting and Analyzing Student Data

The suggestions that follow can help schools become more effective as they collect and analyze student data.

Count carefully. The data that a school collects convey what is important. This sounds simple enough, but problems can occur when emphasis is placed on process data rather than achievement data. For example, one school tried to improve reading scores by rating teachers on the number of minutes per day their students spent reading. This was taken to an extreme, and classrooms were ranked on the number of minutes of reading, with rewards for the highest numbers. This emphasis led to a disproportionate amount of time spent on reading without real improvement in reading ability. The data collected led the school to focus on that single variable. If data are measuring process rather than results, school leaders should be sure that the data correlate to achievement.

Look at distribution, not averages. Averages are the most frequently used and abused statistics. Averages provide a single number that makes comparison easy — perhaps too easy. For example, if the average SAT score of students at school A is 1050, and the average at school B is 1100, it appears that students in school B are performing at a higher level. However, there may be many more individual students in school A who achieve at high levels than in school B. Averages do not reveal this information. The total distribution of actual scores gives a better picture of the achievement of all students. Looking at distribution reveals the number of high-performing students, which could be a source of information for effective learning practices. Similarly, looking at the students at the low end of the distribution will reveal who needs the most attention.

Disaggregate. Just as distributions offer revealing statistics, disaggregation reveals a more accurate picture of total student performance than averages do, and it can expose groups of students who require extra support. Dividing total student scores into subgroups by such categories as gender, teacher assignment, ethnic group, number of years in district, and attendance rate can help to pinpoint the needs of student subgroups.

Study trends. One of the other dangers of relying on any single data source is that these numbers are "snapshots in time." Because many factors may distort one simple average, however, it is better to look at changes over time. Trends provide a more accurate picture than isolated numbers do. School leaders must take care never to place a great deal of emphasis on a single number.

Collect data to answer questions. Schools often collect some data and then try to decide what to do with it. This is backward, for the most useful data are collected to answer specific questions. For example, a district planning committee that wants to assess writing achievement might ask, "How well do our students write?" The first step would be to look for existing data elements related to students' writing. Then, if needed, the committee can develop additional measures, such as feedback from former students, scores on writing exams, numbers of students participating in writing contests, or the amount of instructional time spent on writing.

Use technology. Increasingly, technology is playing a critical role in the compilation and analysis of education data. An article in *Education Week*'s *Technology Counts 2006* report shows that the nation has made dramatic progress in developing computerized data systems that can reliably guide education decision making. However, there is still plenty of work to do before those systems reach their potential to accelerate student achievement. According to a survey of the 50 states and the District of Columbia, two thirds of states provide educators with access to interactive databases through which they can analyze school-level information. Twenty states have data systems that allow educators to compare their schools with others that have similar characteristics. Slightly more than half the states provide access to student test performance results over time through a web portal or other centralized data tool. (Edwards, Virginia, ed., "The Information Edge: Using Data to Accelerate Achievement," *Technology Counts 2006*)

Make data understandable. Anyone can become overwhelmed when confronted by large groups of numbers. When presenting findings, school leaders should limit the amount of data to what is absolutely needed and should convert numbers into charts to show trends when possible. For many people, pie charts, bar graphs, or line drawings are more meaningful than are tables full of numbers.

Go deeper. Looking at initial data should inspire further questions and a deeper analysis to achieve greater levels of understanding of student performance or education processes. Schools that use data regularly in the decision-making process continue to expand the breadth and depth of data collected. This allows them to develop a fuller picture of the learning that is taking place in their schools.

Becoming More Data-Driven

Strategies for district leaders to support data-driven instruction and improve their own data skills:
- Ask for and post public displays of data visibly in schools.
- Ask data-driven questions of leadership teams.
- Ask students to quantify their learning progress.
- Ask teachers to cite data to indicate how they gauge student learning.
- Use charts and graphs to reduce data to useful information by focusing on simple numbers, gaps comparisons, and trends.
- Ask frequent questions to ensure data accuracy.

Using Data to Drive Academic Excellence Through Career and Technical Education

One of the trends emerging from school reform and the implementation of learning standards is data-driven instruction and achievement. Often, the only data considered are the students' scores on standardized achievement tests. If the numbers are low, then schools and districts place tremendous emphasis on trying to improve instruction in order to "get the numbers up." True data-driven achievement involves much more than merely reacting to low test scores. There are many other fundamental pieces of data that schools and teachers must acquire and analyze in order to improve student performance.

Career and technical education teachers should not be fearful that an emphasis on data-driven decisions about curriculum will lead them to distort their teaching and eliminate instructional activities that they feel contribute significantly to student achievement. CTE teachers can continue to deliver essential job skills while improving student academic performance.

Much of what teachers do is to attempt to move a group of students to acquire the necessary skills and knowledge that will enable them to be lifelong learners and successful adults. While student test scores are one measure of progress toward those goals, other important data sets are the match of instruction to (1) the actual standards, (2) to the standards that are tested, and (3) the essential skills needed by high school graduates as identified by educators and the wider public.

In order to plan instruction that gives students the best possible education, teachers must know what the standards are, which standards are tested, and which are deemed essential. The next sections describe these data sets.

Test Data

Test scores get all the headlines, and the local media are quick to post the numbers and compare schools. Results on state tests can give an indication of whether students are developing competence in the standards if three assumptions are met:

- The state tests must be aligned with the standards.
- The tests must be comprehensive enough to cover all of the standards.
- The tests must assess student competence reliably and consistently.

Before educators jump to respond to test scores by changing instruction, it is essential to examine the reality of these assumptions.

Quality Counts 2001 indicated that the match between state standards and tests was not close enough. In particular, state tests measured some standards but not others. They also tended to emphasize the less demanding knowledge and skills in the standards and test that knowledge through simple questions. The report stated (*Education Week: Quality Counts 2001*, Vol. XX, Issue 17, January 11, 2001):

> Forty-nine states include multiple-choice questions on their exams, 38 include short-answer items, and 46 ask students to compose essays as part of writing tests. But only seven require students to write essays or engage in performance tasks in subjects other than English. Two states use portfolios, compilations of students' classroom work.

The 2007 edition of the *Quality Counts* survey broadened its definition of *extended response* in assessments to include multiple-step problems in which students must show and explain their work. With that change, the number of states with extended-response questions in subjects other than English rose to 27.

For schools and districts, state tests may not be the most appropriate vehicle for judging student performance, and they do not address the full range of local beliefs about what a student should know and be able to do. This does not imply that schools should ignore these tests, but rather that simply doing well in state-defined report card categories is not enough to guarantee that students are truly prepared with skills for success.

Essential Skills

The International Center believes that a curriculum needs to prepare Essential Skills students for the world beyond school, not just for the next level of education. To accomplish this objective, the curriculum must reflect what the community believes students should know and be able to do when they graduate from high school.

The International Center developed the National Essential Skills Study (NESS) to help districts identify what educators and the community believe is the most important English language arts, mathematics, and science content in terms of the rigor and relevance needed to prepare students for post-school, real-world experiences. Since NESS was launched in March 2007, nearly 10,000 people across the U.S. have participated, generating a national database on the skills and knowledge deemed most essential for students to possess.

NESS asks participants to identify what they believe are the 20–30 most important topics in each of the three core subject areas. The topics were compiled following a comprehensive review of the national standards established by the National Council of Teachers of Mathematics, the National Research Council, and the National Council of Teachers of English, as well as various state standards. The lists of topics then went through an intensive editing process by subject specialist teachers. In all, 50 English language arts, 70 mathematics, and 85 science topics were identified and incorporated into NESS.

The top-ranked topics are typically skill-based. In English language arts, for example, they typically depict the application of knowledge. These topics traditionally have been considered by many, especially non-educators, as the basic skills within the discipline.

A comparison of the high-ranked topics in the National Essential Skills Study with the highest-ranked English language arts, math, and science standards from the McREL study revealed comparable findings. This is a definitive signal of the nationwide consensus on the importance of practical, skill-based standards that involve the application of knowledge.

Rankings of topics by educators and the general public, which included the business community, correlated highly to each other, indicating that these groups have similar priorities. This may be surprising to those who perceive the public, especially the business community, to have different priorities from educators in general. However, the rankings by subject-matter teachers of topics within their respective disciplines are often substantially different from those of the general public and other educators. This is significant because curriculum and assessment committees typically are composed primarily of subject-matter specialists, who appear to have a unique perspective on what should be included in the curriculum and on the tests.

Topics that typically are considered "basic" skills and knowledge in a discipline are ranked as high priority by all segments of the population with the exception, in some cases, of the educators in that discipline. This is alarming because the teachers who must deliver those basics appear to believe either that these skills are not important or that they are not the responsibility of the discipline. The result is that these basic skills may not be receiving the attention they deserve.

Setting Curriculum Priorities

Data on standards, essential skills, and state tests can be used to set curriculum priorities. The International Center's Next Navigator is a tool that helps districts do so. It compares state standards in English language arts, math, and science with findings from the National Essential Skills Study and a review of the state's mandated assessments in up to four grades in each of the three subject areas.

This type of analysis is a powerful tool for districts as they try to sort through the numerous state standards. Without it, districts must choose between trying to cover all the standards by diluting or condensing them and eliminating some, which runs the risk of leaving students unprepared for the assessments or without the skills considered essential by the community. With it, however, districts can make decisions to place more emphasis or less emphasis on a standard or to delete it completely, confident in the knowledge that the decisions will help students succeed on the assessments and that they are consistent with public expectations. In addition, this analysis can serve as the starting point for planning staff development activities.

Although districts may wish to incorporate supplemental criteria in making decisions to emphasize, add, or delete topics, using Next Navigator data in this manner provides a clear indication of the impact of such decisions.

CTE Alignment Search

The alignment search between standards and career pathways is designed to enable CTE educators to identify the critical math, science, and English skills and knowledge that they can incorporate into their courses. Teaching and reinforcing these test priorities in CTE programs will help these students fare better on the state academic exams.

Chapter 4: Instructional Leadership

What International Studies Data Means for CTE

The 2003 Trends in International Mathematics and Science Study (TIMSS) examined the mathematics and science achievement of students in 49 countries overall. Approximately 300 schools in the United States were sampled at grade 4 and grade 8.

U.S. students scored above the international average in both mathematics and science at both the 4th-grade and 8th-grade levels. In the 1995 study, U.S. 8th-graders performed below the international average in mathematics. In the same 1995 study, U.S. 12th-graders, including our most advanced students, were among the lowest performers in both science and mathematics. The final year of secondary school was not part of the 2003 TIMSS, so it is yet to be seen if the U.S. is catching up or lagging further behind.

The Program for International Student Assessment (PISA) measured 15-year-olds' abilities in reading literacy, mathematics literacy, and science literacy. PISA is conducted every three years. In 2003, 41 countries participated in PISA, including 29 Organization for Economic Cooperation and Development (OECD) countries. Unlike other international studies, such as TIMSS or PIRLS, which focus explicitly on curricular outcomes, PISA attempts to measure the application of knowledge in problems with a real-life context.

The 2003 PISA results tell a story of U.S. students' ability that differs from that of the TIMSS. U.S. performance in mathematics literacy and problem solving was lower than the average performance for most OECD countries. U.S. students exhibited poorer mathematical literacy than their peers in 20 of the other 28 OECD countries and three of the non-OECD countries. In 2003, the average U.S. score in reading literacy was not measurably different from the OECD average. The U.S. average score in science literacy was lower than the OECD average. Eighteen countries (including 15 OECD countries) outperformed the United States in science on the 2003 PISA.

There are several reasons why the U.S. did not do well on PISA overall. We teach many more topics than other nations do; we do little prioritizing of the subjects taught; and we provide virtually no opportunity for students to apply the knowledge gained. We can address these matters in our schools. CTE teachers can and do teach academic knowledge and skills in their curriculum. Students learn the relevance of subject matter when they apply this knowledge in real-world situations in the workplace and in the classroom.

Cultural Practices

Leaders who apply the practices that compose the four quadrants of the Transformational Leadership Framework are working toward establishing a culture that supports significant and sustainable improvement. The use of the practices that are associated with Quadrant D reflect high levels of vision and leadership empowerment.

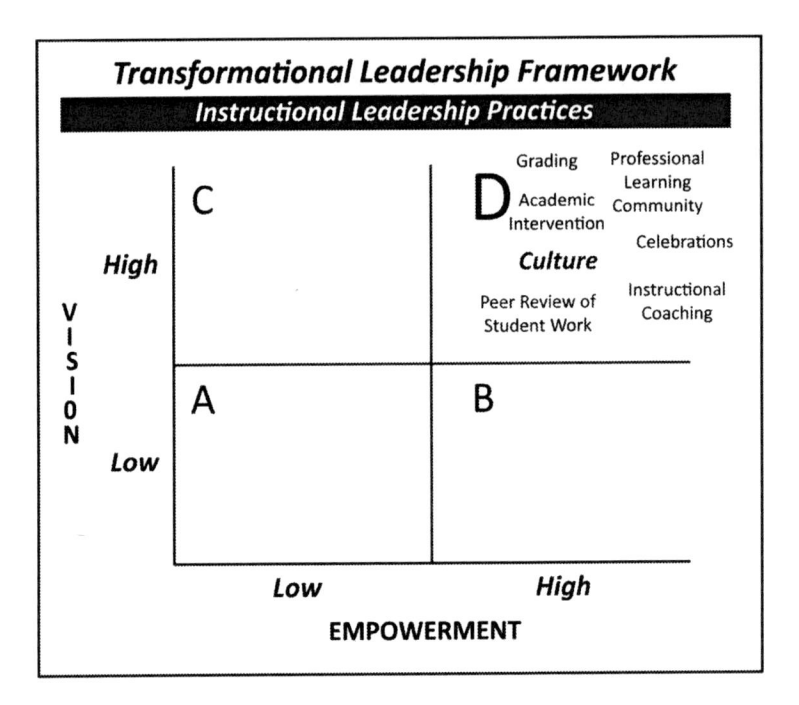

Transformational Leadership Framework
Instructional Leadership Practices

Quadrant C: High Vision, Low Empowerment
Quadrant D (Culture): High Vision, High Empowerment — Grading, Academic Intervention, Professional Learning Community, Celebrations, Peer Review of Student Work, Instructional Coaching
Quadrant A: Low Vision, Low Empowerment
Quadrant B: Low Vision, High Empowerment

Axes: VISION (Low/High) vs EMPOWERMENT (Low/High)

Cultural practices include:
- academic intervention
- instructional coaching
- peer review of student work
- grading
- celebrations
- professional learning communities

Academic intervention. Ensuring that every student succeeds frequently requires intervention in order to provide personalized and timely alternative instruction. The actual intervention may take many different forms. It may simply mean making adjustments to better engage a student or allowing more time for an alternative learning approach. Additional teachers or an alternative program may sometimes be the most effective intervention.

When examining intervention services, administrators need to consider students with disabilities and English language learners. Students in these groups frequently require supplemental services to be successful. With supplemental funding available for some of these students, federal and state regulations come into play. States and districts may also have their own regulations that prescribe intervention for students who are performing at low levels on state assessments. Academic intervention is a complicated but very important practice. The International Center's handbook *Effective Approaches to RTI* provides professional development activities related to this topic.

Leadership strategies. Successful implementation of an intervention philosophy and program requires instructional leadership. If schools are committed to the success of all students, a flexible approach to learning is key, for all students do not learn in the same way or at the same speed. One or more academic intervention strategies may be necessary for students to succeed. To some people, academic intervention means instruction that takes place outside the classroom, such as tutoring or special classes. However, many academic interventions need to occur directly *inside* the regular classroom.

The timing of intervention services is critical to student success. Sometimes general education classroom teachers wait until they reach a point of frustration before speaking out to request that a student be removed. At this point, the student is a discouraged learner as well. In other situations, teachers are too quick to remove students who perform poorly or who cannot succeed because of their disability. Some teachers may even resist having any students with disabilities placed in their classroom. Still other teachers may refer students for alternative placement when they have not even tried preventative or differentiated strategies in the classroom. There are as many different intervention situations as there are teachers and students. It is difficult to prescribe a limited number of interventions that will always work. From a leadership perspective, there are several systemic initiatives to increase the likelihood that education professionals will make the right choices in providing appropriate and timely intervention services that will enable each student to succeed.

Intervention often focuses on reading. Reading proficiency is a gateway to all other learning in school. According to the National Assessment of Educational Progress (NAEP), however, 67% of students in grades 8–12 are not proficient readers. These reading issues are not typically issues with decoding words. The difficulty is with comprehension; 90% of the reading difficulties of students in middle school and high school are difficulties in comprehension.

Response to Intervention. One strand of intervention that seeks to look at intervention in a systems approach is Response to Intervention (RTI). RTI is often associated with students who have disabilities because it is linked to the reauthorization of IDEA (*Individuals with Disabilities Education Act*) in 2004. However, the goal of RTI is to meet the needs of students in the general education classroom and therefore avoid unnecessary classification for special education. RTI is a tiered approach to intervention, often represented by a pyramid.

There are several RTI models, the simplest being a three-tier approach. Tier 1 instruction is preventative: Every child in a classroom experiences this instruction, aimed at preventing learning failure. Such effective, solid, evidence-based instruction meets the nature and needs of the students and maintains fidelity to the content of the curriculum. Its activities include group work, small-group work, individual practice, and assessments. Effective instruction naturally includes preventative intervention when it is conceptually rich and challenging, builds on the student's previous knowledge and skills, includes multiple strategies, addresses the standards of the curriculum, and reflects current research. In the Rigor/Relevance Framework, effective instruction matches the quadrant with the instructional objective and moves toward Quadrant D learning activities. If effective instruction is in place, 80% of the students will be successful with ongoing, preventative intervention.

Supplemental to Tier 1 instruction is Tier 2 instruction. Tier 2 is typically about differentiation and small-group instruction that is designed to meet individual student needs, including steps that the teacher can and should take at the first sign of learning difficulty. Effective instructional practice for Tier 2 interventions occurs at the same time for everyone in the class, as all students are involved in either a small group or in individualized instruction. This time can be used for accelerated and challenging work for those children who are achieving at grade level in the particular unit of study, extra attention to the current lesson for those who are experiencing difficulty, and reteaching of previous skills or teaching those skills in different ways for those who are struggling. Children are not assigned to tiers; rather, they move in and out of tiered instruction as needed. Interventions occur for approximately 15% of the students who do not make adequate progress via Tier 1 instruction.

For some students, Tier 1 instruction and Tier 2 differentiation are not enough. For those students, Tier 3 intervention may be necessary some of the time. Tier 3 is even more targeted, systematic, and explicit than Tier 2. Tier 3 can be aimed at preventing students from needing special education services by providing more flexible, regular education options. Instructional support personnel, such as reading specialists or special education teachers, often provide Tier 3 interventions, but a student does not need to be classified for special education in order to receive this support. Tier 3 intervention is provided for about 5% of the students who struggle, in spite of effective Tier 1 instruction and Tier 2 interventions.

RTI Tiers

Tier 1: Preventative Intervention — instruction that attempts to prevent a certain outcome from happening

Tier 2: Secondary Prevention — instruction that includes steps to take at the first sign of trouble

Tier 3: Tertiary Prevention — instruction that involves steps to take after a problem has manifested itself

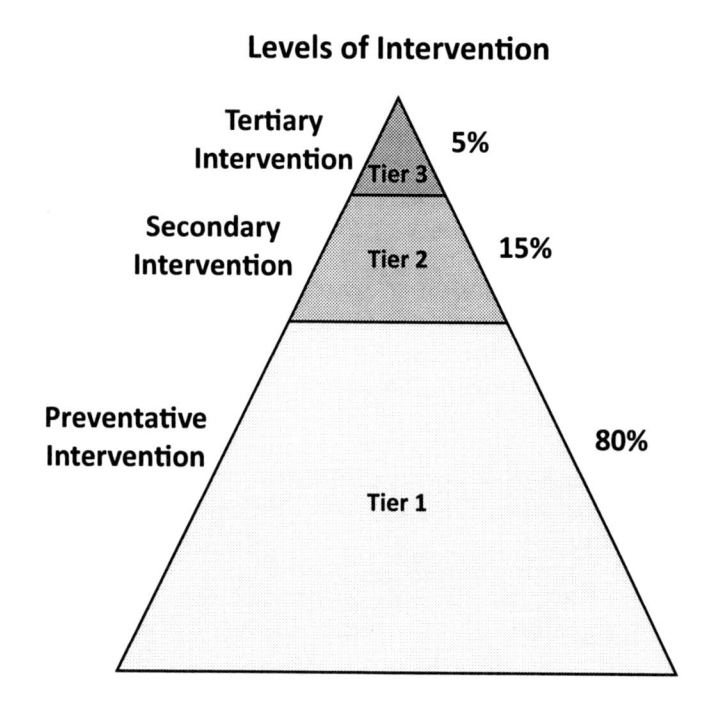

Levels of Intervention

- Tertiary Intervention — Tier 3 — 5%
- Secondary Intervention — Tier 2 — 15%
- Preventative Intervention — Tier 1 — 80%

The groups of professionals who will experience the greatest impact and change related to their professional responsibilities, and who therefore will need the most professional development as school districts plan for RTI, are the general education teachers. RTI is an effort to avoid an unnecessary learning disability designation by giving the student precise, scientific-based assistance as early as possible.

RTI requires the classroom or content-area teacher to focus on data-driven decision making and the collection of quantitative as well as meaningful qualitative data by the general education teacher to aid in intervention decision making. Reading specialists, special education teachers, and literacy coaches are among the best-trained professionals in the school district to help develop, implement, and evaluate new models of intervention strategies. The potential for success of RTI lies in providing teachers and/or paraprofessionals with concrete information on how to vary the instructional level and scaffold the support needed by students.

Supplemental Instructional Time

Through systemic RTI practices, schools should limit taking students out of regular instruction. However, part of an overall system of providing high-quality earlier instruction is providing supplemental instructional time. Supplemental instruction is frequently provided using federal funding resources, such as Title I. Schools should include as many options as are necessary to meet the range of student needs, including the following:

Within-class staffing that reduces student-teacher ratios (e.g., co-teaching, team-teaching). Often the immediate response to providing supplemental instruction is to add onto the class instruction. However, placing additional professional staff within the classroom and class period to provide additional and more individualized instruction can also provide supplemental instruction.

Extra time during the regular school day. Depending on the school schedule, there may be opportunities to create additional instructional time by adjusting lunch periods or time allocated to other subjects.

Extended school day. The most common way to provide supplemental instructional time is extending the school day. This time might be both formal class periods and informal times for tutorials by teachers who are available to work with individual students. Schools may provide transportation services to make extended school-day sessions more convenient to students and families.

Before-school sessions. Many schools are finding before-school options viable. Sessions might be short time periods devoted to instruction, while other students have unstructured time in the morning. Many urban schools that rely on public transportation for students create staggered starts to the school day, in which some students start school earlier in order to obtain supplemental instruction. In this option, staff members might have different work hours or might receive stipends for working longer hours.

Evening and weekend sessions. Evenings and weekends are also options, but they are less popular and usually are reserved for students who have significant behavioral issues that make it difficult for them to participate in school with the larger school population.

Summer sessions. Summer school is the traditional remedial program for high school students who fail courses. Using summer school solely for students who have failed is becoming less popular. However, summer sessions for students are increasingly used for students at all grade levels. Many charter schools are experimenting with a longer school year. Some urban schools have created summer sessions in an effort to lessen the reduction in learning that often occurs during the summer for students living in poverty. The Syracuse City School District in New York recently adopted an 11-month "urban" teacher calendar whereby all teachers are employed for an additional month. Schools are encouraged to create summer supplemental instructional programs for at-risk students, using this available pool of instructional staff.

Intervention Specialists

Intervention specialists are a growing group of educators for which many states now have specific certification. An intervention specialist may assume a variety of roles in the school, depending on the support needs of the students served:

- teaching collaboratively with the general classroom teacher
- serving as a consultant to several classroom teachers
- working with small groups of students in a resource room
- teaching in a self-contained classroom
- providing private tutoring in academic areas for students with learning disabilities

When schools have people in positions like "intervention specialist," "math specialist," or "reading specialist," the tendency may be to schedule them in consistent ways for accountability reasons. For example, on Monday from 9:00 to 10:00 A.M., the math specialist is assigned to work within the 3rd-grade class to support three students who struggle with math. Then the specialist goes to the 4th-grade class to support students in that class. This method rarely works. Depending on the lesson and the concepts being taught, those students may or may not need the specialist to be present in the room.

Intervention specialists should be assigned caseloads of students, preferably no more than 25. They should plan their week around what those children are going to be learning, anticipating areas where they might need preteaching, reteaching, or alternative teaching. Such a schedule requires the establishment of trust: The other teachers need to trust that the intervention specialist is working when he or she is not 100% visible in the classroom, and the administration needs to trust the intervention specialist to plan his or her day in accordance with contractual agreements (one planning period, one lunch, and so on). Trust usually emerges after results begin to become evident. Overcoming the "scheduling hurdle," however, can be difficult. The intervention specialist should not be planning around the teacher; he or she should be planning around the student.

Credit Recovery

A rapidly growing practice in high schools is credit recovery. While credit recovery is not a direct intervention into classroom instruction, it is an alternative form of instruction, which helps to retain students in school and assist them in making progress toward a diploma. Under increasing pressure to increase graduation rates, many schools have turned to credit recovery programs to retain students and improve graduation results. Credit recovery is an alternative to traditional remedial lessons, summer school, or evening programs. Many credit recovery programs are technology based; and, after the initial investment, they provide a cost-effective way for students to complete required coursework, often in an accelerated manner.

Program options available to schools in credit recovery have experienced rapid growth. Many states have virtual school programs, in which students are there specifically for credit recovery purposes. Some of the commercial programs that are popular in secondary schools include Apex Learning, PLATO Learning, Pearson Digital Learning, Know The Net, and Penn Foster. The North American Council for Online Learning (NACOL) produced a summary document in June 2008 that outlined promising practices/success stories and suggestions for operating effective credit recovery programs through online learning. (Watson, John and Gemin, Butch, "Using Online Learning for At-Risk Students and Credit Recovery")

Chapter 4: Instructional Leadership

Credit recovery programs and online learning provide viable options for many students who may be struggling in the regular classroom and become frustrated with trying to accumulate sufficient graduation credits in the regular education program. Other information and ideas related to improving the achievement of struggling or frustrated learners can be found in the International Center's handbook *Motivating All Students in Grades 9–12*.

Instructional Coaching

Instructional coaching, an effective onsite, job-embedded professional development practice of peer assistance, is based on current research and effective instructional practice. The effectiveness of instructional coaching is described in Hattie's *Visible Learning for Teachers*, which cites research by Joyce and Showers that shows a powerful positive impact of instructional coaching. Instructional coaching creates collaborative professional learning and provides sustained support for individual teachers and school improvement efforts. An instructional coach educates teachers about strategies and classroom routines that have been validated through research. The coach assists the teacher in a specific content area while integrating the goals of the school and district, focusing on and improving instructional practice and student achievement.

Leadership Strategies

Instructional coaches act as onsite professional developers who assist teachers in implementing proven instructional practices. The instructional coach and the individual teacher (or team of teachers) form a partnership to analyze the teacher's (team's) needs and discuss research-based ideas and solutions. They also work together to find ways to meet those needs. Considerable knowledge is gained on the job.

The coach frequently models the instructional practice for the teacher and then observes the teacher engaged in the same practice. Action research can be used as the mentor and mentee share ideas, identify problems, create solutions (research-based practices and interventions), model the suggested modifications in instruction, and observe and provide feedback. The mutual supportive relationship created by the coaching model enriches not only the professional learning but also the collegiality, friendship, and collaborative spirit of the coach and teacher.

Although the format of the peer review process differs from school to school, the objective is always the same: to help teachers improve instruction. Coaching involves using one's peers to examine aspects of teaching and learning. Staff can use the opportunity to reflect on strengths and weaknesses and to work together to make improvements. The overall goal is to establish a culture of self-study that stimulates continuous inquiry, reflection, information sharing, and success.

There are many variations in a coaching program; however, several common practices ought to be in place in any successful program. A strong focus on professional practice and improving the effective instructional strategies that lead to student achievement is essential.

Since instructional coaching is a job-embedded task, taking place within the school day, it does not significantly interfere with the instructional process or remove teachers from the classroom for outside workshops. Conversations related to coaching are conducted within planning periods, designated team meetings, or after school.

Coaches should see themselves as collaborators with teachers to guide the discovery implementation and support the introduction of new instructional strategies. It is important that the coach not become an evaluator — nor be perceived to be an evaluator — in judging the quality of teaching. The role of the coach is to discuss teaching practices with colleagues in a nonjudgmental way. The nature of conversations and reporting about coaching should be confidential. These are professional conversations as teachers attempt to improve strategies; they should not draw attention to a specific teacher's performance. Therefore, coaches need to be excellent communicators who can listen respectfully, ask thought-provoking and reflective questions, and keenly observe instructional practice and student engagement in the classroom.

Elements in a successful coaching program include the following:

Clear focus and continuity. Everyone should understand the purpose of coaching, and every effort should be made to maintain consistent coaching over a significant period of time.

Strong personal relationships. It is important for coaches and teachers to get to know one another, to build strong relationships, and to create an atmosphere in which teachers feel respected and comfortable about taking risks to introduce new strategies. An environment in which teachers are frequently ridiculed for poor practices will likely result in an avoidance of risk taking and innovation.

Strong principal support. Within the school, coaching should be seen as an extension of overall improvement efforts. Messages from the principal should be supportive and consistent with the efforts underway in school coaching.

Clear roles. Clear roles for the coach and each teacher are necessary in understanding what a coach does and does not do. The coach does not replace some of the functions of school administration and supervision; he or she is there primarily to support and guide the introduction of new strategies among the teaching staff.

Time. Since coaching takes time, schools need structures for teachers that provide available time to meet with coaches, discuss teaching practices, and reflect on their own practice.

Continuous learning. Both coaches and teachers need to be involved in and have a mindset for continuous learning. Coaches will learn a great deal about teaching practices by observing many different classrooms and then sharing skills with other teachers. Teachers also need to recognize the need for continuous learning and the value of improving strategies for student achievement.

Many myths circulate about coaching, as in these examples:

- **Myth:** Adult brains are fully developed and do not change.
- **Reality:** A human brain has plasticity. It is able to create new neural connections throughout an individual's life, allowing a person to learn novel ideas and obtain new knowledge at any age.

- **Myth:** Coaches cannot impose on teachers since they have no supervisory responsibilities.
- **Reality:** Although a coach is not a supervisor and should not be confused with evaluating teachers, coaches can expect teachers to connect their instructional strategies and priorities with the school's vision and mission, and they can ask questions that cause teachers to reflect on the quality of instruction and student achievement within their classrooms. Coaches are expected to be nonjudgmental; however, they need to be proactive advocates for improving instruction within the classroom.

- **Myth:** Teachers resist change.
- **Reality:** Many teachers are perceived as resistant to new ideas, but change is really what empowers individuals and offers the greatest rewards. Most people resist change, but they often welcome the opportunity to change when they can develop their own ideas and are recognized for their innovation. Coaches need to empower individuals to reflect on their practice and to take control of the changes necessary in the classroom to increase student achievement.

- **Myth:** The work of coaches is to support teachers.
- **Reality:** The work of a coach might be considered as supportive, but the coach is in the classroom to improve student achievement. The needs of the students are most important, and the purpose of the coaches is to guide the teacher in ways that will improve instruction and benefit the students. While the coach attempts to develop a good working relationship with the teacher, a coach must never lose sight of the fact that he or she is there for the students.

- **Myth:** Once coaches are accepted, they have more leverage to work with teachers.
- **Reality:** Although coaches must develop solid relationships with teachers, they should never overemphasize being accepted by the teacher and never lose track of their agenda to improve classroom strategies in student achievement.

- **Myth:** Helping teachers know about or learn how to implement new instructional strategies is a coach's primary responsibility.
- **Reality:** Again, the primary purpose is student learning, not improving instructional strategies. Teachers must know how to use effective instructional practices and when and where to implement them to increase student achievement.

Summary

Instructional leadership is critically important in schools. It is used to address a variety of challenges, leading to improved instruction and increased student achievement. Instructional leadership is based on the concepts of context, target, and management practices. Data are used to drive decisions that relate to instructional leadership.

Reflection Activity

1. The text described three questions that instructional leaders should consider as they attempt to address an adaptive problem. Think about each of the following questions. Then write a short summary of what your responses would be if the questions were asked about your school.

Chapter 4: Instructional Leadership

- Which parts of the "instructional DNA" must be altered or discarded in order to achieve the school's vision for learning?
- Which parts of the school's DNA must be preserved?
- How will creativity and innovation be stimulated to create a new, more adaptive DNA and school culture?

2. This chapter contains a chart that compares and contrasts opinion-based decision making and data-driven decision making. Reflect on a recent leadership situation in which you made a decision based on opinion rather than data.
    - Would your decision have been different if you had used data-driven decision making?
    - What steps can you take to move to using data in your decision making?
    - How can you reinforce the use of data-driven decision making by other leaders within your school?

Chapter 5

Leadership Through Empowerment

Defining Leadership

The definition of *leadership* can be complicated, even elusive. Traditional definitions that consider leadership to be the province of one person who is empowered to make decisions, tell others what to do, and move an organization forward are too limited. On the other hand, simply saying that everyone in a group is a leader is too amorphous. Seeing leadership as having a set of beliefs, a way of acting, and a sense of empowerment to act, however, leads to a more useful construction of leadership. Leadership is the willingness to take action and the means to do so.

Developing leadership throughout a system — distributed leadership or leadership density — involves changing the manner in which the members of the system work with one another. In schools, this means a shift in how educators relate both to their colleagues and to students, parents, community partners, and other stakeholders. The concept of "power over" must become the concept of "power to," as educators begin to realize their own leadership potential. When members of the system are empowered, the system allows them to make decisions for optimizing resources and learning experiences. Empowered professionals have the power to do what they need to do, not the power to control others. This basic shift applies to all levels of a school, from empowering the student body to empowering the community at large. Building leadership capacity is a key focus of the DSEI, which emphasizes the need for existing leaders to identify and cultivate the development of existing leaders.

The focus of this chapter is empowerment: embedding and distributing leadership throughout the organization. When all members of a community are empowered to act, then leadership can emerge in anyone, at any time or in any place. Sustained leadership demands empowerment. Educators should strive to empower students to take control of their own lives. In order for this to happen, schools must empower teachers to make decisions in their classrooms about what is best for their students.

Total Leadership

A report produced by the British National College for School Leadership defines the concept of *total leadership* as "leadership provided by many sources — individual teachers, staff members, parents, central office staff, students, and vice-principals — as well as the principal or head teacher." Total leadership is akin to what the International Center for Leadership in Education calls leadership density. In a claim that goes straight to the heart of this chapter, the National College report notes:

> Total leadership accounted for a quite significant 27 percent of the variation in student achievement across schools. This is a much higher percentage of explained variation (two to three times) than is typically reported in studies of individual head teacher effects.

In addition, the report states that "the relationship between total leadership and teachers' capacity is much stronger than the relationship between the head teacher's leadership alone and teachers' capacity." (Leithwood, Kenneth, et al., *Seven Strong Claims About Successful School Leadership*)

Leadership Turnover

Leaders, in the traditional sense, come and go. In fact, according to an October 2009 article in *Education Week*, "Data available from a handful of states suggest that only about half of beginning principals remain in the same job for five years and that many leave the principalship altogether when they go." Often people feel deserted when a leader leaves and may worry about how the system will carry on. (Viadero, Debra, "Turnover in Principal Focus of Research")

A publication of the British National College for School Leadership suggests that "unplanned head teacher succession is one of the most common sources of schools' failure to progress." If leadership resides throughout the institution and an organization's members feel empowered, however, then there will be a minimal gap in leadership between official leadership appointments.

Empowerment creates a system wherein each professional has room and resources to do what he or she does best. Empowered individuals have the knowledge and beliefs to maintain an organization on its path of continuous improvement without specific direction from someone else. One or more people eventually must fill administrative positions, but that does not mean that those positions have a monopoly on leadership and on how the system continues to grow and learn.

Components of Leadership Through Empowerment

Leadership through empowerment includes six major components:

- Leadership always includes the potential to say "yes."
- Leadership operates from truth.
- Leadership tolerates delayed gratification.
- Leadership demands the ability to remain peaceful, even during times of chaos.
- Leaders do not engage in "I'm right, you're wrong" thinking.
- Leadership nurtures humanity by valuing knowledge as well as personal, social, and emotional skills.

Cultivate the Potential to Say "Yes"

Empowered people know that their ideas are valued. In organizations in which members are not empowered, an individual may share an idea with colleagues or supervisors, only to be met with discouragement. Others may decide quickly that an idea will not work. This is typical of institutions that are comfortable with the status quo. It is a common condition of school boards, faculties, or parents who want to know absolutely that a new idea will work before approving or trying it.

For example, a school board in a small town had very clear ideas about what principals should do. They believed that the principal's job was to run the school, which primarily meant managing the school in a traditional sense. When the principal explained that a major function of the position was to nurture professional growth through supervision, especially for new teachers, the board was incredulous. What did that have to do with running the school? Institutions can erect walls to preserve simple routines of comfort and stability by maintaining fixed, concrete definitions of roles and functions. When this happens, innovation — which thrives in a culture of empowerment — withers.

Individuals do not wish to pour their thoughts, perceptions, and suggestions into an abyss. When there is the potential to say "yes," there is greater potential that one's colleagues across the organization will listen to ideas, consider them carefully, and engage in conversations about them. Empowering others means not dismissing ideas as they emerge. Empowered people know that they have a voice, and they are more likely to use it.

Operate from Truth

Truth here is not referring to larger philosophical or religious belief systems. Truth in this context is honesty, the courage to face and accept what is as a starting point. Leaders must be honest with themselves and others about the situations with which they are dealing. Statements such as "Our entire community supports the school" or "We have no resources" are not realistic.

The power to act does not mean anything without a true, clear understanding of what is. Effective leaders do not act on the basis of believing that the world is the way they want it to be; they act on the world as it is in order to bring it closer to the way they want it to be. For example, all of a school's teachers may say that they believe that every student can learn, but that does not mean that all of the teachers are acting on that premise. A leader's job is to nurture those within the organization to move beyond the saying and into the doing — from the truth of what is toward the way they would like it to be.

Tolerate Delayed Gratification

Empowered individuals can tolerate delays. Insecurity begets panic, shooting from the hip, and the feeling that all is lost if the situation does not change immediately. One way to think about delayed gratification is to see it as confidence. Those who are empowered know that their ideas will be heard, and they have confidence that the situation will improve as a result of their and others' efforts. Growth and change can be messy and slow.

Chapter 5: Leadership Through Empowerment

This can be fine if the process is sound and people are able to make carefully considered, informed decisions.

Frustration at delayed success can destroy the possibility of forward motion. "I told you it wouldn't work" may be the response to an idea that has been in place for only a few months. Until a new idea is well underway, there is no way to know exactly how well it will work. Inevitably, adjustment and fine-tuning will be required. Patience with and careful nurturing of innovation are necessary for ultimate success. Effective leaders see improving a system as a process of evolution, not of achieving conclusion. If members of a group demand proof that a new idea will be absolutely successful before they will implement it, they will never try anything new.

Courage to withstand the wait for gratification is also necessary when a leader makes an unpopular decision. He or she knows that the action is sound and justified, but to others it looks negative or frightening. Only after some time has passed will everyone see the virtue of the original action. For example, staff members agree that a particular teacher is not up to par; in fact, they frequently talk about this teacher's lack of ability. Community members know about the problem, as does the administration. However, when the principal and school board successfully make the case for the teacher's dismissal, the other teachers circle the wagons. Instead of feeling relieved that the standards of their profession are being upheld, they see threatening and frightening power in the administration's actions. In time, however, most members of the organization accept the fact that the decision was for the best and that the action was necessary. The administration has to withstand the negative feelings and scrutiny of the staff in the short run, and that takes courage. When people demand that success be immediate or even guaranteed, then empowerment suffers, because the disposition to act is constrained. Good leaders need not only courage but also patience.

A well-known study by a team of psychologists at Columbia University linked delayed gratification to such qualities as social competence, the ability to handle stress, and higher cognitive ability. The longitudinal study examined the behavioral choices of a group of 4-year-olds who self-selected into two groups: those who demonstrated an ability to delay gratification and those who did not. Ten years later, the research team asked parents to rate these children on a variety of traits and factors. The self-control of the young subjects was measured using a variety of scenarios, but all essentially involved each child's being given the choice between a smaller, immediate reward, such as a single marshmallow, versus a larger reward that was delayed, such as two marshmallows for waiting 15 minutes. In the follow-up, the researchers found that, among other characteristics, the young children who had demonstrated greater self-control by delaying gratifica-

A Systemwide Approach to Leadership

tion tended, when older, to be more future-oriented and goal-oriented, attentive, able to concentrate, socially competent, and able to cope with frustration. (Mischel, Walter, et al., "Delay of Gratification in Children")

The characteristics associated with a willingness to delay gratification are precisely those desired in empowered individuals, so it behooves a system to create the necessary environment for the empowered to act productively. If power is a disposition to take action, then there has to be climate that supports that disposition.

When a leader is patient about seeing results, it is empowering to those who are producing those results. If people feel that they must constantly be producing rapid results, however, then they will likely choose to aim for short-term gains to meet the expectations. This is not unlike the problem with high-stakes testing. Is the larger goal really to get the students ready to score well on the test tomorrow without regard to what they remember a month after the exam? Educating for the long term is not the same as prepping for a one-time event. The long run should be what matters.

Empowered leaders know that they have the institution's trust, which enables them to work toward long-term improvement, even if there are false starts and failures along the way. If every new idea has to be perfect from the beginning, then people are likely to do nothing rather than risk short-term disappointment. Leaders must be very careful not to punish individuals for trying new ideas that may fail; it is a sure way to squelch creativity and hinder empowerment. Failure is an integral part of forward motion. People who are empowered to take action and try new approaches understand this and give innovation time to succeed. And, if an innovation fails, they are more likely to examine carefully what went wrong so that they can use that information to make informed decisions in the future.

When a leader forgoes short-term success to achieve more significant long-term gains, he or she is essentially banking reward capital. Once a short-term award is received, the implication is that the job is done. If individuals are expected to work for more powerful, long-term payoffs, the system must support them along the way. Leaders have a responsibility to shape an environment that is patient and supportive, thereby empowering others to engage in the system without the constraints imposed by an overeager timeline.

Maintain Peace in Chaos

Maintaining peace in chaos relates to delayed gratification. Empowered leaders understand that proceeding with knowledge and with deliberate action will always yield better results than simply reacting in the moment. Indeed, sometimes chaos is productive: Ideas and emotions swirl around for a while but then settle down to organized inquiry and reflection.

A great example of maintaining peace in chaos is the emergency landing of U.S. Airways flight 1549 in January 2009. Pilot Chesley "Sully" Sullenberger might have panicked when he realized that his commercial airliner had hit a flock of geese and was going down. Instead, he remained calm. Doing so allowed him to assess the situation in the few minutes he had and then to act deliberately as opposed to reactively. He successfully landed the airplane in the Hudson River, saving everyone on board. Not only was Sullenberger empowered to make decisions, but he also had the necessary information, equipment, and confidence to do so with thoughtful intelligence. He was ready to take responsibility for the people on board, and he was willing to act. He could not have done this had he not felt empowered. Additionally, numerous boats in the Hudson immediately turned toward the sinking plane without having been told to do so; the captains and crews simply acted. This extraordinary set of actions occurred through calm, purposeful decisions.

Moving too quickly can lead to misjudgments and mistakes. Being peaceful can help stabilize a situation, modeling good grounding and thoughtful action. Remaining calm allows a center, or eye of the storm, to form. This is a deliberate place from which to watch, thoughtfully, what is happening. Sometimes the best thing to do is nothing — to give the situation time to unfold and reveal all of its nuances. Empowerment means having the confidence in yourself and others to consider the options and make thoughtful decisions rather than panicking.

Avoid "I'm Right, You're Wrong" Thinking

Again, individuals who are not empowered generally are reluctant to share ideas. When an organization operates as a zero-sum system, one idea succeeds at the cost of another, rather than ideas informing one another on the way to the best solution. National politics offers a clear example of the lack of progress that results when opposing factions refuse to acknowledge anything positive in each other's ideas.

The fear of being dismissed or discounted can be very powerful, shutting down numerous sources of energy and thinking. The collective voice is generally wiser than any one individual's. Successful leaders know that, in the final analysis, there are no winners and losers, but many stakeholders. Data determine direction, not a debate of how people feel about an issue. The British National College study offered this finding: "There is no loss of power and influence on the part of the headteachers when . . . the power and influence of many others in the school increase." (Leithwood, Kenneth, et al., *Seven Strong Claims About Successful School Leadership*)

Sharing leadership does not mean giving everything away. Rather, it means collaborating, working together, and honoring and respecting others' perceptions and talents. Ultimately, sharing power requires recognizing that collective leadership can accomplish more than individual leadership can.

Sharing leadership requires the ability to hold opposing ideas in one's mind simultaneously. Roger Martin, dean of the Rotman School of Management at the University of Toronto, calls this *integrative thinking*. Integrative thinkers do not operate in either-or systems; instead, they look at all aspects of an issue, taking what is best from every side as they formulate a solution. If the obvious options are not acceptable, these leaders continue until they find an option that is.

Value People as Much as Knowledge

Leaders can have all the technical skills and knowledge in the world, but that can mean nothing if they do not know how to interact positively with others. Effective leaders never forget that students, teachers, administrators, and other stakeholders are people, regardless of their roles and labels. People have emotional and physical needs. They need acceptance and understanding. The British National College study holds that (Leithwood, Kenneth, et al., *Seven Strong Claims About Successful School Leadership*):

> [T]he most successful school leaders are open-minded and ready to learn from others. They are also flexible rather than dogmatic in their thinking within a system of core values, persistent . . . resilient and optimistic.

The article also underscores the importance of leaders "understanding and developing people" as well as addressing functional demands.

When leaders are empowered and, therefore, confident, they are not ashamed to show emotion, to be openly caring for others, and to take responsibility for the people around them as well as the formal institution. Anyone can give orders, but not everyone has the compassion necessary to understand people, build trust and loyalty, and bring individuals together.

Good leaders need what internationally known psychologist and science journalist Daniel Goleman calls *emotional intelligence*. Emotional intelligence includes self-awareness, empathy, self-regulation, compassion, and the intuition to understand others' emotional states. Individuals who demonstrate strong emotional intelligence are balanced and emotionally healthy, and they understand their own biases. Through carefully listening and responding to others, emotionally intelligent leaders can construct emotionally safe situations. Feeling safe supports empowerment, because people who feel emotionally protected are more likely to show initiative and take risks.

One New England high school adopted a three-year cycle of supervision and evaluation that centered on trust and empowerment. Formal teacher evaluations occur once during the cycle. During the other two years, teachers work with their supervisors to develop their own professional development plans. During the professional development years, the only documents that go into the permanent record are the original goals and a summary paragraph of progress that each teacher writes. One teacher at the school, whose work exemplified what empowerment through trust can achieve, wrote this in his summary statement: "Much of what I tried failed, and much of what I learned I learned too late to help my students this year." Empowerment to take action and take risks, along with strong trust among the teacher, the supervisor, and the system, allowed this extraordinarily honest professional growth experience to occur.

The Role of Courage in Empowerment

The difference between being a good leader and a great leader is courage, and the greatest courage is moral courage.

The Courage to Do the Right Thing

An act of courage is not an act of reckless abandon. For many people, the word *courage* conjures an image of the person who runs into a burning building to save a child. Such a person is considered an individual of great courage. To be sure, this is one type of courage in action, and it is to be admired. The courage discussed in this chapter, however, is a more thoughtful and less instinctive type of bravery. A leader with moral courage can do the right thing even if it potentially means the end of a professional career. The courageous leader knows that he or she may very well be the loser by doing the right thing but then does it anyway. So, if the hero who ran into the burning building to save the child was conscious of the fact that he or she had a far greater chance of dying than living, and an even smaller chance of saving the child, and yet chose to go ahead with this selfless act, he or she showed the highest level of courage.

A Systemwide Approach to Leadership

Moral Courage in Schools

Moral courage is a necessity in effective leadership. Throughout history, there have been many times when school leaders' moral courage has been exercised particularly strenuously, such as during school integration. Some of the issues that have challenged leaders' moral courage in the past persist today. At the same time, new challenges have emerged. One new challenge, for example, is the increasing level of danger that schools have faced over the past few decades. Once unimagined, schools must now consider such dangers as an individual with a weapon, an explosive, or simply a desire to create mayhem laying siege to a school. As a result, most schools now have emergency lockdown procedures in place.

A Modern-Day Moral Dilemma: School Lockdowns

No matter the school, lockdown procedures tend to follow the same basic steps once a triggering event has occurred: (1) The teacher immediately closes and locks the door, (2) the teacher covers the window in the door, (3) the teacher groups the students in an out-of-the-way area of the classroom while instructing them to stay quiet and calm, and (4) the door remains closed under all circumstances until the principal or some other authority opens it from the outside.

When schools train their teachers in this procedure, one question inevitably arises: "What do I do if one of my kids knocks on the door to be let in after we have gone into our quiet space?" The official answer is that the door stays shut, based on the assumption that a shooter (or an otherwise threatening individual) is right behind the child. Of course, this is not a popular answer.

This is the moral dilemma of the lockdown. Does it take more moral courage to open the door, or to keep it closed? The reason that the group is discussing the situation in the first place is to help people understand the various consequences before there is a situation that requires this intense decision making. The decision to open the door or not is complex. There are many unknowns. There will be a winner and a loser, and the teacher's actions will be second-guessed by the media and peers, regardless of the decision.

Discussing the situation in advance is a way of working toward a common set of beliefs before empowering anyone. If all the players have a thorough understanding of why and how the system operates the way it does, then they will be more likely to make a sound decision, one that is in line with the organizational mission. Empowerment does not lead to rogue actions. In fact, it leads to just the opposite: It leads to decision making within

© International Center for Leadership in Education

a well-understood framework. Leaders promote the shared vision and well-understood framework, thereby empowering others, even in very difficult situations.

Building Up to Moral Courage

When a leader empowers others, then he or she is trusting them to make the right decisions. Life is fraught with difficult choices, and we all make mistakes. However, once the leader has brought the institution to a place of a common philosophy, beliefs, vision, goals, and mission, the time has come to trust others. That takes moral courage as well, because there is risk. Still, it is the right thing to do. Not surprisingly, a key component of success in developing and exercising moral courage is self-knowledge. Understanding one's own shortcomings and being honest about them with others is essential. No one is infallible, and a good leader must recognize and admit when there is a problem. By not admitting weaknesses or mistakes, or by placing the responsibility for poor decisions on others, a leader relinquishes control.

Sometimes it is hard to be honest even with oneself, so getting objective feedback can be helpful. It can be difficult to face one's weaknesses, especially if one has always viewed a characteristic as a strength. A leader has to find the courage to face the truth about his or her shortcomings. Third-party observers can be useful here. An outsider has less personal investment in a situation than does someone on the inside and can point out weaknesses from a position of relative objectivity. Identifying places in an organization where greater support is needed is part of beginning the dialogue for improvement and change.

It is important to remember that a leader cannot actually empower others. He or she can create the climate with trust, communication, and agreed-upon values to allow empowerment to happen; in the end, however, the person has to decide whether or not to pick up the power.

Courage and Responsibility

The courage to act cannot exist without accountability or responsibility. As Betty Velthouse, an associate professor of management and communications in the School of Management at the University of Michigan-Flint, once commented: "Make individuals accountable and responsible for tasks, for themselves, and they tend to behave responsibly."

If an individual wants the empowerment that will allow him or her to act independently, then that individual has to take responsibility for his or her decisions and actions. Too often, people do not want empowerment because they do not want responsibility. Criticizing others is easy, but taking responsibility demands courage. The issue of responsibility is critical in the empowerment process.

An Experiment in Shared Governance

Not all decisions can be — or should be — made by committee. The courage to empower others also requires the courage to say "no" when necessary and the good sense to define the decision-making process well in advance. Will there be a committee meeting to decide whether or not to pull the fire alarm? Can there be a committee meeting to define how teachers will be evaluated? These are two very different situations. Is an interview committee making a decision about whether or not to hire a new teacher, or are the members making a recommendation? Does an empowered teacher still have to take direction from his or her supervisor, or is that teacher independent by virtue of being empowered?

A crucial aspect of empowerment is defining what individuals are empowered to do. If the answer to this issue is not clear from the beginning, then there likely will be trouble along the way.

Too Much Empowerment

If everyone in an organization is a free agent, then there can be no organization, and any attempt at being an organized system will fail. A leader needs the courage to be honest and to let people know from the beginning what empowerment does and does not mean. Too often, ground rules are not made explicit from the start of a project, inevitably leading to hurt feelings, anger, and cynicism.

G. William Dauphinais, a PricewaterhouseCoopers partner and author of several books about business management, recounts a story about Kiwi Airlines as an example of what can happen when there is too much empowerment throughout an organization (Dauphinais, G. William, "Forging the Path to Power"):

> The case of Kiwi Air Lines provides a perfect example of empowerment that turned to anarchy without involvement limits and strong leadership . . . At first, employee involvement seemed to be working well . . . Gradually, however, involvement turned to contention and then to anarchy. The employee-owners perceived no limits to their empowerment. The managers hired to run things did not respond to senior management suggestions because they were, after all, owners. Flight attendants

began to disregard certain management requests, such as offering products in flight. Pilots refused to fly charters or meet with travel agents. Meetings became nightmares because everyone wanted to be part of the decision.

Thus, courage has two functions in empowerment. First, to be empowered demands the courage to accept responsibility for actions taken. Second, leadership has to have the courage to be honest with everyone involved and to establish limits to empowerment. In fact, different roles in an organization may have different levels of empowerment. Dauphinais touches on the need to define responsibility (Dauphinais, G. William, "Forging the Path to Power"):

> Assigning decision rights includes deciding which are the most difficult and important decisions faced by the organization and who should make them. The answers are not as obvious as they sound. Leaders must take the time to identify various types of decisions and to get agreement on who must decide what, when, and how.

A Formula for the Courage to Act, Power, and Responsibility

Imagine that the courage to act (C), power (P), and responsibility (R) are linked in a mathematical formula: $P \times R = C$, or power times responsibility equals the courage to act. Power and responsibility are factors of courage. If an individual has no power, or $P = 0$, then the equation would read $0 \times R = 0$. In other words, acting independently would have no effect and basically would be foolish. Acting without taking any responsibility, or $R = 0$, is easy and takes no courage; in this case, the equation would read $P \times 0 = 0$. Power without responsibility is also a bust. Both power and responsibility must be present to enable substantive action, and taking substantive action requires some level of courage.

Think again of a lockdown situation. The teacher is responsible for what happens when he or she decides whether to open the classroom door. In part, the teacher has the power to make the decision because no one will be on the spot to direct his or her actions. The decision requires courage precisely because of the responsibility and power associated with the action.

A person cannot accept empowerment without also taking on responsibility. Doing so is an empty gesture. There are principals who are unwilling to leave their schools for other district obligations because they do not think that the schools can operate in their absence. These principals do not have the courage to empower their staff by giving them the responsibility and ability to take action. Handled judiciously, empowerment leads to leadership density and a more efficient, responsive organization.

When the parameters and expectations of empowerment are clearly outlined from the outset, leadership density makes everyone's job easier. This is because there are a number of people responsible for acting in various situations instead of just one. Empowered individuals do not have to act in isolation, nor do they always have to be told what to do.

The Courage to Be Who You Are

Trust requires honesty, and honesty requires transparency. A leader should frame his or her professional identity by being warm and supportive, while at the same time having the courage to do the right thing based on the transparency of his or her beliefs and values. When leaders share a common set of values with everyone else in the institution, then they can safely let go of power, secure in the knowledge that others can be trusted to do the right thing. This emphasizes the importance of creating a shared vision and aligning organizational structures and systems to that vision.

Emotional Detachment and Fear of Change

One of the most difficult aspects of moral courage is the ability to detach emotionally from a decision based on a clear understanding of what must occur to enable the best outcome. Emotional detachment does not mean that an individual has to be cold and unfeeling; it means that personal emotional attachments should be resisted and not allowed to fog a clear vision of what to do. The question during a lockdown is "Do I open the door during the lockdown, or leave it shut?" Obviously, there is an extremely emotional aspect to this difficult question, no matter who — besides the threatening individual — is on the other side of the door.

Relationships are an essential backbone of school climate and community. However, there are circumstances in which the attachment is heightened, which is one reason why supervisors should not be married to or otherwise deeply emotionally and personally involved with anyone whom they supervise.

Sometimes, if a leader has past experience with a particular type of situation, then he or she will be more likely to know what to do despite the emotional quality of the circumstances. For example, if there is a reduction in force, someone will have to leave. That someone may be a young teacher who just bought a house and has a baby on the way. Letting that teacher go challenges a leader's emotional intelligence to the limit, but the decision must be made free of emotional strings. If the leader has been in the unfortunate position of having to let staff go in the past, he or she may be able to move forward with less of an internal emotional debate than would a leader who has never had this type of experience.

Power comes with responsibility. At times, this means that an individual must put the system or institution ahead of personal gains, popularity, and emotional discomfort. If a person is true to the vision and acts in a dispassionate manner, it is likely that the action taken will be the right one and defensible. When the vision and mission are clear, the data are there, and emotions are in check, all the ingredients are in place to empower individuals to act. Staff members will know what to do despite emotional tugs of the heart.

There is always some call for educators to change in some way: "Be more student-centered." "Use constructivist techniques." "Students should sit on the school board." The usual complaint about change is that people resist and sabotage the change process in order to protect their emotional comfort zones. The leader must always return to the base of philosophy, vision, and mission, and ask himself or herself, "Does the change support these value statements? Does the current situation fly in the face of these value statements? Are we fulfilling our mission? Are we acting according to our philosophy?" This is where emotional detachment can become a hindrance rather than a help. Change takes courage, leadership, and personal investment. It is difficult to feel personally invested if one is emotionally detached.

Emotional Attachment and Fear of Change

People often are willing to take on enormous responsibility if they feel an emotional attachment to what they want to do. If a leader can create an emotional story to go along with the change, then people are more likely to accept the change and actually implement it.

Imagine a pair of newlyweds. They are young, and they have their whole lives before them. They are free from many of life's obligations. Now, think about offering them a life of constant interruptions to their sleep, being vomited on, and having to clean up someone else's mess all the time. Who would want to trade the first situation for the other? Still, many couples want to have children. There is a strong emotional attachment to the idea of a family. All of the work and heartache of having children pales next to the joy associated with having a family. In such a case, the newlyweds do not simply accept the challenge; they actually embrace it.

The emotional precursor to successful change is a unified commitment to the school's philosophy, vision, and mission by everyone involved. Once a culture of high expectations has been established, a shared vision has been formulated, and leadership capacity has been broadened, impediments to instructional effectives can be changed. Change is never easy, and change without emotional commitment is just about impossible.

Courage to Act Outside the Rules

Little if any progress can happen without risks. There is risk associated with delayed gratification, but there is also the risk of being wrong or making a mistake along the path to results. A leader needs moral courage to deal with this situation. Leadership demands a certain tolerance for trial and error and a belief that through errors come learning, correction, and, ultimately, success. A leader knows empowerment when the system not only allows risk taking but also sees it as entrepreneurial rather than random, renegade action.

The ability to take skilled action is an asset in any leadership, but a leader must be willing to perform "without a net," at least sometimes. An example of this type of action occurred at a comprehensive high school in Vermont several years ago, where bold action by a leader led to some broad changes in the school to benefit students. Many students at this school were being challenged by a number of problems, including the need to hold jobs, a rigid curriculum and teaching structures, and general incompatibility with the way that the school delivered curriculum and instruction. The principal could see that in order to keep students from dropping out, the school would need to offer alternative methods of earning credits.

The principal made some courageous and bold decisions. Instead of going through the usual channels, which were slow, cumbersome, and tricky to negotiate, the principal chose to act independently, which allowed greater expediency. What developed was an outgrowth of independent study that the school called The Family School Partnership. A student, parent, or educator could initiate the process, which entailed the family, school, and specific curriculum department head working together to devise an alternative method for the student to earn credit. Students entering the program were monitored closely, and their work ultimately had to be approved by a teacher in a relevant area. But the work could be done on or off campus, often under the supervision of a community mentor. For example, a student might work in a local art gallery for art credits toward graduation.

The principal took a number of risks in instituting this program. There was a danger that community members, school board members, and parents might feel that students were doing too little and avoiding school requirements that they did not like. Teachers might feel the same way and resent being replaced by experiences outside of the classroom. Students might see the program as a way to skip out on school without dropping out. In fact, all of these challenges arose as the program was implemented. The principal and program's governing committee dealt with each in turn. In the end, the program was a resounding success. As a side benefit, it sent a strong message to some teachers and programs, because students continually found ways through the partnership program to avoid certain classes while still earning the required credits.

The risks were real, but the success of the program was worth it. Students who otherwise might have dropped out or failed to fulfill graduation requirements found success. Some exceptionally gifted students found ways to exercise their talents in challenging experiences outside of a traditional program.

A key to The Family School Partnership was not only that it saved students from difficult situations, but that it also helped students avoid those situations in the first place. Such solutions require creative thinking and the courage to act in unexpected ways to address unpredictable situations.

Broken Field Running

In football, when something unexpected happens, players are compelled to think on their feet and bring together instinct, experience, and creativity to figure out what to do next. Such a scenario is described as "broken field running."

Even if a school leader is not a football fan, he or she is probably familiar with the idea of broken field running. There is no set of rules and consequences that will cover all possible events and situations. Unexpected situations always will arise. Leaders need to be able to enter the mode of invention, which is largely the result of Quadrant D thinking, and find the courage to turn that thinking into action.

Responses here are not predictable, but rather designed to fit the particular case. The leader's actions are driven by the commonly held values — philosophy, vision, and mission — the written rules, procedures, and policies and the specific circumstances, experience, and self-knowledge. These factors, along with creativity, empower leaders to act in new and thoughtful ways.

Nothing disarms a student more than not living down to his or her expectations. Imagine that a student who has a reputation for getting into trouble ends up in the principal's office. The student expects the principal to confront him or her with some sort of charge and to mete out a punishment. Instead, the principal and student work out a system to keep the student out of this kind of trouble in the future. Meanwhile, the offended teacher keeps questioning why the student has not been suspended from the school for the infraction, as is the rule. After several weeks, while the teacher is making the usual complaint, the principal asks, "Has the offensive behavior stopped?" When the teacher answers affirmatively, the principal replies, "Then I have done my job." Solutions do not always have to look exactly like the rules, and leaders must be able to risk doing the right thing, not just the prescribed consequence, when taking action. This is empowerment. Empowerment and the courage to do the right thing are at the heart of the adaptive style of transformational leadership. In order to lead from Quadrant D, leaders must find the courage to venture out of their comfort zone, accept their own empowerment, and empower others.

Creativity and Empowerment

Creativity and empowerment are linked because taking independent action naturally involves being creative when deciding how to proceed with problem solving in a new situation. In the following chart, note how the organizational factors that contribute to empowerment and those that support creativity overlap and complement one another:

Linking Empowerment and Creativity

Factors Contributing to Empowerment	Factors Supporting Creativity
Open communication	Providing resources and support
Network building	Encouraging creative problem solving
Access to decision-making	Minimizing supervision
Control of resources	Inviting participation in goal setting
Participation	Assigning challenging work
Expanded awareness	
Attunement to organizational goals	

(Velthouse, Betty A., "Creativity and Empowerment: A Complementary Relationship")

Creativity and empowerment are "individual expressions of independence, risk taking, confidence, and commitment . . . fostered by similar environmental characteristics." Empowered individuals are expected to be creative in solving problems as they arise. Staking new territory requires courage. Once again, empowerment is not about simply letting people do what they want; it is about supporting a specific set of behaviors that align with a philosophy, vision, and mission.

The leader who empowers staff to be creative and independent must demonstrate self-assurance and the courage to put key leadership issues and decisions into others' hands. Empowering others is a courageous act, one that is new to many organizations. A leader cannot expect others to be creative, take on problems, take risks, and have the courage to act if those individuals are tightly supervised, if they do not have access to good information, and if they do not have the means for communicating ideas.

Empowerment helps individuals or groups to develop the confidence to be creative. All schools employ best practices, but developing a new generation of best practices — "next practices" — requires creativity and courage, both of which are enabled through empowerment. If change is a goal, then even the most tried and true best practices will eventually need to evolve as the system evolves. Otherwise, change will not be possible.

Imagine a school that has entered corrective action, for example, and that is struggling to change its systems and processes to support student success. At first, the school will want to identify and implement some best practices that have helped schools in similar situations move beyond their challenges. Some of the best practices will lead to good results. This will generate some confidence. Confidence is empowering, and it supports courage. Some of the practices, however, may be only minimally successful, and others may not be successful at all. With some confidence from the successes that the best practices have brought about, however, the school may feel empowered to try some creative new approaches. Doing so takes courage. Some new approaches will be successful, and some will not. The successes further shore up confidence; the failures provide learning opportunities. Eventually, some of the successful creative approaches — the "next practices" — may evolve into the new wave of best practices.

Transformational Leadership and Empowerment

Transformational leadership, discussed in Chapter 3, is an effective blending of vision and empowerment that involves an adaptive process by which leaders, staff, and students take action to improve teaching and learning in their school.

A Systemwide Approach to Leadership

Effective leadership does not reside in a single position; rather, it encompasses the diversified skills of many. It is this distributed leadership that defines successful schools. The Transformational Leadership Framework gives leaders a way to guide their daily actions and reflect on the growth of leadership in sustaining school improvement and long-term student achievement.

Obviously, transformational leadership is empowering. In fact, this type of leadership cannot exist without empowerment. If everyone is to be involved, then everyone will need authority, information, and trust. All members of the institution can be leaders. They all have the power to solve problems and bring about change. They all are moving in the same direction, based upon a shared vision.

Ironically, not everyone wants to be empowered. There are those who look to the administration to solve their problems. Often, people who do not want the responsibility of empowerment complain that they are not included in a decision. They undermine the decision and then complain that the decision makers have failed. On the opposite end of the spectrum, there are those who try to take over the decision-making process. They want to control what happens to ensure that they get what they want. Sometimes these individuals want to have the ear of the institutional leader so that their needs are met, but they do not want to have responsibility for the ultimate solution.

Of course, there are those who genuinely want to help and be part of the solution. These individuals can work collaboratively and put aside their egos for the greater good of the school and the students. They want and need the information and skills necessary for empowerment as they devote themselves to improving the school.

The intersection of leadership and empowerment is crucial. The movement toward sustainable transformational leadership depends on how the development of leadership is handled. To take advantage of the momentum toward empowerment means providing everyone with training in skills such as consensus building, decision making, collaborative action, data analysis, effective communication, and human relations. In addition, these individuals and groups need data, freedom to act, and trust. They must also be willing to accept responsibility for their actions.

In Practice: Cambridge Middle School

Cambridge Middle School (CMS) in Cambridge, Minnesota, is a comprehensive public middle school located about an hour north of the metropolitan Minneapolis/St. Paul area. CMS serves about 600 students in grades 6–8 with a staff of 35 teachers, one principal,

Chapter 5: Leadership Through Empowerment

one assistant principal, and two counselors. Cambridge is a close-knit community that is supportive of education. Key elements in the school's strategy for empowerment include positive, supportive human relationships and involvement of the entire community, both within and outside of the school. The description below emphasizes both of these aspects of the school's philosophy. The leadership at CMS describes itself as "positive, positive, positive!" Staff members receive positive feedback in myriad ways, including a weekly refreshment cart, upbeat notes, gifts to use in their classrooms, compliments at faculty meetings, and e-mails that end with the ubiquitous "Thanks for all you do for kids." The administration at CMS is respectful to staff and students.

Classroom observations are geared to the positive. In addition to regularly scheduled, district-required observations, the principal visits classrooms weekly for informal walk-throughs, charting activities and getting a feel for the nature of instruction. These observations shape quarterly and monthly training meetings, because the principal knows where more time needs to be spent and what could be emphasized more in instruction. The principal is the lead instructor in the Rigor/Relevance Framework and focuses instructional goals on factors that will make a difference for students. The principal strives to keep the staff and students focused on what is important for learning.

CMS uses a shared leadership model, with grade-level teams and their facilitators meeting with the principal to discuss concerns and develop proactive strategies. Planning for staff development is done by staff in keeping with district and school improvement plans. The student council is active in the school and is included in decision making, which is key in developing leadership skills among students.

Teacher/student relationships are emphasized at CMS. Students work with the same advisor for all three years. The advisor facilitates parent contacts and conferences and provides education interventions when needed. Teachers are trained in using the language of instruction to raise the odds of compliance and reduce oppositional behavior. They are also trained to interact with students in a way that will strengthen their relationships.

Parent and community involvement is considered integral to the school. CMS uses computer technology to ensure that parents are well informed. The school nurtures education and community partnerships whenever possible. A partnership with St. Cloud State University, for example, focuses on improving instruction in algebra, while a partnership with the local community college focuses on science. Local businesses help with donations, fundraising, and student incentives.

Getting Everyone on Board

What will entice everyone to get on board with empowerment and distributed leadership? Some people will be ready, but others will need a little push. The most resistant will need to be part of small successes, building to greater and greater commitment. To paraphrase Shakespeare, some are born empowered, some become empowered, and some have empowerment thrust upon them. Administrators must be honest and open. The process of developing a vision must be inclusive and then must be publicly implemented and pursued. There is no room for hypocrisy. As Cribb points out:

> In all collaborations, a key strategy is to anticipate and avoid barriers through developing a culture of "taking people with you," taking every opportunity to explain what is being done, why it's being done and demonstrating the key benefits. (Cribb, Ben, *Working Better Together: A Practical Guide for Embarking Upon In-school Collaborative Development*)

Individual or group deviation from the vision cannot be tolerated. Members of the institution need to develop the habit of questioning constructively rather than simply pointing out flaws or developing reasons not to do something new. There can be no place for lobbing grenades and then sitting back to watch. The challenge of persuading people to accept empowerment and leadership roles entails developing a climate of dedication, of embracing a cause bigger than oneself, of accepting responsibility, of willingness to take risks, and of learning from mistakes as opposed to citing mistakes as reasons not to try anything.

Being empowered requires hard work and dedication. It means joining with others, and it means trusting and being trusted. Empowerment brings joy, purpose, and meaning to one's work beyond what could be attained without it. When every member of the school community is empowered to be a leader, the institution never lacks for leadership. The school builds this climate one step at a time, beginning with small projects and working toward a sense of group ownership and pride. Success becomes possible when teachers and students not only are expected to be active participants in teaching and learning but also when they are empowered, supported, and given the tools to make that participation possible.

Vital Factors: Self-Knowledge, Philosophy, Mission, and Vision

Along with the exhortation that the unexamined life is not worth living, the ancient Greek philosopher Socrates offered this advice: "Know thyself." This is the most basic tenet of effective leadership. Before leaders can lead and empower others to lead, they must first empower themselves. If leaders have not fully examined their own beliefs, it will be difficult for them to make consistent and meaningful decisions. In *The Art of War*, ancient military strategist Sun Tzu observed:

> So it is said that if you know others and know yourself, you will not be imperiled in a hundred battles; if you do not know others but know yourself, you win one and lose one; if you do not know others and do not know yourself, you will be imperiled in every single battle.

Why Educators Do What They Do

Knowing oneself involves thinking about one's motivations, values, beliefs, strengths, and weaknesses.

Driving Forces

Take a step back for a moment and ask yourself, "What are the driving forces in my life as an educator? Why did I become an educator?"

A Principal Speaks: Driving Forces

Kathy Weigel, when principal of Atlantic Community High School in Delray Beach, Florida, reflected on what drives her teaching, actions, and decision making. Her belief that everyone has value was a driving force for her when she was a teacher, and she carried that attitude with her when she assumed a leadership position. She believes that every teacher must embrace this concept and that the best teachers find the gift in each student.

Her actions as a leader are a reflection of a desire to push everyone "into the light." For Kathy, this means leading people into situations in which they can do their best, understanding that there will be mistakes. The more mistakes a person makes in nonthreatening situations, she feels, the stronger an individual becomes.

In her decision making, Kathy tries to consider all of the school's stakeholders. She strives to take direction from all players and works to ensure that everyone feels a sense of ownership for the final decision. One example of her commitment to including all stakeholders in the decision-making process is her inclusion of students on interview committees.

Motivation for Leadership

Not every teacher chooses to make the transition from the classroom to an administrative office. The process and motivation is different for each who does.

A Principal Speaks: Motivation for Leadership

Sue Szachowicz, principal of Brockton High School in Brockton, Massachusetts, has a great deal to say about what motivates her as a leader. Ironically, her primary motivation for becoming a principal was a negative one. When she was a beginning teacher, Sue worked in a school that lacked good leadership. The principal was not student-centered. Sue saw numerous issues that she felt needed improvement, but she had no power to act. She witnessed students in her own classes being driven out by the system. First, she became a department leader, involving herself with the development of the state's standards. In that capacity, she had the opportunity to visit other schools, where she saw how strong leadership could make a difference.

What drives Sue now is student and school success. The school's public image was terrible for a long time, so Sue makes the school's reputation — backing up words with action — a priority. Brockton High celebrates every accomplishment, and Sue's team makes sure that the public knows about every triumph. Sue's commitment to ensuring that no student falls through the cracks has shaped her administrative style.

Sue's experiences as a teacher helped her understand the importance of strong, supportive leadership. She is determined that the teachers in her school not suffer from the same lack of support that she experienced early in her own career. As a result, the culture that she has created at Brockton High benefits teachers and students alike.

Core Beliefs

An individual's beliefs, ethics, and understandings shape his or her core values. Core values help leaders determine what they feel is worth fighting for or whether they are willing to compromise on a particular issue. Through self-examination, effective leaders develop an understanding of their core values. With this knowledge, leaders can stay true to their beliefs. Without it, leaders are left to make decisions based on expediency instead of on a solid foundation of deeply rooted personal and professional integrity.

A Principal Speaks: Core Beliefs

Aaron Hansen, principal of White Pine Middle School in Ely, Nevada, is clear about his core beliefs. He believes that good educators have a desire to make the world a better place and that there is no better way to do this than through teaching.

By becoming an administrator, Aaron believed that he could expand his influence in this respect. He believes that all students have the right to feel safe, to be listened to, and to have at least one positive relationship with an adult. He realizes that educators cannot expect all students to come to school with the same set of traditional middle-class values. He asserts that schools can no longer be valueless but that they must teach a common set of values and then expect them from every person in the organization, including administrators, teachers, staff, students, parents, and even spectators at school events.

Empowerment is crucial to Aaron's core beliefs. When some of his teachers felt marginalized by the school's leadership team, Aaron instituted a new decision-making process. There are now six "cabinets," each devoted to a different challenge. Membership to every cabinet is open to anyone who wishes to participate. Each cabinet is charged with framing the issues, brainstorming solutions, and presenting ideas to Aaron, who finds that he generally can approve them with little to no alteration. One great example of distributed leadership at White Pine is that a group composed of a member from each cabinet, not the principal, has presented the semiannual school status report to the school board.

What will Aaron not compromise about? Doing what is best for students and relationships. What is he willing to let go? Power and trying to do something about those things that are out of his control, such as the economy. He is willing to let go of small issues when there is a larger or more positive context to consider. For example, he may choose not to reprimand a teacher for occasional lateness when he or she is otherwise excelling at the job.

Strengths and Weaknesses

Another imperative piece of self-awareness for leaders is recognition of their strengths and weaknesses. No one can do everything well. This is one basis for empowerment: allowing people's various talents to come into play through collaboration instead of competition. So, when leaders identify what makes them anxious, they can gain control of those issues rather than be controlled by them.

A Principal Speaks: Strengths and Weaknesses

Brockton High School Principal Sue Szachowicz has reflected on her strengths and weaknesses. She sees strength in her energy and enthusiasm for the organization and in helping people to become successful. She also knows that she has strong emotional intelligence, which helps her read the emotional cues of the people in her environment. She understands context and is able to motivate others. Sue has a strong personal work ethic and the ability to stay focused on the vision while remaining adaptable. Sue listens well and knows how to gauge the climate of an organization.

On the other hand, Sue is aware of her own impatience. She becomes frustrated when others do not move as quickly as she does. She has to remind herself that not everyone has the same drive as she does, so she strives not to push others too hard. Sue has to work at not imposing her personal standards onto other people. She likes to respond with humor, but she has come to learn that humor coming from the principal has the potential to be misinterpreted; thus, she is mindful of her position and her audience and considers both carefully before she uses humor.

Mindfulness, Self-Knowledge, and Empowerment

The more aware or mindful leaders are, the more they are on top of a situation. Leaders need to guide a situation to a successful conclusion, not be pushed around by it. To be empowered means to know what you are all about.

For a school to build a successful and sustainable education system, it is not enough for only the leader to understand personal strengths and weaknesses. When all members of the school community go through similar exercises — each person identifying his or her beliefs, strengths, and weaknesses — the entire school benefits.

To empower others, a leader must help them to know themselves. Through this awareness, the leader can help organize belief systems around a single set of beliefs and goals for the school. Individual values and beliefs must be balanced against community values and beliefs, but the goal is to establish a clear vision that all members of the community can embrace, even if they express their common beliefs in a variety of ways.

Self-knowledge and honesty are two of the basic tools of those who want to be leaders. As individuals look inward to discover who they really are, they can share their values and beliefs. When there is a clear understanding of values and beliefs, both individual and organizational, there is assurance that each individual has the capacity to take on leadership responsibilities within the institution.

Philosophy

Any group that intends to empower its members must develop a philosophy that everyone can embrace. Too often, school philosophies are documents that are produced to satisfy accreditation organizations rather than statements of commonly held, inviolable beliefs that guide the actions of the people in the system. The typical philosophy statement is put away until the next accreditation sequence.

A Philosophy for Empowerment

The kind of philosophy that leads to empowerment is one that is in evidence everywhere, every day. When members of an institution can summarize the organization's common beliefs at any time, and when their actions support these beliefs, then there likely is a philosophy in place that has meaning and that empowers people to take meaningful action without direct supervision. When they know that they are expected to act in accordance with the philosophy, there is little concern about divergent actions that might be detrimental to the school's work. Aligning organizational structures and systems to a vision, or philosophy, is a key aspect of leadership as outlined by the DSEI. All members of a group must ask themselves whether they belong in that system and whether they can support the agreed-upon philosophy. If they cannot, the organization probably is not a good fit for them.

Of course, creating such a set of beliefs is no easy task. It is daunting to consider how to include all the constituencies: students, parents, community members, businesses, teachers, administrators, and local government. Empowerment is about giving people real voices; and if those voices are not heard and considered seriously, any statement of philosophy is bound to fail. One way to show people that their voices count is to provide opportunities for all stakeholders to participate in all stages of creating the philosophy. For example, when developing agendas or questionnaires, schools can send out draft copies to participants, who are encouraged to ask questions or suggest topics to include.

Developing a Philosophy

A philosophy is a collective statement that belongs to everyone in an organization. Developing a philosophy is not a short project. Whoever is responsible for overseeing the process of developing a philosophy might begin by sending out a questionnaire designed to find out what people believe, what they feel is important, what their vision of education is, and the like. By nature of the topic, such surveys should be open-ended, which means their results may be difficult to distill.

Nonetheless, the system should devote sufficient resources to organize survey results into a few well-considered statements of belief. These statements should be short, concrete, and in simple language. For example, instead of "We will all treat each other with respect," a more useful statement might be "People should listen to one another carefully, disagree without anger, and take care of one another." In this way, the philosophy illustrates expectations for behavior.

University of Georgia educator Lew Allen asserts that most mission statements, or philosophies, are too general. There is no way to tell what they might look like when implemented. He also points out that such statements tend to be too long and complicated. Often, not enough people are involved in developing the statement. (Allen, Lew, "From Plaques to Practice: How Schools Can Breathe Life into Their Guiding Beliefs.")

The philosophy development process should incorporate empowerment. Everyone should know that his or her voice has been heard and taken seriously. An important message for the group to hear is that listening to, respecting, and honoring each voice does not mean that every idea will be included in the final product. The process of developing a philosophy statement necessarily involves compromise and consensus.

One exercise that can be useful when developing a philosophy statement is the "World Café." Meeting in a large space, faculty are broken into small groups. Each group has a sheet of paper with the same key questions about core beliefs, driving forces, and other topics. The groups discuss the questions until they come up with a list of answers. When each group is finished, all of the ideas are collated into a single list, which is distributed to the entire faculty. In this way, each individual sees his or her responses along with all the others. No ideas are left out, so everyone is heard and taken seriously. From here, further distillation of the responses begins.

Chapter 5: Leadership Through Empowerment

Strategies

Planning a strategy to develop a meaningful statement with a supporting set of beliefs requires some important strategies and tools. It also requires time.

For a team to work well, several areas need to be addressed at the outset of the process. First, there must be a clearly defined purpose and goal; team members need to understand what they are trying to accomplish. The second step in the process is to ensure that team members understand the task in the context of the organization. Parameters, such as for timeline, budget, resources, and the like, need to be established in advance of the first meeting. Third, the team should assess what vital skill sets are needed among the members to accomplish the task.

Next, the team must settle on the members' roles and other team logistics: Who will lead the team? What responsibilities will each member have? When, where, how often, and for how long will the team meet? Finally, the team must establish a communication system so that all members are clear about how the team will get and use data, what the team's responsibility will be with respect to communicating outside the committee, how technology needs will be evaluated and met, and more. Keeping a team running smoothly and efficiently requires some tools and techniques, which should be explained to all participants. These include the following:

- Agenda development and the agenda itself are very important. The agenda should include the purpose of the meeting, topics, the lead person for each topic, and time estimates. Members of the committee should know how the agenda is developed and how they can request that items be added.

- A system for evaluating the meeting is also important. This should be simple and quick. Some teams simply use a "thumb system": "Thumbs up" means good, "thumbs down" is negative, and "thumbs sideways" signifies neutral in response to evaluative questions such as these: "Was today's meeting productive?" "Did the meeting move at a good pace?" "How well did we follow our ground rules?" and "Did we make good progress in this meeting?"

- Discussion techniques, such as brainstorming to encourage creativity and multi-voting to establish a priority ranking, should be familiar, as they are effective tools for getting ideas out and keeping discussion items to a manageable number.

Decision making is the most important, and at times the most difficult, task for a committee to tackle. There are two basic decision-making methods that groups can use: voting and consensus. Voting is used when it is unlikely that consensus can be reached in the time allowed. Consensus, however, is the better way to make a decision, especially if a decision will impact many people. Understanding consensus is very important:

- Consensus does not mean a unanimous vote or everyone's getting his or her way.
- Consensus requires time, active participation by everyone, and great listening skills.
- Consensus means that everyone understands the decision and why it was made. All members agree that they can support the decision.

During the consensus-building process, the group leader should ensure that all members listen carefully and participate actively in the discussion. Members should probe for alternative viewpoints and check frequently to ensure that they understand one another's ideas.

Revising and Refining

Once a committee or the individual designated with leading the creation of a philosophy has reduced the input to as tight and useful a statement as possible, the rounds of revision begin. All stakeholders receive a copy of the draft document, and all are given the opportunity to submit written comments, additions, disagreements, or changes. This process may result in many new ideas and refinements to consider. The process of seeking comments and revising should happen at least three times. Again, the very activity of developing a philosophy is empowering and a starting point for creating a system of shared beliefs.

With a refined draft in hand, the conversation can commence. Anyone who cares to do so should have an opportunity to discuss the refined draft. This can occur in faculty meetings, student council meetings, parents' group meetings, whole-school meetings, and open meetings for the community. It is vital that everyone understand the ground rules. First and foremost, the process is a consensus-building operation. No single philosophy can reflect every belief of every individual, but everyone must know and believe that he or she has a voice that is considered seriously. The individual or group presenting the proposed philosophy should be prepared to explain why some ideas did not make it into a final decision or document.

Most likely, there will be numerous meetings about the philosophy, which will result in further revisions. Ultimately, there should be a culminating meeting, at which the process leader or group presents the final product and answers any remaining questions.

When "No" Is the Answer

Michael Fullan, author and international leader on education change, and Andy Hargreaves, the Thomas More Brennan Chair in Education in the Lynch School of Education at Boston College and author of numerous books about education leadership and change, maintain that one of the most important skills a leader must develop is the ability to say "no" and "yet maintain, indeed enhance, one's reputation and the respect others have for that individual." (Fullan, Michael and Hargreaves, Andy, *What's Worth Fighting For in Your School?*)

Saying "no" is a delicate aspect of empowerment, for it involves helping those who are empowered understand that they will not always get their way. When soliciting ideas for the philosophy, one inevitably will find some mutually exclusive suggestions. Some ideas simply must be let go. The key is to assure those whose ideas did not make the final cut that they are still empowered, that their ideas were seriously and fully considered, and that their voices are as strong as anyone's.

In his seminal book, *The 7 Habits of Highly Effective People*, international leadership authority Stephen Covey states that "communication is the most important skill in life." He also counsels to "seek first to understand, and then to be understood." Saying "no" relates to both of these points. Rather than dismissing another's point or suggestion out of hand, the leader must let that individual know that he or she has heard and understood the idea fully. Repeating an idea back until the listener is confident that the leader has a full and accurate understanding of the thoughts presented shows supportiveness and respect.

Having truly heard a suggestion, a leader can explain why he or she believes that the idea may not be the best route to take. Even if the person making the suggestion is disappointed, he or she at least knows that the idea has been heard, understood, and considered. The person also knows that the leader has real, thoughtful reasons for disagreeing. Hopefully, this kind of experience, repeated over time, will create an atmosphere of trust and mutual respect, which allows for good decision making without winners and losers.

Saying "No"

Even if a leader takes all the right steps when saying "no," the person whose idea has been rejected may be unhappy, especially if the notion of empowerment has not taken hold fully. An example of this scenario occurred in a large high school English department in which teachers were encouraged to suggest new senior electives and did so regu-

A Systemwide Approach to Leadership

larly. One teacher proposed a course in minority literature to the department chair. The chair rejected the idea, but not without giving a full explanation.

Over the years, the chair had been working to integrate minority literature into all English classes. In this way, she hoped to establish minority literature as part of literature in general, not as something outside the mainstream. In her opinion, having a separate course would continue to marginalize the genre, rather than support its place as part of the traditional canon. She did not dismiss the teacher's idea; instead, she put it into a larger context that moved toward a long-term solution, not just a politically correct quick fix. Unfortunately, the teacher did not take the "no" well. He demonized the chair with the student minority group. He was not able to see the bigger picture, which in fact honored the genre and the students who wished to study it. The chair stuck to her point, however, and continued working in the broader context. The teacher's unhappiness was the result of a long history of mistrust, the need to be a hero with the students, and his inability to understand that not every idea can be implemented in the way one individual would like. In this case, the chair had taken the appropriate steps, but the leadership in this school clearly had work to do in helping people understand that empowerment did not mean that every idea would be implemented.

The process of saying "no" can be distilled into a series of steps:

1. Understand the suggestion or request by repeating it back to the speaker.
2. Acknowledge the individual's willingness to participate.
3. Acknowledge the person's expertise in the relevant area, commitment to the overall mission, and commitment to the area being explored.
4. Acknowledge the individual's willingness to be a problem solver and to seek creative solutions.
5. Respectfully, clearly, and logically explain the reasons for not following the suggestion.
   a. Take the time to acknowledge, respect, validate, and integrate the ideas of the individual.
   b. Explain the aspects of the idea that align or do not align with the established value system, philosophy, vision, and mission.
   c. Search for venues for which the suggestion might be appropriate, rather than simply rejecting it.
   d. Seek ways in which the suggestion can be honored, such as in a classroom or within a specific department.

Decision-Making Frameworks

When it comes to saying "no," it is helpful to have a well-established process for decision making with which all members of the organization are familiar. A decision funnel is one framework for describing how decisions are made at various levels of team participation. A leader should always make clear what everyone's role in the process is and who will make the final decision. The following diagram explicitly defines responsibilities and roles at different levels of the decision-making process.

Decision Funnel

Manager/Leader	Level	Team Member
Lay out process and criteria by which decisions are to be reached. Embrace the decisions.	1	Accept responsibility for decision-making process.
Participate in and acknowledge consensual process.	2	Work on outcome until it feels right. Embrace the decision.
Listen and discuss participant's input. Make decision.	3	Active participation. Voice opinions. Support decision.
Listen to input. Make clear decisions.	4	Voice opinions on time.
Give a direct command.	5	Listen carefully.

Time Needed ↑ (increases toward Level 1)

Commitment to Decision ↑ (increases toward Level 1)

Butler Technology and Career Development Schools of Hamilton, Ohio, has designed a simple format for deciding whether a new idea is worthy of consideration and potential implementation. The format demands that participants examine several factors when making decisions. This system applies to all levels of decision making. The following questions inform the decision making:

- Is it ethical?
- Can we afford it?
- Will it improve student performance?
- Will it improve student satisfaction?
- Will it improve stakeholder satisfaction?

Conflict Resolution and Decision Making

Conflict can be the result of poorly implemented empowerment initiatives or the result of a general lack of empowerment. A principal must put the institutional environment in order before even thinking of implementing an empowerment model with faculty, staff, and students. If the organization is rife with contentious conflict, it will be far more difficult for the school to make any progress toward empowerment or change (Short, Paula M., and Johnson, Patsy E., "Exploring the Links Among Teacher Empowerment, Leader Power, and Conflict"):

> Dysfunctional conflict creates chaos and interferes with job performance and productivity. It tends to lessen communication among members of the organization . . . Withdrawal and distancing of the participants decreases problem solving and effective interaction. Under these circumstances implementation of the empowerment process may be impossible . . . Empowerment strategies are dependent on all of the organizational functions that dysfunctional conflict inhibits.

If individuals are to be empowered and thus look to themselves first when problems arise, then the organization must build the necessary scaffolding for this to happen.

The Empowered Voice

Perhaps nowhere is the empowered voice heard more clearly than in decision making and conflict resolution. These are the activities through which all voices can and should be heard and recognized. This significance cannot be overstated. Empowered people know that their voices count, that they are listened to, and that they have influence in the final outcome of the process.

Of course, leaders must be willing to give up some of their control in order for other voices to become empowered. The benefits of doing so, however, are clear (Short, Paula M., and Johnson, Patsy E., "Exploring the Links Among Teacher Empowerment, Leader Power, and Conflict"):

> Business organizations have found that empowered workers contribute more to the profit motives of the company at less cost. Education leaders faced with similar productivity concerns and cost constraints are also exploring empowerment strategies for their personnel.

When teachers are empowered as partners in decision making, they have the opportunity to have a direct impact on their work environment. School leaders are wise to encourage this, because teachers have different perspectives about student needs and their own needs.

Power and leadership are about relationships. The character of a leader's power, and how those working under that leader perceive of it, plays a large role in how successful the leader is in empowering others. One research team found an empirical correlation between a principal's leadership influence and teachers' perception of empowerment.

The Faculty Meeting

The faculty meeting has long stood as an icon for poor productivity, rancor, and a forum for rehashing old issues. All voices should be equal in a faculty meeting, but some voices overpower others, and others choose not to participate. The net product is a sloppy process that pits ideals against practical matters. The loudest or most intimidating voices control the debate. The principal is a participant-observer, running the meeting while watching and inserting his or her opinion from time to time.

Faculty meetings are notorious for being too lengthy, but even the longest meetings may not yield answers because a great deal of time is frequently spent with little insight gained. The voices of individuals are not empowered when they exist in a context of poor listening and a general sense of confusion. When this happens, staff members can become cynical and disillusioned, which is not conducive to high productivity or morale.

School leaders can help lessen some of the potential for contention by inviting staff to make suggestions for the agendas, creating clear agendas with specific topics and time limits, keeping discussions on topic, and ensuring that all ideas are voiced and given proper due, among other strategies.

Empowered Student Voices

Many of the same issues that plague faculty meetings apply equally to classroom dynamics. When teachers ask students for their ideas about classroom rules, assignments, and curricular decisions, they are empowering their students' voices. But if the teacher then turns around and ignores all of the students' ideas, the students will see that the process is a fake. Their voices do not count at all. When this happens, students disengage. It is very difficult to bring back a student who has lost all interest in the class.

Many adults think of young learners as not yet developed, and they assume that students do not know what they need or should have. These adults tend to have a preconception of what students are moving toward as adults. Since the students are not there yet, their voices count less, in these adults' opinion. Think of the parent who tells a child that he or she could have earned A's instead of B's on a report card if only he or she had tried harder. Is it not possible that the child has tried his or her hardest? The student's voice is worth listening to, but many parents (and teachers) are skeptical when a child says that he or she already has expended maximum effort.

Schools might do well to take a recruitment point of view with respect to students. If students were not a given, but rather were customers to attract to the institution, then the school would take a much different view of them. Student voices would take on new meaning, since students would have the choice about where they spent their classroom time.

Students need to have a voice in their schools now, not "someday," when they have matured. The student viewpoint is relevant and valid. Students should be considered credible now — maybe not on all issues, but on many. Adults should not tell students how to feel or what to think; doing so denies students a voice. Some districts and states validate the student voice by including students on their boards. Although those students do not have a vote, their inclusion is a powerful confirmation of the student viewpoint. The International Center's handbooks, *Personal Skills — Leadership, Communication, and Collaboration for Grades K–6 and Grades 7–12*, provide provides more information about the development of student leadership skills as an important aspect of a meaningful school experience.

School Boards and Policy Issues

School boards give voice to the public at large. Open meetings empower the voices of anyone willing to attend. Principals bring teacher voices to the board table; superintendents bring principal voices to the board table. This is part of the cycle of professional conversation, discussed in Chapter 4. A great debate is great only when all the voices are empowered and included in the conversation.

The Bill & Melinda Gates Foundation published a set of briefs based on a series of cooperative planning processes that examined strategies for reforming teacher training and for hiring and retaining highly effective teachers. The process was inspired by research that indicates that:

> A teacher's effectiveness has more impact on student learning than any other factor under the control of school systems, including class size, school size, and the quality of after-school programs.

A specific focus for determining school readiness for reform in this area is policy. The Gates Foundation report concludes that "A school system's readiness to undertake teacher effectiveness strategies will depend on the extent to which policies assist or impede hiring, evaluation, tenure, compensation, and placement." (Bill & Melinda Gates Foundation, *Empowering Effective Teachers: Readiness for Reform*)

In order for schools to be successful in this, they must change the ways in which things traditionally have been done. Board and school policies, as well as laws, can easily interfere with this direction. Perhaps a school has inflexible policies in place that govern decision-making processes and hiring practices. This school will have to examine these issues carefully as it moves to empower teachers and students. As already noted, a disconnection between decision-making power and responsibility for that decision can be disastrous for an organization.

A Systemwide Approach to Leadership

Data Is King

A high school math department chair used to introduce hard discussion topics by saying, "In God we trust. Everyone else bring data." When dealing with a controversial topic, data makes the best tool.

The *We Survey* suite, described in Chapter 4, can provide the necessary data for a school to figure out where to ask questions and what questions to ask. Since its development in 2008, the *We Learn — Student Survey*, which has versions for students in grades 3–5 and grades 6–12, now includes the responses of 230,000 individuals. The *We Teach — Instructional Staff Survey* represents the opinions of 21,000 educators. The *We Learn* and *We Teach* surveys are designed to provide a basis for comparison between the attitudes and perceptions of students and those of teachers, as in the following example, which presents student and teacher responses to a question about the relevance of the curriculum as it is taught.

Teacher-Student Comparisons	
Teachers Students can apply what I am teaching to their everyday lives.	92%
Students I can apply what I learn to my everyday life.	59%

Clearly, there is a large gap between student and teacher perceptions on this issue. These data generate the question of whether the material being taught really is relevant to students' lives. Why are the perceptions so different? What do teachers need to change to make what they teach more applicable to students' lives? These are not evaluative questions; they are questions that guide an understanding of the obvious discrepancy.

An empowered educator would not be defensive about this information; instead, he or she would welcome the knowledge as a starting point for improvement. Being empowered means facing situations as they are and having the necessary information to deal with them. Power is the disposition to act, and action can be meaningful only when supported by sufficient data.

With the *We Survey* suite, all voices are empowered. Survey responses help define an issue so that schools can determine how to begin addressing it. In the example, it is the student voice compared to the teacher voice that begs the question of relevance.

Meaningful Conversations That Lead to Empowerment

For a conversation to be clear, productive, and empowering, all participants, including the group leader, must:

- listen to everyone carefully and thoroughly
- ask questions
- seek advice
- gather information
- consider various opinions

The Rules

Conversations are more successful when a group's rules and roles are clarified at the outset. The group should outline the process for decision making for the situation under discussion. Participants must know how their group fits into the larger picture. Is the group intended to generate ideas, offer advice, or make decisions, or is there more than one purpose for the group's work? If a group is intended to be advisory, but the members think that they have the power to make decisions, trouble lies ahead. It cannot be overstated: Be clear about roles and purpose from the start!

When a committee is formed and meets but does not use participants' ideas, the situation damages relationships and the chances for empowering others now and in the future. "Destructive consequences occur when [team] members feel powerless, alienated, and oppressed and become passive and combative." (Short, Paula M., and Johnson, Patsy E., "Exploring the Links Among Teacher Empowerment, Leader Power, and Conflict")

As a leader, think about the teams you create to aid in decision making. How do teachers and students figure into these committees? What authority are committees given? Consider these additional questions:

- Do hiring committees give advice, or do they make the decision?
- Do textbook adoption committees give advice, or do they make the selection decision?
- Do discipline committees make recommendations, or do they mete out consequences?
- Do policy committees set policies, or do they simply make suggestions?
- Do building issue committees set a course of action, or do they just offer options?

Respect

Most educators know about respectful techniques, such as active listening, but knowing and doing are not the same thing. When a person knows that his or her ideas are carefully considered, then that person feels empowered. An empowered person is willing to continue offering ideas at subsequent meetings. Ask clarifying questions until everyone, including the group leader, is satisfied that all ideas are understood.

Ignorance

The only bad question is the one that is never asked. If a leader — or anyone involved in a process — does not know an answer, he or she should not be afraid to ask questions. Asking questions is not a sign of stupidity. It is important to take the time to gather good information, as opposed to opinions. Data should be checked for accuracy and relevance. If advice is needed, a good leader should find a reliable source and ask for the advice.

To ensure understanding, a leader must facilitate a free flow of ideas and viewpoints. Slow down if there is time; it is a good idea to proceed slowly to ensure that all voices are heard and all ideas are understood. Group and individual reflection are imperative; the best solution or idea may result from either process.

The Paradox of Freedom

Chaos, not freedom, ensues when there are no rules. Chaos allows the bigger, stronger, and louder to dominate. In order to maximize everyone's freedom, there must be rules, including rules of engagement.

A general conversation about a topic is not always fruitful. An individual can get lost, buried by louder or more aggressive group members. Sometimes, members are afraid to speak, especially about delicate or especially difficult issues. One way to combat this potential problem is to ask group members to write down their thoughts, discuss them in small groups, and then present them to the larger body. Written thoughts may be collected and posted, without names, as a means of focusing the discussion. This approach can empower all voices.

A Constructivist Approach to Meetings

A constructivist believes that knowledge is not certain and that individuals make their own meaning by making sense out of lived experiences. When confronted with information that does not fit with his or her understanding of the world, an individual is forced to rethink the framework and construct a new meaning that incorporates fresh data or ideas.

Change the Presentation

The typical faculty meeting debate is a series of individual position statements, such as "Should we allow students to wear hats in school?" One by one, teachers offer their answers and reasons for their opinions. Often, the first or most strident speaker sets the conversation's tone and direction. When this happens, new discoveries or ideas may never make it to the table because ideas are introduced as full-blown and fixed. In some instances, a conflict arises, and the process of "defending positions occupies the thinking space; this position of advocacy closes down the space for listening." (Zimmerman, Diane P., "The Linguistics of Leadership")

Presenting an issue using a different question can change the process entirely. As one research team points out, "It is in framing the question that we have an opportunity to seek lasting and significant solutions to school dilemmas." In the case of hats, the leader could ask, "Why do you think kids like to wear hats in school?" Since this is not a yes-or-no question, quick, fixed answers are more difficult to produce. In fact, by asking the question in a new manner, the principal has maneuvered staff into reflecting on the issue rather than simply rushing to answer. (Lambert, Linda, and Walker, Deborah, "Constructing School Change: School Stories")

Constructing Meaning

When a principal poses a reflective question, he or she empowers the group by creating an opportunity for a more substantive discussion. A good next step is to have teachers form groups, each of which creates a list of suggestions for solving the problem or making a decision. The lists are then shared and become a starting point for meaningful dialogue.

By using this process, the principal opens some space for discussion. Black-and-white topics do not allow for such space. This space is where the group will construct meaning by accepting, modifying, melding, and shaping all of the ideas offered. As Zimmerman states, "Constructing shared knowledge and understanding is the essential work of a leader." (Zimmerman, Diane P., "The Linguistics of Leadership")

The hat issue will not be solved in one meeting, but the leader has enabled faculty to establish a rich collection of ideas to consider regarding the broader issue of student expression in terms of dress, social habits, and more. In addition, the constructivist dialogue builds trust and efficacy in the institution.

With practice, a school leader can begin to find ways to turn most questions into opportunities for constructivist conversations. It is essential for a leader to construct — or guide construction of — shared knowledge.

Think about how a leader could change the following meeting agenda items into discussion starters:

- Should the school have a half day the day before Thanksgiving?
- Should effort grades be added to report cards?
- How should the school set limits on the number of students using the library during study hall?
- Would faculty like to create common rubrics for evaluating assignments in all classes?

Making Empowerment Possible

A beautiful flower appears to the viewer as a complete, freestanding entity, but it is not. In fact, the flower is actually a part of a long process, one that started before the blossom bloomed and will continue after it has faded. The presence of the flower indicates what happened prior to its appearance, even though there may not be any direct way of measuring what preceded it.

First, the soil had to be adequate for the seed to germinate and to support the flowering plant. This means that there were sufficient nutrients and moisture to allow the plant to grow. Without sufficient water, the growing plant would have withered. Too much water might have rotted the roots. Insufficient minerals and other elements in the soil would not support plant growth, but too much fertilizer could burn the vegetation.

The plant had to be in a spot that received the proper amount of sunlight. It needed protection from footsteps, invading weeds, nibbling creatures, and insect invasions. Perhaps pollination by insects or birds was necessary.

As the flower blooms, bees may collect its nectar and transform it into honey. Perhaps it will feed a butterfly or hummingbird. Maybe the flower will be picked to become part of a bouquet or tucked behind an ear for a bit of beauty. If left alone, even as the flower withers, the process continues. The petals fall and rot into the ground, adding nourishment to the soil for the next round of blooming.

Empowerment is like a flower. There are many conditions, forces, and causes that precede its blossoming. There is no specific formula that someone follows to ensure that it takes hold and flourishes. The same holds true for leaders and other members of an institution, who must be cultivated to accept empowerment so that it becomes a natural part of the everyday life cycle of the organization.

The Uniqueness of Each Situation

As for a flowering plant, there are a vast number of variables that need to work together in just the right amounts for empowerment to take root. This chapter has illustrated the nature of many of these variables, showing what is necessary and how different organizational aspects work together to produce the right conditions to support empowerment.

The elusive aspect of this process is the lack of a specific formula or recipe for putting everything together. Just like gardens, every institution is unique, a singular instance of just such a combination of factors. The superior leader knows how to analyze his or her environment; then, like a good gardener, he or she knows what to add and what to take away.

The actions of a particular school may be inspirational, but it is important to remember that those events did not just happen. Through sensitive leadership and after a great deal of development and cultivation of the school culture or climate, the school came to be a place where empowerment could flourish as a result of a shared mission, vision, and values. Culture and climate, by their very natures, are qualitative, difficult to measure in quantities. How can a number describe how a school feels?

Some people believe that if you cannot easily measure something, it must not be important. Effective leaders, however, understand that what is difficult to measure is often the most significant. Society is fixated on pure quantitative data. We have become overly focused on predictability and test scores. Yet, if straight data are so important and so useful for making predictions, how did the stock market crash? Why were the accountants responsible for AIG unable to see what was coming? There is no way to measure things like deceit, love, and passion for the work, but they are likely more important than pure quantitative data.

Empowerment at Work

Brockton High School in Massachusetts offers a good example of what can happen in a school when all of its members feel empowered. In January 2010, print and broadcast media featured a heartbreaking story about the suicide of a student in South Hadley, Massachusetts. The apparent cause of the student's self-destructive behavior was bullying.

Brockton High students wanted to respond to this tragedy by showing their disapproval of bullying in general and in this specific situation. Through research, the students discovered the "Day of Pink," which started in Nova Scotia in support of a male student who had been bullied for wearing a pink shirt to school. Representatives of the student body approached their principal, Sue Szachowicz. She told them that they could mount a peaceful demonstration but that they had to work their actions into the normal flow of the school day.

A technique called "quick writes" is already a standard part of the school's teaching and learning strategies. Peer mediators developed five questions, one for each period, which would help gather information about how students felt about the issues of harassment, discrimination, and bullying. Each quick write was collected in an envelope labeled only with the period, not the name of the class or teacher. Here is the assignment given to students during first period:

> Day of Pink is a day of action, born when a youth in a high school in Cambridge, Nova Scotia, was bullied because he wore a pink shirt to school. His fellow students

decided to stand up to bullying and hundreds of students came to school wearing pink to show support for diversity and stopping discrimination. What do you feel makes you different or unique? Have you ever felt this puts you at risk for being bullied or harassed?

The administration read and tabulated the responses to this and the other questions. The next day, Brockton High held its own Day of Pink, for which the majority of students wore something pink to school.

The students at Brockton High School were empowered to act when they felt that there was a need to do so. This could only have happened as a result of many hours of hard work to create a climate and culture that would support such independent action. Student empowerment did not result in chaos. Students channeled their energies through the proper institutional hierarchy and structures.

The result was tremendously positive. In Sue Szachowicz's words, "What a GREAT day … GREAT!!! I have the BEST job in the world!!!" (Susan Szachowicz, personal communication, April 2010) The students' actions were a win for them, a win for the school, and a win for the community.

If Sue were asked what made this event possible, she probably would have some difficulty answering, for there was no one thing that allowed students to be empowered. Any number of causes, conditions, and forces had to be in place for the appropriate values and attitudes to develop and for the event to occur. Each school starts where it is and travels its own journey to empowerment.

Ordinarily, the response to bullying is administrative actions, such as stricter rules, hiring a consultant, or asking staff to be more diligent in policing students. At Brockton High School, as a result of the climate of empowerment, students were able to lead the way in making a statement about bullying without the administration's having to step in beyond the support that was offered. Students were empowered to act — and to act preemptively.

Inspiration Is Not Transferable

That which is inspirational cannot simply be picked up and dropped into another situation. An inspiration reflects an individual school's long journey toward a culture that supports the empowerment of its membership. The journey will necessarily differ from one school to the next, but each will contain some combination of the factors, attitudes, conditions, values, and causes discussed throughout this chapter.

Empowerment is essential for sustaining the school improvement process. Most systems that are trying to improve are riding on the heels of an administrator who came in to transform the school; however, when that talented leader leaves, the system often falls apart. In schools where staff, students, parents, and the community are empowered to lead, the system survives, because the beliefs are deep and inform the work and because everyone knows what is going on. The formal leader is just one of many leaders in the system.

Revisiting the Key Questions

Several key questions are helpful for leaders to reflect on as they look for ways to empower others.

Why are some leaders successful and others not? Successful leaders see leadership as a disposition, not a position. They see the need to listen and to share the positional power they have. These leaders understand that everyone has something of value to contribute. They are flexible, and they understand the need to change leadership strategies depending on the situation, as is characteristic of transformational leadership.

Leaders who see leadership as a power-wielding opportunity tend to be less successful. They insist on adhering strictly to the rules and imposing regulations on others regardless of the nuances of a situation. By refusing to relinquish power to others, they deprive the organization of the richness that comes through creating leadership density.

How do successful leaders build a common cause? The common cause results from the shared mission, vision, and values of the system. In too many systems, the administration does not know where the system is heading, and it has not empowered members of the organization to understand and act on the mission. Building this common cause takes time and deliberate action on the part of the organization's leadership.

How do successful leaders communicate? The key here is that successful leaders *do* communicate, and they do so often. They understand that communication involves giving out information, taking in information, and understanding what is communicated to them. Effective leaders employ the entire scope of communication skills, verbal and nonverbal, expressive and receptive.

How do successful leaders deal with conflict? To the effective leader, conflict is potentially helpful, not something that must be avoided at all costs. Conflict can become a way to enter into a situation and allow everyone to be empowered to work toward positive movement.

How do successful leaders build resolution? Successful leaders consider all points of view and special interests in their thinking. Everyone is assured that his or her suggestions and needs are considered before a final decision is made, which leads to empowerment. All stakeholders have empowered voices; and, whenever possible, consensus is the method for reaching a resolution.

How do successful leaders move beyond "that's not the way we do things around here" thinking? Leaders who understand that working through challenges is an iterative process are more likely to find success. They know that no single answer always leads to a solid solution, so they invite others to share their ideas. They are also sensitive to the fact that no two situations are identical. While there may be strong patterns, there is never exact duplication.

What is the role of courage in being a successful leader? Courage is connected to mission, vision, and values. If a leader has helped all members of the organization to come to agreement on the "why" of the work, then the courage to act comes more easily. When a leader knows what must be done and the reasons for doing it, then he or she can call upon moral courage. Confusion about purpose dilutes courage.

How do successful leaders support the human resources in their schools? Successful leaders understand the needs of the people in the system. They know that in order to accomplish great things, people need to know that they are valued and connected. Teacher support, selection, and evaluation are identified in the DSEI as key roles of leadership.

What is the difference between license and empowerment? Having the license to make decisions and take action through a position title does not rise to the level of being empowered to do the work. Empowerment brings a sense of understanding and connectedness to the system. Where license can be seen as unbridled freedom, empowerment is an earned right to act resulting from an understanding and acceptance of the institutional philosophy, vision, and mission.

When should leaders act, and when should they just sit with an issue? In some situations, a leader's best action is no immediate action. Sometimes, in order to determine if an issue requires any action, a leader must observe. An issue may resolve itself without any intervention. Obviously, this does not apply to health or safety concerns, but it is a valuable approach when there is no clear way ahead. Pausing to listen, watch, and think before taking action can provide the leader with stronger understanding and sense of purpose.

Is adaptive leadership the same as just thinking on one's feet? Adaptive leadership is synonymous with the athletic term "broken field running," which is akin to instinct or thinking on one's feet. In some circumstances, a good leader can feel the direction in which the system is headed and intuitively make decisions to avert a situation. At other times, a leader will run up against a new situation. At that point, he or she must apply the system's philosophy, vision, and mission to the situation to make rapid decisions about the best actions to take.

A Summary of the Power of Empowerment

Imagine a school that is working hard but just cannot seem to achieve adequate yearly progress (AYP). Something has to be done to move the situation along. In this case, leadership needs to employ a tight-tight system of reform.

The term *tight-tight* means that there is little discussion and that the focus is on the fidelity of implementation across the system. Reform is attained by mandating specific, research-based strategies for success. Such action will ensure that student learning increases so that the school can achieve AYP. However, this cannot be the final step, especially if the goal is continuous improvement.

Once leadership has shown staff one way to success, it can back off a little as teachers apply the new, successful strategies. Over time, though, the institution will reach a critical point where progress flattens out, and once again AYP will be in jeopardy.

At some point, the entire school has to be empowered. Otherwise, teachers will eventually go back on automatic pilot, completely relying on the administration for direction. Doing so has two deleterious effects: (1) teachers become bored and uncreative, and (2) everything depends on the administrator. If the person directing the system leaves, then the whole house of cards falls.

The solution is to move from a tight-tight approach to a tight-loose approach. Once a school has met with some success, which establishes credibility, then there is room for empowerment and professional freedom. This means that everyone remains in agree-

Chapter 5: Leadership Through Empowerment

ment with the goal of making AYP. Maintaining a consistent focus on the goal is the tight part of the approach. Everyone understands the value of research-based strategies when striving for improvement; however, instead of defining the goal and approach externally, the teachers now can experiment with strategies of their own. The method for this is loose, and this approach becomes possible when staff are empowered.

At first, as some of the leadership is ceded to the staff, a school may experience an implementation dip. Whenever there is change and new ideas come into play, there is a period of adjustment and a need for fine tuning. Over time, however, teachers will make the necessary changes, and progress will resume. When teachers are empowered, leadership is no longer the sole province of leadership or the administration, thus enabling the transition from the tight-tight approach to a tight-loose system.

This process of innovation-implementation-dip-innovation will continue in cycles. Once individuals have been empowered, the system will naturally reinvigorate itself in cycles of reform and adjustment. The difference is that the reforms will come from within the institution instead of in a top-down manner from the administration.

Another significant result of empowerment is leadership density. When staff members are accustomed to making decisions and taking bold action, then they are less reliant on the guidance of the administration. Remember, the whole idea of cycles of improvement must be jump-started by leadership who employ a tight-tight approach. But once staff members have been empowered, they can carry on with minimal supervision. This is leadership density — the point at which the departure of the principal or other official leader will not spell disaster for the institution. When there is enough embedded leadership and empowerment, the institution can continue moving in a positive direction during the transition to new leadership.

In essence, empowerment makes it possible for an institution to largely lead itself. Of course, there will always be specific individuals in designated official institutional roles — principal, dean, department head, teacher, coach, and so on — but leadership will be spread throughout the organization. When there is leadership density, there is more leadership and more power in the system.

By giving away power, those who originally hold it multiply it. They do not lose authority, but the members of the institution gain the ability and necessary skills to take effective action without having to wait to be told what to do or to ask for permission. If there is an honestly shared and held philosophy, vision, and mission, then any worry about maverick action is minimized.

A Systemwide Approach to Leadership

Summary

Building the leadership capacity of the school community requires empowering others. Transformational leaders who have a clear understanding of their own motivations, strengths, and weaknesses, along with a clear vision for the school as a whole, are in a position to empower others. Courage plays a key role in empowerment. When many individuals are empowered to act on a shared vision, needed changes are more readily accepted.

Reflection Activity

1. Examining your motivations, values, beliefs, strengths, and weaknesses as a leader can help you empower yourself, opening the door for empowering others. Think about the following questions:
   - How do my beliefs about teaching and learning drive my actions and decision making?
   - Why did I choose to become an education leader?
   - What am I willing to really fight for?
   - What specific actions do I carry out that lead to the empowerment of others?
   - How do I build leadership in my school to complement my strengths and support my weaknesses?

   Discuss your answers with others. How do individual differences among leaders shape the ways in which people lead and share leadership?

2. Think of a time when, as a leader, you did the right thing, but the results took considerable time to manifest. Reflect on these questions:
   - What was it like to wait for results?
   - What pressures did you feel from others, including peers, supervisors, parents, students, the school board, and community members?
   - What did others think of your actions?
   - Were you forced to discontinue your actions before they bore fruit?

   In a "quick write," record your responses, especially how the past experience has shaped your willingness to wait for long-term results from others in your school community.

3. A school leader may be faced with many types of moral challenges, each with its own set of consequences for the leader, for the others involved, and, sometimes, for the school community or community at large. As a school leader, think about the moral courage needed in each of the following situations. What would you do?

- You have to fail the superintendent's child.
- The school board demands the use of corporal punishment.
- You find out that a student is pregnant.
- You see a colleague berate a student in front of the class.
- A star student or highly regarded teacher is accused of wrongdoing.

After you have reflected on each, think about how empowerment (of yourself and of others) is involved in resolving these situations.

Chapter 6

Leadership Skills for a Positive School Climate

Effective leadership is propelled by many factors, including the personal, social, and emotional skills of those in leadership positions. These skills (for example, kindness and honesty) influence a school's climate and can lead to strong relationships among administrators, staff, and students — and these, in turn, can lead to empowerment.

Climate and Relationships

What do we mean by the term *climate*? Numerous authors and scholars offer various definitions for this somewhat elusive concept, but there is agreement that climate involves the interaction of many different factors and that it is associated with effective schools. Climate has been described as consisting of "shared values, interpretations of social activities, and commonly held definitions of purpose." (Kottkamp, Robert, "The Principal as Cultural Leader")

Elements that influence school climate include the following (Marshall, Megan L., "Examining School Climate: Defining Factors and Educational Influences"):

- the number and quality of interactions between and among adults and students
- students' and teachers' perceptions of their school environment
- environmental factors

- academic performance
- feelings of safety and school size
- feelings of trust and respect for students and teachers

Instructional leaders are responsible for establishing the school climate. They do this, in part, by ensuring that members of the school community understand the vision and by developing strategies to implement the mission. The DSEI emphasizes these elements of school leadership. Imagine how the influence of a single leader can be intensified if everyone in the system is empowered to have a leadership role and is invested in these issues.

Administrators to Teachers, Teachers to Students

A great deal of research places the teacher-student relationship at the crux of school climate. Relationships between leaders and staff are analogous and are, therefore, also inextricably linked to school climate. If teachers are empowering students, and leaders are empowering teachers, it is easy to see how relationships create multiple leaders — or leadership density — throughout an organization. Building the leadership capacity within the school is a key element of leadership, as outlined in the DSEI.

Every teacher knows that the purpose of education is to empower students with the skills, knowledge, and attitudes necessary for success as independent and interdependent members of society. The teacher-student relationship is a vital element of education success. Typical positive aspects of this relationship are high expectations, respect, and a caring sensitivity. Is the situation any different with respect to a principal and his or her staff — or, indeed, in any relationship between leaders and the group they are charged with leading? Whenever there is a superordinate/subordinate dynamic, there is an opportunity to empower. If a teacher can empower a class, then how much more significant is an administrator's empowerment of an entire school community?

In his 1970 book, *Crisis in the Classroom: The Remaking of American Education*, education journalist and scholar Charles Silberman wrote, "What tomorrow needs is not masses of intellectuals, but masses of educated men — men educated to feel and to act as well as to think." Silberman is suggesting that the purpose of education is to empower individual students, an idea that is easily expandable to the entire education community. Effective leadership is not about using power to demean or control others; it is about empowering others, which means helping them to understand how to act in thoughtful ways. (Silberman, Charles E., *Crisis in the Classroom: The Remaking of American Education*)

Education innovator Dennis Littky sees education as a means of empowering learners — if educators embrace the opportunity — as his discussion about teaching democracy explains (Littky, Dennis, and Grabelle, Samantha, *The Big Picture: Education Is Everyone's Business*):

> [The United States Constitution] is very cool stuff to know. But while they're learning these things, most kids are not making one democracy-inspired decision throughout their entire 12 years of schooling. Most kids either are not allowed to or don't believe they have the right to make decisions about anything significant during the years they are in school. So, to me, if we're trying to teach kids about the importance of democracy . . . we really should be giving kids the opportunities to make real decisions and take real responsibility for what is going on around them. They should actually *be* voting, not just talking about it.

The Role of Climate in Empowerment

Littky has described 14 overall goals of education. Among these, several relate closely to the concept of empowerment:

- taking risks
- solving problems
- thinking critically
- working in groups and independently
- having moral courage

Kristen B. French, a literacy teacher in an urban Montessori school, offers an interesting perspective about climate and empowerment (French, Kristen B., "Teaching for Empowerment, Love, and Mentorship):

> Empowerment can be a loaded word, as if one person can empower another. I don't want to presume that I have the ability or power to empower anyone other than myself, but the possibility for empowerment can be created when a foundation is provided. And hopefully, within the process of dreaming and imagining a just community, students [or staff] will take an active role to become agents for change in their own lives.

A leader cannot change anyone or force someone to do something that he or she does not want to do. However, a leader can change how he or she treats others, and a leader can develop a climate that will encourage and maximize the ease with which people can become empowered. Building the right climate for empowerment is absolutely crucial for success.

There is a self-perpetuating quality to a positive, empowering school climate. People who are empowered are likely to feel more positive about themselves and their organization, thus contributing to the positive climate. The results can include greater satisfaction, higher productivity, and longer length of service.

Communications, Relationships, and Climate

A positive school climate is associated with fewer emotional and behavioral problems among students and increases in the academic success of high-risk populations in urban schools. Some research indicates that because a positive climate supports healthy development and avoidance of antisocial behaviors, it may be particularly helpful for male students and high-risk students. (Marshall, Megan L., "Examining School Climate: Defining Factors and Educational Influences")

Another benefit appears to be increased job satisfaction for employees. This results when teachers perceive that their interactions with school leaders are positive and are based on such factors as effective communication, advocacy, inclusive decision making, and fair evaluations.

A leader must pay attention to how he or she communicates with staff and faculty. It is equally important for a leader to develop an understanding of how faculty and staff perceive his or her communication style and effectiveness. One tool for achieving this perspective is the *We Lead — Whole Staff Survey*. Part of the *We Survey* suite, which was discussed in detail in Chapter 4, the *We Lead — Whole Staff Survey* elicits feedback from staff and faculty about their perceptions of factors related to school climate and the school community, including communication between and among colleagues and leadership. The qualitative data gathered using the survey offers leaders insight about their schools' and their own strengths and weaknesses. As of June 2010, 35,000 educators had taken the survey.

Empowerment and a positive climate are something of a chicken-or-the-egg phenomenon, each contributing to the success of the other. The influence that a principal's leadership qualities have on school climate cannot be understated; but, again, imagine how much greater the influence on climate is when an entire community is empowered.

When a school leader can envision what teachers need, he or she can provide the appropriate tools and support to empower them to act confidently and independently, trusting them to do the right thing, without close supervision, as part of the decision-making process. Empowering others involves ensuring that people have the information they need and treating them as competent individuals whose ideas and contributions have value.

Most educators would agree that encouraging students to be active members of their communities through political or social activities helps form habits of caring, involvement, curiosity, and commitment. Supporting students in such endeavors involves forging and nurturing relationships with others. The International Center studied schools that were successful despite confronting challenges such as poverty, high student mobility, and diversity. The study showed that relationships were an important factor in the positive movement in these schools (McNulty, Raymond J., and Quaglia, Russell J., "Rigor, Relevance, and Relationships"):

> In these schools, relationships among students and staff are deliberately nurtured and a key reason for student success. Students believe the staff genuinely care about them and encourage them to achieve at high levels. If there is not a high level of positive relationship, students will not respond to higher expectations.

Understanding the positive role of relationships in student success makes it easy to understand how relationships between staff members and school leaders are also imperative. Hattie's meta-research confirms that teacher-student relationships have a positive impact on student achievement. (Hattie, John, *Visible Learning*) Research on examining factors contributing to the success of top-performing companies draws similar conclusions about the need for strong, positive relationships between leaders and staff members. Employees who are encouraged to be innovative and who understand their organization's goals, mission, and values are more productive and satisfied in their jobs.

Strong relationships are the vehicle for encouraging innovation and connection to organizational goals, mission, and values. Empowerment is the destination. Perhaps no one states the importance of relationships with more power and compassion than Nel Noddings, a leading educational philosopher and a professor of philosophy and education at Columbia University's Teachers College:

> The most basic idea of relational caring is to respond to each individual in such a way that we establish and maintain caring relations. My particular philosophy of education is important to me, and I am committed to it for my own practice. But the living other is more important than any theory, and my theory must be subordinate to the caring relationship. (Noddings, Nel, *The Challenge to Care in Schools: An Alternative Approach to Education*)

A Systemwide Approach to Leadership

Bending the Rules: Some True Stories

When individuals are empowered, they are trusted to make the right decisions at the site of a problem. Sometimes the decision must be made because there is no one to consult about the next steps to take. Sometimes there is no need to consult someone else, because the individual who is taking action has the knowledge and skills — and the leadership's trust — to make appropriate choices. In some instances, a situation may call for breaking, bending, or interpreting the rules in new or different ways to get a job done.

There is always a risk involved in trying new interpretations within a system without the lead time to mount an inclusive review or decision-making process. In such situations, a leader needs moral courage, a characteristic discussed in greater detail in Chapter 3. Following is an example in which school leaders flexed the rules to support positive outcomes for students and a positive school climate.

Testing and Troubled Students

One state's former education commissioner operated by the motto "no exceptions, no excuses." This worked when everything was running smoothly. With absolutely no room for discretion, however, problems were inevitable. Rules can be crystal clear, but eventually a situation will arise that calls for an adaptation of the rules.

One state testing day in this commissioner's state, an elementary school principal called her superintendent with a problem. Two students had seen their father taken out of the house in handcuffs the previous evening. There had been abuse in the home, and the two children had spent the rest of that night in temporary care outside their home. The principal told the superintendent that he could not justify making these two students take the high-stakes test. As he saw it, those two youngsters had given all they had to give by showing up to school at all.

The superintendent agreed and called the state department. Although the commissioner's office responded with the "no excuses, no exceptions" motto, the superintendent and the principal exempted those two children from taking the test that day. There was no further action on anyone's part.

Results of Empowerment

In the school profiled above, leaders felt sufficiently empowered to do what needed to be done. They worked in a climate that supported empowerment and trust. Adults forged positive, productive relationships with students and with each other in order to solve problems in innovative ways. Education leaders must develop and maintain such climates if they hope to empower others and invite them to act independently as agents of the institution as well.

Situational Adaptations

Leadership is necessarily situational. Some people will need more direction than others. By adapting to the needs of each individual, a leader can support the empowerment of each individual at a level appropriate to his or her readiness to accept the responsibility and the work of being empowered.

The following chart illustrates how a teacher can shift responsibility to students systematically. If the leader is the teacher and the teacher is the student, the chart works equally well for the gradually increasing stages of empowerment.

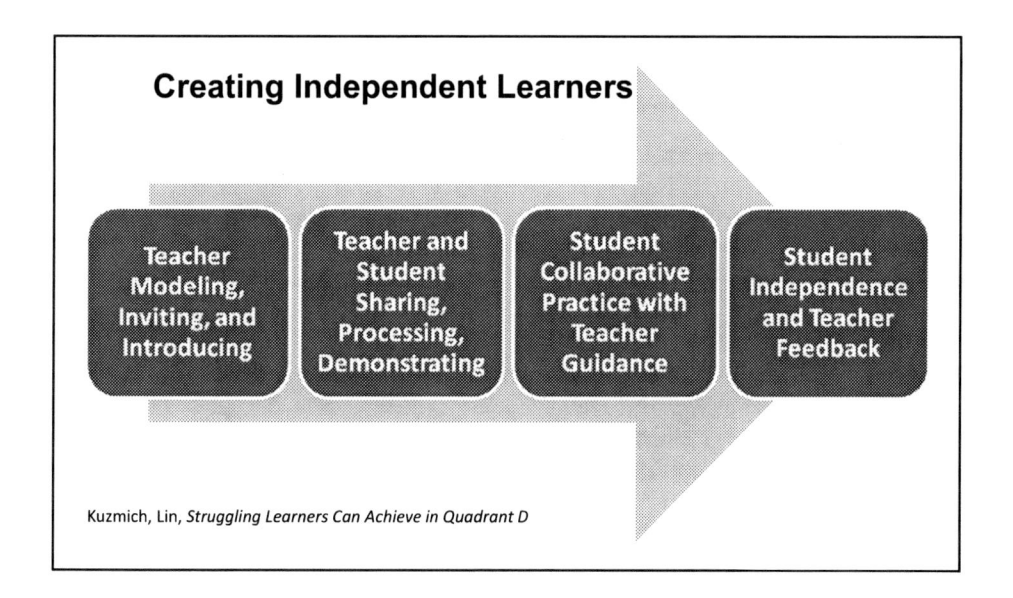

Creating Independent Learners

Teacher Modeling, Inviting, and Introducing → Teacher and Student Sharing, Processing, Demonstrating → Student Collaborative Practice with Teacher Guidance → Student Independence and Teacher Feedback

Kuzmich, Lin, *Struggling Learners Can Achieve in Quadrant D*

If empowerment is talked about to a faculty member, and that faculty member then is expected to act in an empowered way, the prospect of success is thin. The intervening steps of sharing the work and then fading into the background as teachers begin to adapt to the approach are vital for empowerment to become a regular, productive element in the system. The point is that people cannot sally forth from a workshop equipped to take on the world. As with any learning, there is a need for scaffolding and gradual move toward autonomy.

Every institution must establish clear rules of behavior, oversight, and the like in order to function smoothly. A problem can arise with respect to empowerment if those rules are too rigid, however. Effective leaders often use what is described as a tight-loose approach. The "tightness" involves carefully establishing the vision, setting learning standards and developing systems to support students in achieving them, and implementing strategies to ensure that faculty and staff have the tools and resources to support students. The "looseness" involves staying flexible in order to encourage creativity and trusting that faculty and staff will strive for the standards. This type of approach hinders micromanagement and encourages the formation of leadership density. A tight-loose approach in leadership creates fertile ground for empowerment. There may be clear beliefs, behaviors, and vision for the system; and through this approach, teachers have the freedom to exercise professional discretion in applying those shared beliefs in their own classrooms.

Empowerment and Trust

Perhaps the most important foundational aspect of empowerment is trust. Administrators need to trust that individual staff members will do the right thing, in accordance with the school's philosophy, vision, and mission. At the same time, staff members, the community, and students must know that they can trust administrators and each other to be supportive, honest, and direct.

In a climate of empowerment, there can be no place for saying one thing and doing another. The members of the school community cannot proceed productively if they do not trust the administration to support them; back-room decisions, breaches of confidentiality, and undercutting others' efforts are strictly off limits. These characteristics support an empowered group of people, and empowerment supports these characteristics.

Russell Quaglia, an expert education researcher, has spent more than two decades examining the factors that support student success. In his work, Quaglia has identified three guiding principles — (1) self-worth, (2) active engagement, and (3) purpose — that, when supported, create conditions for students to achieve personally, socially, and academically. These principles are supported by what Quaglia describes as 8 Conditions That Make a Difference™, which must exist in order for students "to strive for, and fulfill, their academic, personal and social promise."

While each of the three guiding principles and all of the 8 Conditions are related to empowerment and a positive school climate, two in particular stand out in relation to this discussion (Quaglia, Russell J., "8 Conditions That Make a Difference"):

- **Leadership and responsibility**, which is supported when students (or staff members) are given the support and power to make decisions and take responsibility for their actions
- **Confidence to take action**, which describes the extent to which students (or staff members) believe in themselves, are motivated to set goals for themselves, and are encouraged to imagine their future successes

Again, creating a climate that empowers students is analogous to creating a climate that empowers all members of the school community. In other research, Quaglia asserts that a well-developed school climate can foster a sense of self-worth in people, allowing individuals to feel that they belong to the larger community while retaining their personal uniqueness as individuals. In addition, climate can help develop a sense of purpose — being responsible and accountable for choices, behaviors, and actions — by providing people with real leadership roles that have significant responsibilities. This is empowerment. (McNulty, Raymond J., and Quaglia, Russell J., "Rigor, Relevance, and Relationships")

Noddings would likely agree, albeit in different terms. She rejects the idea of some educational theorists that teachers are interchangeable instructional treatments. Instead, she asserts that educators need to have the power to examine themselves, their students, and what they are trying to accomplish, separately and together, in order to design specific instruction for the current conditions. She posits "an argument against an ideology of control — one in favor of shared living and responsibility." (Noddings, Nel, *The Challenge to Care in Schools: An Alternative Approach to Education*)

Building Trust

Trust is not an automatic condition. Experience leads many people to be mistrustful of both themselves and others. This can lead to an "us versus them" attitude between teachers and administrators or between teachers and students. Leaders need to be sensitive to this phenomenon and deliberately work to build trust. There are many strategies, including trust-building exercises and games; however, the most basic and powerful method for building trust is for leaders to prove through their actions that others can trust them.

Trust does not mean holding others or oneself to a standard of perfection. People make mistakes, and a mistake should not lead automatically to a breach in trust. Part of believing in someone is to understand that his or her motives are in the right place, even if that individual may misjudge a situation or make a poor decision.

Trust is an extremely delicate entity. It can take months, even years, to build and only seconds to destroy. As with anything, taking a few minutes to reflect before reacting can save a situation or a relationship. Waiting before reacting is an essential tool.

Attributes of Leaders Associated with Positive School Climate

The attributes of school leaders can greatly influence the climate of the school.

Honesty

Is empowerment possible if there is no atmosphere of honesty? Honesty and trust are inextricably linked. If one individual does not trust another to be honest, a climate that is rife with paranoia, isolation, and little risk taking develops. If the goal is empowerment, then honesty is crucial. Each person will have to believe that what others tell him or her is sincere, that the information and data received are reliable, and that the espoused support by the administration is genuine. In the absence of these assurances, it is difficult for people to feel sufficiently confident to make decisions and take actions on their own.

Positive Attitude

For leaders, maintaining a positive attitude surely supports institutional health and individual empowerment, but being a Pollyanna is not necessary. An endless smile and constant cheerleading can become empty gestures. Approaching difficult situations with an open mind and the belief that there is a solution to be discovered, however, can do wonders for one's attitude and the school climate.

Pessimism and worst-case-scenario thinking undercut the very idea of empowerment. People who consider conditions hopeless cannot be empowered; they have already given in to the external world, declaring themselves powerless.

There are many real-world situations in which it would have been easy for those involved to give up, yet a positive attitude helped them to forge ahead. For instance, in the world of sports, we often see teams facing overwhelming odds, yet emerging as winners. The opportunities that are opened up by adopting a positive attitude are endless and rewarding.

Kindness and Respect

Without kindness and respect, imagining a system of empowerment is futile. Although there are many technical aspects and definitions of *empowerment* to be studied, leaders cannot forget the enormous foundation of affective characteristics needed to build empowerment. These habits begin when those in leadership positions demonstrate and support such behaviors publicly every day. Kindness and respect for others is in everyone's best interest.

Kindness: Strength or Weakness?

Sometimes people who are seen as kind are also seen as weak. Sometimes people who are seen as kind are also seen as plotting. There is a synergy of kind-and-honest-and-trustworthy that makes the kindness real. Indeed, kindness can be seen as a sort of pandering; however, if it resides alongside honesty and trustworthiness, there is a much greater sense that the kindness is sincere.

Someone who is honest would naturally show honest characteristics as opposed to self-serving ones, and doing so would engender suspicion. When someone asks, "How are you?" does that person really want to know the answer, or is the question a hollow social convention?

A Systemwide Approach to Leadership

To take a page from Shakespeare, kindness (herein referred to as "mercy") is a commodity in great demand:

> The quality of mercy is not strained;
> It droppeth as the gentle rain from heaven
> Upon the place beneath. It is twice blest;
> It blesseth him that gives and him that takes.
> 'Tis mightiest in the mightiest; it becomes
> The throned monarch better than his crown.
>
> — *The Merchant of Venice*, Act IV, Scene I

In many ways, empowerment involves risk taking. It does not flourish in a "gotcha" environment. People need room to make mistakes and learn from them. Every individual is both a learner and a teacher. In schools, this includes the principals, superintendents, and other administrators. Empowerment demands that there be a safe place in which the necessary skills can be learned and practiced. This is where kindness and respect come in. Inspirational educator Ron Clark describes the process of developing a respectful climate in the classroom. His words could apply at any level within a school:

The transformation of a group of unfamiliar students into a caring and respectful community doesn't happen in an instant. But by consistently modeling respectful behavior from day one, you can expect to see a change by the end of the first month of school.

Clark goes on to offer five techniques to help foster respect:

- Do not laugh at the ideas and opinions of others.
- When a classmate is talking, no hands should be raised.
- When a classmate is talking, turn and face that student.
- Before giving your opinions, talk about others' ideas.
- Clap for great answers, ideas, and opinions.

Perhaps one of the best means of developing kindness and respect in others is by living it and modeling it oneself. Noddings corroborates this idea: "So we do not tell our students to care; we show them how to care by creating caring relations with them." When individuals — students, staff, faculty, leaders — feel safe, they also feel empowered to take risks and bold actions to solve emerging and future challenges. (Noddings, Nel, *The Challenge to Care in Schools: An Alternative Approach to Education*)

Kindness and Trust in Action

One day, a frustrated high school teacher sent a difficult student to the principal's office. The first thing the principal did was to read the referral carefully. Then he asked the student to tell him what happened. The student started by using an unflattering metaphor to describe the teacher. The principal did not comment; he simply repeated the metaphor back to the student. This was empowering to the student, because his words were not judged. The student then proceeded with his version of the incident and his feelings about the teacher. The principal simply sat and listened while the student spoke. In the administrator's opinion, the student was more in the right than the teacher, but this was not the time to undercut the teacher's authority without talking with him about the situation first.

When the student had finished talking and had calmed down, he and the principal discussed the situation at greater length. Ultimately, they came up with a plan: The student could come to the office whenever he felt that he was going to act out from frustration. The principal agreed to cover any attendance issues related to such needs, and he later informed the teacher of the plan. There were no further incidents.

The student graduated two years later, on time with his class. This principal had shown respect for the student and the teacher. In particular, he had treated the student with kindness, respect, and empathy as a person, not as a discipline issue. "Why on earth would we add to the stress that already exists by being unkind to one another?" he commented when recounting the story.

An environment characterized by knowing how kindness and trust can lead to powerful results, such as the free exchange of ideas, creativity, speculation, and experimentation. When such a climate — an empowering climate — exists, individuals and groups are able to think broadly to determine the best skills to use to resolve an issue. People are empowered when they learn to work collaboratively to solve complex problems.

Humor

Humor can enhance success in building empowerment. Laughing at oneself and finding the humor in a situation, when possible and appropriate, can lessen stress or anxiety, enhance well-being, and boost self-confidence. It behooves people to avoid taking themselves too seriously.

Effective leaders can "take themselves lightly but take their work in life seriously as they encourage others to do likewise." Fear of making an error or being laughed at can easily arrest any possibility of moving forward. A storyteller once said, "You can go kicking and screaming, or you can go quietly, but life will have its way with you." Perhaps a third choice, laughing, is the best of all. (Pollack, Judy P., and Freda, Paul D., "Humor, Learning, and Socialization in Middle Level Classrooms")

Humor can lighten the mood in even the worst of situations. As long as humor is not used as a weapon, it can serve as a release valve, relieving tension, disappointment, discouragement, and the desire to quit. For a leader, the ability to laugh at himself or herself engenders a sense of humanness.

A teacher or leader who has made a mistake has several options, but not all options are equal in terms of creating credibility and the climate of risk taking necessary for empowerment. Denying a mistake is never a good choice. Making light of one's own foibles, however, allows someone who has made the mistake to relax, reduces some self-imposed pressure, and demonstrates to others an acceptance of his or her own shortcomings. It is even better if a leader can laugh with — but never at — those around him or her.

Humor has the power to bring a whole group together in an instant. Imagine a room full of people arguing. Then someone says something funny about the situation, and the disagreements stop while everyone laughs together. When tension is defused, a group is better able to refocus on the task at hand, be it planning, problem solving, decision making, or the like. Humor can also create a reference point, especially when there are incompatible viewpoints to be considered. In an article about humor in the classroom, an author calling himself Snotty Girdlefanny asserts (Girdlefanny, Snotty, "Using Humor in the Classroom: Learning May Be Serious Business, But That Doesn't Mean You Can't Have a Little Fun along the Way"):

> Recent studies show that a sense of humor is the most consistent characteristic among executives promoted in major companies and that managers showing a sense of humor advance faster and further than those without one.

Humor, and the encouragement to share humor, can be very empowering. If humor can help prepare individuals for career advancement and growth in business, why not use its power in classrooms and faculty lounges? Effective leaders understand the power of humor to defuse a situation, to lighten the moment, or to bring people together. This is why so many meetings begin with fun icebreaker activities that help people get to know one another, or why a wise remark (especially about oneself) that is made at a heated point in a discussion can ease the decision-making process along.

Empathy

While knowing oneself and others is an essential ingredient for empowerment to be successful, caring for one another — or showing empathy — creates the safe environments that allow empowered individuals to take action. Hattie identifies empathy as a quality found in teachers who are "adaptive experts." (Hattie, John, *Visible Learning*) Daniel Goleman, leader of the emotional intelligence movement, notes (Goleman, Daniel, *Emotional Intelligence*):

> All rapport, the root of caring, stems from emotional attunement, and from the capacity for empathy. That capacity — the ability to know how another feels — comes into play in a vast array of life arenas, from sales and management to romance and parenting, to compassion and political action.

Without the trust and sensitivity of empathy, a climate that supports empowerment is extremely difficult to create, and perhaps impossible to sustain.

Collecting Qualitative Data

Studying school climate entails gathering and studying characteristics of the system that may best be described as qualitative. Too often in education there is such an intense focus on the quantitative data gathered through formal assessments that essential factors, such as climate and relationships, are overlooked. Quantitative data may be useful for measuring performance and progress toward specific standards, but qualitative data reveal a great deal about how performance and progress come about — or fail to come about — in a school.

Understanding how members of an organization feel about specific factors is essential if any sort of change is to occur and be sustained. In schools, it is crucial to know how the faculty, students, community, and administration perceive the institution. The ways in which the perceptions of each group intersect or contrast can help shape the strategies that will lead to successful change.

One of the most effective instruments for assessing schools is the *We Survey* suite, which was mentioned earlier in the chapter and described in detail in Chapter 4. Data from the surveys offer a multidimensional view of the school climate, based on school community members' attitudes and experiences.

Developing and maintaining a positive school climate, especially during times of change, can be very challenging. Leaders need to know whether individuals are ready for empowerment, and evaluating qualitative aspects of the school is imperative. In the process of building a philosophy, vision, and mission, qualitative data will help leadership begin to align thinking. This will result in greater coherence, understanding, and trust, all of which provide the necessary base for empowerment.

Summary

School climate has an impact on all members of the school community. The personal, social, and emotional skills of a leader can contribute greatly to the establishment of a positive school climate.

Reflection Activity

1. Littky has described 14 overall goals of education. As a leader, how would you connect each of the five goals in the following list to empowerment and school climate?
   - taking risks
   - solving problems
   - thinking critically
   - working in groups and independently
   - having moral courage

   Write a one-sentence response for each of the five goals.

2. Communication between administrators and teachers can help establish a positive school climate. As a school leader, reflect on your communication style. Review your written communications and meeting minutes from the past month. Overall, how would you characterize your communications with members of your staff? In what ways could you have improved these communications? Write a brief summary of your thoughts.

3. Trust, honesty, kindness, respect, and empathy are attributes that can enhance leadership and encourage the empowerment of others. Use the following ques-

tions to reflect on how these attributes play a part in your role as a leader. Discuss each in a small-group format.

- How does trust enhance leadership? Can there be true leadership without trust?
- Think of a time when you thought that someone was not being honest with you. Did you feel comfortable, as a school leader, about raising your concerns with the individual? Why or why not? Did addressing your concerns enhance leadership, school climate, and empowerment?
- How does showing kindness and respect for others produce results in your own best interest as an education leader?
- What are some of the ways in which you publicly model kindness and respect as a leader?
- As a leader, how do you demonstrate empathy for staff and students? How would you rate the importance of empathy in the school climate?

Chapter 7

Leadership and Community Engagement

Engaging the community is a function of effective school leadership. The DSEI emphasizes the establishment of a culture of high expectations that is communicated not only to staff and students but also to community stakeholders, including parents, community groups and businesses. In this chapter, effective strategies for involving various components of the school community are examined. Specifically, the chapter describes ways to engage parents, community groups, and the business community. The chapter concludes with examples of interesting approaches to community engagement.

Who Is the Community?

At first thought, a school community comprises administrators, faculty, staff, parents, and students, all functioning within the school complex. More broadly, a school community could extend to the neighborhood residents and the neighborhood in which the school is located, outside service providers (such as bus drivers and therapeutic services professionals), the central administration, other schools in the district, the central office, and the board of education. Then there are businesses, families with grown children or no children, and the local government.

A little thought could make the list continue to grow. The point is that while many schools define *community* as the people within the school building and on the grounds — administrators, faculty, staff, parents, and students — there are stakeholders beyond those in the immediate school surroundings who want their voices to be heard.

Some stakeholders, students and teachers among them, need to be empowered; others, such as local, state, and federal agencies, have statutory power. Still other stakeholders have a vested interest in education, such as institutions of higher learning or businesses that are working to ensure the qualifications of the future workforce. All stakeholders place upon schools pressures that must be addressed.

Educators recognize that schools benefit from connecting with their communities. Mavis Sanders, an assistant professor of education in the School of Professional Studies in Business and Education at Johns Hopkins University and a research scientist at the Center for Research on the Education of Students Placed at Risk, and Adia Harvey, an assistant professor of sociology at Georgia State University, write:

> Current educational reforms emphasize the need for schools, especially those serving poor and minority students, to partner with families and communities to create more challenging, responsive, and supportive learning environments. (Sanders, Mavis G., and Harvey, Adia, "Beyond the School Walls: A Case Study of Principal Leadership for School-Community Collaboration")

There is a pervasive attitude that school personnel, with all of their specialized training and experience, are the best people to make decisions about the school system. This may not be as true as it seems. When highly specialized individuals join together as teams to find solutions, conflicts may arise.

A *Harvard Business Review* article explored the concept of collaboration and concludes that complex problems demand complex teams of specialists to solve them. Such teams are typically "large, virtual, diverse, and composed of highly educated specialists." These same characteristics, however, can be roadblocks to collaborative problem solving. Team members have individual specialties and may not move easily in and out of other fields. They may see their own viewpoints as critical, without valuing those of the others. (Erickson, Tammy, and Gratton, Lynda, "Eight Ways to Build Collaborative Teams")

Consequently, a team of school specialists may not be the only way, or even the best way, to solve problems. There are many more viewpoints and ideas within the larger school community. School leaders are wise to listen to those voices.

The Philosophy of Open Sources

The online encyclopedia *Wikipedia* is an example of an open source. Anyone can add to an item to the online data collection. This setup may invite some misinformation and outlandish responses, but it also captures the unusual ideas and points of view of the entire online community. A team of experts and specialists could never amass such a wide lens.

The philosophy of open sources is to promote practices in production and development that provide broad access to source material for the end product. A person with a question or problem invites ideas for a solution from a network as broad as the entire population of Internet users.

Although the pool of potential ideas and opinions may not always be on the scale of the Internet, the open source concept can be beneficial in problem solving. There is value in opening up the field of potential ideas by turning to a community. For instance, if a school has poor test scores, a leader traditionally might bring together teachers, administrators, and counselors to share ideas and try a combination of known strategies. However, posing the question to the entire school community can add richness and freshness to the idea pool. At the same time, the community is empowered to be part of a solution.

Remember, it takes courage to empower others. School officials may not like hanging their problems where everyone can see them, but doing so can be an excellent means of empowering the community. In a way, this strategy breaks all the rules — but it can deliver great results.

A Goldmine

With the advent of electronic communication, the available community of ideas has become enormous. The owner of a goldmine sent out a request on the Internet. He was looking for ideas about how he could find more gold, as the mine appeared to be running thin. Normally, a mine owner would never put any information about a goldmine online — it flies in the face of business competition — but this strategy worked. The mine owner empowered anyone and everyone to make suggestions. He paid for the suggestions he used. He had been running a multimillion-dollar business; but following his e-quiry, he was running a multibillion-dollar business.

This is a lesson for all schools: Use your school community! A good solution may come from an obvious advisor, but an unexpected source sometimes can yield an even better option.

We Support—Community Survey

The *We Survey* suite (see Chapter 4) developed by the Successful Practices Network in partnership with the International Center, includes several tools for gathering crucial data from students, teachers, and staff about their experiences and attitudes regarding their school. The latest addition to the suite is the *We Support — Community Survey*, which is designed to assess parent and community perceptions of the school experience as well as their expectations of the school system. The *We Support — Community Survey* is designed to give voice to families and the general community and is an excellent tool for identifying community outreach needs.

Like its counterparts, this *We Survey* takes about 10 minutes to administer. Respondents are asked to rate items on a Likert scale from "strongly agree" to "strongly disagree." The survey, which comprises parallel items to enable comparisons to data from the student and instructional staff surveys, includes such statements as these:

- The schools help students develop healthy attitudes for success in life.
- The school system helps students make informed decisions about post-high school plans.
- The schools use resources in the community to make education relevant to students.

The survey breaks out data in two ways. First, respondents are separated into three categories: (1) those who live and work in the community, (2) those who live in the community, and (3) those who work in the community. Second, data are organized by the extent to which participants agree or disagree with specific statements in relation to the themes of rigor, relevance, and relationships.

Data about attitudes and perceptions are an essential element in creating opportunities to empower parents and the community. This *We Support* survey's greatest value is that it offers educators a unique opportunity to view their school or district through the eyes of the community.

As of June 2010, some 2,500 individuals had completed this *We Support* survey. Some of the responses point to areas in need of investigation. For example, 84% of respondents agree with the statement "Small class size is important for student learning." However, only 34% agree with the statement "The school board acts in the best interests of the taxpayers." A school board that saw similar data would be wise to investigate why a community supports a cost increasing concept such as smaller classes while questioning the board's responsibility to the taxpayers. Perhaps the board needs to improve communications to help people fully understand the costs, choices, and sacrifices involved in staffing a school. Maybe the board has not listened well to what the community wants. It is possible that the board is spending on something that the community sees as having little value and could redirect those funds to support staff increases.

Another example from the survey is the statement "Teachers are respected by the community." Of those who live and work in the community, 74% agreed with this statement. People who live in the community but do not work there agreed with the statement at the rate of 77%. However, only 45% of people who only work in the community agreed that teachers were respected. What are members of this group seeing that others are not? What does this discrepancy tell a school about its community connections, and how can the school use these data to its advantage to increase support and involvement?

The Mistake of Forgetting About the Community

A school ignores the community at its own peril. Derek Pierce, founding principal of Casco Bay High School in Portland, Maine, describes what happened when establishing connections with the community was not made a priority in the process of launching his school (Derek Pierce, personal communication, March 23, 2010):

> Before Casco Bay High School opened, I remember approaching a principal who had launched two high schools and asking him what was the most important thing for a new school to do in the first few years. He said it was to gain the trust of the community . . . Within six months of our opening of Casco Bay, there was a petition circulated at the Portland Town Dump, demanding an overthrow of the school's progressive approach. Eventually, there was an official referendum and town vote that included a vote of confidence/no confidence in me and my superiors.

This happened, according to Pierce, because he and other educators had not paid sufficient attention to the community while establishing the school.

> During the launch of the school, we had been so inwardly focused on getting to know the kids and curriculum — we had ignored the parents and had done little to include, educate, and engage them, even as they trusted us with their most precious possessions, their children and their tax dollars.

Engaging Parents

Parents comprise the largest directly influential group of the school community. They have hopes and dreams for their children, and they expect the school to support them and their children in reaching those goals. Parents can be demanding, but schools cannot overlook this powerful constituency. Hattie's research supports the value of parent involvement in schools and its positive impact on student achievement. (Hattie, John, *Visible Learning*) Further activities for parent involvement are found in the International Center's handbooks *Engaging Parents in Student Learning — Grades K6* and *Engaging Parents in Student Learning — Grades 7–12*.

Parent Involvement: A Working Definition

Reaching agreement on the definition of *parent involvement* is an important step in ensuring that all individuals understand the parameters of the effort, and it allows those involved to place the program in an acceptable context. Reviewing the literature on parent involvement revealed several different definitions, depending upon the particular focus or purpose of the study.

To some, *parent involvement* means the establishment of close, sustainable relationships between parent and child. Others define it as involving parents in school activities such as coming to parent meetings and conferences with teachers and becoming involved in PTA/PTO functions such as meetings and fundraising activities. Some researchers believe that parent involvement may also take the form of parents working with children at home to complete assignments or talk with their children about future plans or courses.

For our purposes, we have defined *parent involvement* as follows: parents participating in activities, both at school and in the home, that promote parents' desires for the academic and social development of their children and the agenda of the school. (Davies, D., "Schools Reaching Out"; Henderson, et al., *Beyond the Bake Sale*; Su-Chi, H. and Willms, D.J., "Effects of Parental Involvement on Eighth-Grade Achievement"; Feuerstein, A., "School Characteristics and Parent Involvement")

No matter what the definition, educators and administrators are on a mission to increase parent involvement and understand how to make relationships with parents pay off in increased student success. (Keith, C., "Parent Involvement and Achievement in High School")

Educators' Assumptions About Parents . . .

. . . That Hinder Collaboration	. . . That Facilitate Collaboration
Parents who don't attend school events don't care about their children's school success. Parents who are illiterate, non-English speaking, or unemployed cannot help their children learn. Parents from different ethnic and racial groups don't understand how to help their children. It is up to the parents to find out what's going on at school. Parent involvement is not worth the educator's effort.	Not all parents can come to school or feel comfortable about it; that doesn't mean that they don't care. All families have strengths and skills that they can contribute to their children's school success. Parents from different ethnic and racial groups may have alternative and important ways of supporting their children. Schools have a responsibility to reach out to all parents. Parent involvement pays off in improved student achievement, improved school effectiveness, and increased parent and community support for education.

(San Diego Schools, 1991)

Six Types of Parent Involvement

Researchers at Johns Hopkins University developed a comprehensive program designed to address the issues and concerns expressed by many teachers and parents about how to comprehensively address increasing parent involvement. This program was incorporated into the National Parent Teacher Association Standards in 2001. Partnership is viewed as an essential component of the school program, not an optional activity carried out by a select group of parents and teachers.

Epstein's "Theory of Overlapping Spheres of Influence" explains the relationship among the home, school, and community in providing for the child's development and academic learning. These three areas "interact" and "overlap" with each other, providing common ground for action. The student is placed at the center of the model.

Epstein describes both external and internal models. The external model notes the family, school, and community as interacting together for the benefit of the child. The internal model describes where and how patterns of influence lie between the parent and child at home, at school, and in community interactions. Activities are designed to assist students in energizing themselves, with guidance from adults, toward the path to academic and social success in school. School partnerships are designed to create more "family-like schools," which recognize the individuality of each child, and more "school-like homes," where the home also recognizes each child as a student. (Epstein, J.L., et al., *School, Family and Community Partnerships*)

Epstein describes six types of parent involvement:

Type 1. Parenting
- helping all families to develop home environments that support learning
- helping families with information about important issues such as child development, "child-rearing" skills, and setting home conditions that support children

Type 2. Communicating
- designing more effective forms of communications between the home and school
- providing information about school expectations, curriculum, and state tests in a language that parents can understand

Type 3. Volunteering
- recruiting and organizing parental help
- providing training and flexible scheduling in schools or other settings

Type 4. Learning at Home
- providing information to parents concerning how to assist their children at home
- providing information and workshops about how to assist their children

Type 5. Decision Making
- including parents in school decision making
- providing information and training about how to serve on PTO and shared decision-making teams

Type 6. Collaborating with the Community
- involving the local community in the life of the school
- providing and coordinating the resources of the community to provide services in the school

Chapter 7: Leadership and Community Engagement

These six types of involvement broaden the definition of *parent involvement* even further. Schools that use these categories to improve the level of various types of involvement will make progress in increasing the visible level of involvement in the school.

Hidden Parent Involvement

Much of what we see as parent involvement is visible only from the school level. However, the most important influence made in this arena is that of the parent and child together at home. When parents talk with their children about school, the importance of education, educational aspirations, homework, and going to college, research shows that children do better in a wide variety of areas. (Caldas, S.J. and Bankston, C.L. "The Effect of School Population Socioeconomic Status on Individual Student Academic Achievement"; Keith, T., Singh, K., Bickley, P.G., Trivette, P., and Keith, T.Z. "The Effects of Four Components of Parental Involvement on Eighth-Grade Student Achievement: Structural Analysis of NELS-88 Data.")

The magnitude of effective parent involvement that takes place in the home and is not observable by the school can be compared to an iceberg, where only a small portion of the mass is observable.

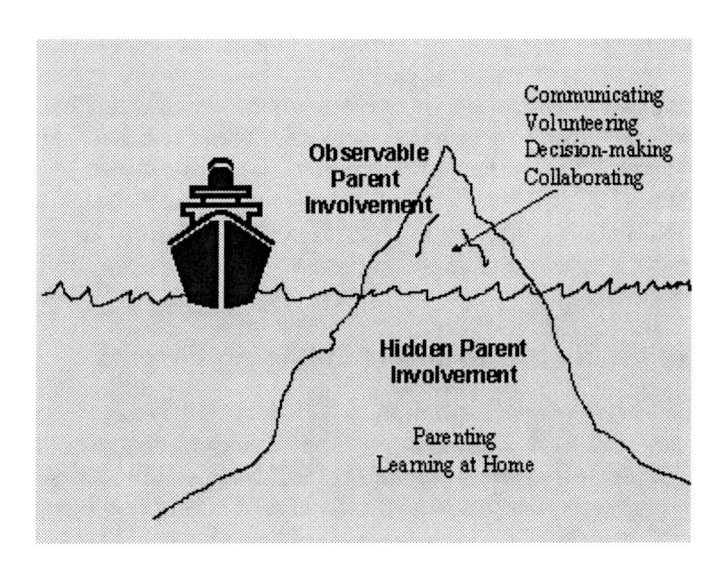

When schools take a one-dimensional view of parent involvement and see it only as parents participating in school, they miss one of the most important aspects of assisting the families. Schools must strive to assist parents in working with their children at home by making sure that they are equipped with the tools to help their youngsters succeed. To do this, schools must ensure that parents are provided with information on such topics as the following:

- school rules and the reasons for them
- homework assistance
- school curriculum
- state standards
- grading policies

Schools also need to offer workshops in areas such as the following:

- child development
- specific strategies to help children at home
- college requirements

A significant challenge for schools endeavoring to improve parent involvement is involving the entire school community. Many parents are well connected to the schools: They attend all school events, participate in teacher conferences, serve as homeroom parents, and so forth. There is another group of parents whom we call the "hardest-to-involve" parents. They are rarely involved in school activities, come to school only when there is a problem, and do not attend parent conferences on a regular basis. This behavior often leads school personnel to assume that the parents do not care about education or the progress of their children. Nothing could be further from the truth. To encourage engagement with this group, barriers to engagement must be examined and broken down.

The Role of *No Child Left Behind* in Engaging Parents

The federal *No Child Left Behind* legislation, which reauthorized the *Elementary and Secondary Education Act* (ESEA) in 2001, put into law sweeping changes designed to ensure the success of all students. Section 1118e of the NCLB legislation describes a number of changes that districts are required to make in the area of parent involvement.

The Title I regulations in *No Child Left Behind* bring many new ideas and opportunities to involve parents in the education of their children. The regulation mentions the key word *parents* 102 times. Parents must be involved in the Title I program in significant ways and must be consulted when planning related programs and activities.

Many educators may not be familiar with all facets of these sweeping requirements, including the parent involvement regulation. Every school receiving Title I money is required to (NCLB Section 1118e):

- develop with parents a written parent involvement policy that is then distributed to parents and made available to the local community
- hold an annual meeting of parents to inform them of the policy and their right to be involved
- conduct, with the involvement of parents, an annual evaluation of the content and effectiveness of the parent involvement policy in improving the academic quality of schools
- offer a variety of times for parent involvement meetings and, if necessary, with Title I funds provide child care, transportation, or home visits
- involve parents in an organized and ongoing way in the planning, review, and improvement of school programs
- develop with parents a school-parent agreement that outlines actions to be taken to improve student achievement
- increase opportunities for parent involvement in the school by helping parents understand state academic standards
- provide materials and training for parents, teachers, pupil services personnel, and other staff to foster greater parent involvement
- integrate activities with other programs
- identify barriers to greater participation by parents at the school
- coordinate and integrate parental involvement strategies
- build the school's and parents' capacity for involvement through the implementation of required parent involvement activities

Over the last decade, the federal government has begun to address the need to increase parent involvement in the school community by passing national goals and legislation designed to address these concerns. The *Educate America Act* states, "By the year 2000 every school will promote partnerships that increase parent involvement and participation in promoting the social, emotional and academic growth of children." The U.S. Department of Education has indicated a commitment to increasing parent involvement in education and has published results of studies and articles showing the link between parent involvement and student achievement. The reauthorization of Title I in 1994 required that school districts spend at least one percent of their funds on parent involvement activities and programs if they received more than $5,000 in funding from Title I. (Solomon, Z.P., "California's Policy on Parent Involvement"; Stein, M.R.S., and Thorkildsen, R.J., *Parent Involvement in Education*; Baker, A.J., "Parents as School Partners." Numerous studies document the link between increased parent involvement and increased student achievement; see Bempechat, 1992; Epstein, 1987; Epstein and Dauber, 1991; Haynes et al., 1987; Henderson and Berla, 1994; U.S. 103rd Congress, *Goals 2000: Educate America Act* of 1994; U.S. Department of Education, *Partnership for Family Involvement in Education*, 2000)

The federal Title I program, in existence since 1965, promotes additional assistance for struggling students, many of whom live in poverty. As this program evolved, it incorporated the concept of involving parents in the education of their children. The Even Start and Head Start programs, which began in the 1960s in connection with Title I efforts, were developed to produce stronger parents with the knowledge and the skills necessary to make a difference in the schooling of their children. The Even Start program often utilizes home visitors who meet with parents regularly, providing information about a wide variety of issues facing parents. (U.S. Congress 6362, Title I of the *Elementary and Secondary Schools Act*, 1965; Even Start Program, 1988)

Strategies to Increase Parent Engagement

There are many strategies that schools can use to encourage family involvement. What mechanisms — e-newsletters, website, notices sent home with students, community bulletin boards, and so on — does the school use to notify families about opportunities? What forums — individual parent workshops, series of parent workshops, teacher-parent conferences, grade-level meetings for parents, and the like — are used to educate families about important topics?

Which of the following topics does your school address with parents?

- school rules and the reasons for them
- homework assistance
- school curriculum
- state standards

- grading policies
- child development
- specific strategies to help children at home
- college requirements

Kathleen Hoover-Dempsey and Howard Sandler, both of Vanderbilt University's Peabody College of Education and Human Development, note several reasons why parents choose to become involved with their children's schools (Hoover-Dempsey, Kathleen V., and Sandler, Howard M., "Parental Involvement in Children's Education: Why Does It Make a Difference?"):

> We present a model suggesting that parents become involved primarily because (a) they develop a personal construction of the parental role that includes participation in their children's education, (b) they have developed a positive sense of efficacy for helping their children succeed in school, and (c) they perceive opportunities or demands for involvement from children and the school.

They also note that the parents' positive sense of efficacy spreads empowerment down the line. The school can and should take an active role in developing the factors that determine levels of parent involvement in the school, as increased involvement reflects increased empowerment.

Unfortunately, in many cases, parent voices are effectively silenced by the school's general operation. This prevents them from engaging in meaningful and productive dialogue about education, concerning both their own children and all students in general. The exclusion of parents from the conversation deprives both families and schools.

Even if a school is doing everything possible to encourage parent involvement, there are many reasons why parents may not engage in the school at all or as much as they could. Increasing numbers of families either have only one parent or have both parents working, which can make finding time to come to the school difficult. Some parents had bad experiences in school when they were young, and they are intimidated by the idea of visiting the school. A percentage of parents have little education and may feel embarrassed or intimidated. Parents of poverty can be loath to visit because of their social status, or even because of their clothing.

Administrators, faculty, and staff must find ways to empower all parents. This may mean offering events or scheduling conferences or workshops in the evenings or during weekend times. They may need to be especially careful to speak to parents respectfully and as equals, even as they are educating them about unfamiliar topics or issues. No matter how a school chooses to do it, they must deal with the many permutations of parental reluctance to engage with the school.

William H. Jeynes, a professor of education at California State University—Long Beach, reviewed research on the subtle factors that affect parents' willingness to work with schools. His findings may surprise many educators (Jeynes, William H., "The Salience of the Subtle Aspects of Parental Involvement and Encouraging That Involvement: Implications for School-Based Programs"):

> Although specific practices to enhance parental participation doubtlessly have some degree of value, the more subtle expressions of love, such as expectations, communications, and mutual respect, are usually more important than the actual techniques that school leaders incorporate into their parental outreach. In most cases, if educators *show love, consistently possess high expectations of students and parents*, even if they do not expressly practice certain techniques to enhance parental involvement, their efforts will yield significant results. [emphasis added]

Jeynes's review suggests that back-to-school nights, parent conferences, parent-teacher conferences, bake sales, parent-teacher organizations, and other obvious points of contact are not as effective as is the attitude that the school takes toward parents and the clear communication of that attitude. Schools, through all of their contacts with parents, need to communicate love and respect. This message empowers parents through their knowledge that they are valued and that the school sincerely welcomes their ideas and opinions (Hoover-Dempsey, Kathleen V., and Sandler, Howard M., "Parental Involvement in Children's Education: Why Does It Make a Difference?"):

> Optimally, the school and parent would work to fit *each other's* expectations; that is, each family-school "pair" would negotiate a common set of expectations, appropriate for child, parents, and school.

Amodeo and Amodeo recommend that each school develop a parent partnership team. Such a team would comprise a cross-section of parents, plus the principal and perhaps others from the school. The group would study, develop, and implement strategies for connecting parents and the school. In essence, this means that the team's goal is to empower parent voices.

In studying the subtle aspects of parental involvement, William Jeynes concludes (Jeynes, William H., "The Salience of the Subtle Aspects of Parental Involvement and Encouraging That Involvement: Implications for School-Based Programs"):

> First, educate parents to comprehend, and then act on, the fact that it is probably some of the more subtle aspects of parental involvement, such as high expectations and communication, that are among the most important. Second, educate school leaders, teachers, and staff to understand that raising parental participation may be more a function of subtle but important demonstrations of love and respect than a matter of instructing parents to apply particular methods of helping children.

One thing is clear: Parental and community empowerment and involvement do not just happen. There need to be inservice trainings for teachers and workshops for parents and community organizations. Individuals need specific tools and information to become empowered. It is also essential that communication between and among the school, home, and community be clear and free of jargon. Such information needs to accommodate non-English speakers as well as those who cannot read. Communications from the school should be frequent, friendly, informative, and useful. Home visits may be necessary in some cases. Schools are more able to accommodate to outside constituencies than the other way around.

Schools need to take the lead in educating parents about the school system, improving their knowledge base on such issues as curriculum, discipline, standardized test scores, and more. To empower parents, schools need to provide them with information and training in the skills required for full involvement. Amodeo and Amodeo note (Amodeo, Charles J., and Amodeo, Suomi Erin., *Reaching the Hard-to-Involve Parents: Powerful Partnerships Under NCLB*):

> Building the skills of all participants associated with the school is a crucial component of any effective parent involvement program. Skill building, or capacity building as it is commonly called today, is an important part of creating a strong team at the school and in the home.

The Effect of Parent Engagement on Student Achievement

Research has shown that involving the parents of students in their education and the life of the school can pay dividends in raising student achievement. A comprehensive effort to improve parent involvement in education enhances the school program and can bring improved results. Although many factors in involving parents are hard to influence, reaching out to parents pays benefits in improved home-school communications. Feuerstein found that schools influence parent involvement by contacting parents more often, asking them to volunteer in school, and inviting them to attend and serve on the school's parent-teacher group (PTA/PTO). (Epstein, J.L., "Parent Involvement: What Research Says to Administrators"; Epstein, et al., *School, Family and Community Partnerships*; Feuerstein, A., "School Characteristics and Parent Involvement")

Cultural differences can impact the personal resources available to address the needs of families. According to Bourdieu's theory of "cultural capital," teachers are often associated with middle-class and upper-class values and mores. These teachers may have difficulty relating to and working with lower-income parents, many of whom are minorities. Since the dominant culture of schools represents the middle-class culture, parents may have a difficult time adapting and communicating their needs to school personnel when they come from backgrounds that differ from those of school staff members. (Bourdieu, P., "Cultural Reproduction and Social Reproduction")

Social class can impact parents' involvement in the school, especially when the school does not reach out. Parents from homes of low socioeconomic status may believe that teachers do not want them to be involved and may feel "negative vibrations" from teachers. Some parents lack the opportunity to come to school because of work schedules, daycare, and transportation issues. (Ramirez, A.Y., "Parent Involvement Is Like Apple Pie"; This view was also expressed by some parents interviewed by Clark [1983].)

Caldas and Bankston argue that the traits of individuals in the school, as well as school characteristics, must be considered "significant influences" on academic performance and achievement. A family's social status has a positive effect on achievement. A parent's education level and occupational status have a related impact on achievement, as well. (Caldas, S., and Bankston, C., "Effect of School Population Socio-economic Status on Individual Academic Achievement")

A group of researchers analyzed the National Educational Longitudinal Study (NELS) data of 1988 and found that the educational aspirations of parents had a powerful influence on student achievement. (Jimerson, S.R., et al., "A Longitudinal Study of Achievement Trajectories"; Keith, T., Singh, K., Bickley, P.G., Trivette, P., and Keith, T.Z., "The Effects of Four Components of Parental Involvement on Eighth-Grade Student Achievement: Structural Analysis of NELS-88 Data.")

Fan studied the NELS data to examine the potential differences in parent involvement that might hold for various racial groups. The findings showed that, after adjustment for socioeconomic status, parent involvement was comparable. Parents' educational aspirations for their children had a consistent, positive effect on students' academic performance. (Fan, X., "Parental Involvement and Student's Academic Achievement")

In another study of the NELS data, Simon examined the data from 11,000 parents and 1,000 high school principals. She found that, after controlling for race, ethnicity, and other factors, when parents attended college-planning workshops and school functions, students were more likely to improve academically, have higher standardized test scores, and have better attendance, behavior, and preparedness for school. (Simon, B. "Family Involvement in High School")

Different racial and ethnic groups have differing expectations about their children's pursuit of higher education. White parents had the lowest expectations regarding their children going to college. Minority parents, particularly Asian-American, however, had much higher expectations that their children would go to college. (Schneider, B., and Coleman, J.S., *Parents, Their Children, and Schools;* Desimone, L., "Linking Parent Involvement with Student Achievement")

When students reported that their parents involved them in conversations about school, all groups were positively correlated with improved grades. Educational researchers have shown that there is a link between parent involvement and improved educational achievement of children. (Baker, 2000; Epstein and Dauber, 1991; Henderson and Berla, 1994; Kohl, et al., 2000; National Center for Education Statistics, 1998)

A ten-year study of 20,000 high school students and their families found that when parents participate in their children's education, the result is an increase in student achievement and an improvement in students' attitudes. Increased attendance, fewer discipline problems, and higher aspirations are correlated with increased parent involvement. Early involvement by the parents in the child's school program can pay dividends in higher reading achievement in upper grades and lower retention later in their school career, according to Miedel and Reynolds. This was further supported by the work of Sui-Chu and Willms, who found a small positive gain in reading performance for 8th-grade students when parents participated at the school. (Steinberg, L.D., et al., *Beyond the Classroom;* Stevenson, D.L., and Baker, D.P., "The Family-School Relation and the Child's School Performance"; Miedel, W.T., and Reynolds, A.J.; "Parent Involvement in Early Intervention for Disadvantaged Children"; Sui-Chu, E.H., and Willms, D.J., "Effects of Parental Involvement on Eighth-Grade Achievement")

Parent involvement in schools has been widely studied throughout the world, with comparable results. Epstein and Sanders offer an international perspective on the status of parent involvement in other countries. Their findings are strikingly similar to the results of researchers in the United States. They find that the "extent of parents involvement varies widely"; that "fathers are less involved" than mothers; and that when schools and teachers reach out to parents, parental involvement improves and relationships between home and school grow. (Epstein, J.L., and Sanders, M.G., "What We Learn from International Studies of School-Family-Community Partnerships")

The effect of parent involvement in Title I-funded math and reading programs was investigated by Shaver and Walls. They studied 335 Title I students receiving math, reading, or both services. They found that parents who attended parent information, training, and discussion sessions on a regular basis had children who made greater academic achievement gains in reading and math. However, achievement gains for lower-income children were not as great. (Shaver, A., and Walls, T., "Effect of Title I Parent Involvement on Student Reading and Mathematics Achievement")

Other types of activities, such as homework, have proved to be important factors in the academic achievement of at-risk students. Clark also noted that parents must understand what their children are doing in school so that they can assist them. He further stated that parents should be provided training in order to assist their children. (Balli, et al., "Family involvement with middle-grades homework"; Clark, R.M., *Family Life and School Achievement*; Dixon, A.P., "Parents: Full Partners in the Decision-Making Process")

Parent involvement in schools was less important than high-quality home-school relationships that lasted over time. Parent involvement practices produce varying results, split along income and race attributes, according to Callahan. (Callahan, et al., "The Effect of Parent Participation in Strategies to Improve the Homework Performance of Students Who Are At Risk")

Dr. James Comer, an educational researcher, noted that there are three reasons for parents to become involved in schools: (1) Parents have knowledge of their children; (2) having parents in the school can improve accountability; and (3) parents become more involved in school programs and provide support for school budgets. He stated that this is particularly critical in lower socioeconomic schools in the inner cities. (Comer, J.P., *School Power: Implications of an Intervention Project*)

Barriers to Parent Engagement

Parents face many real and perceived barriers that hinder the development of parent-student-school relationships. Parents may have had poor experiences in school. They also may have transportation issues, inflexible work schedules, financial constraints, insufficient time, safety concerns, and language barriers. Teachers may lack training in how to work with parents. The U.S. Department of Education found that parents cited time as the biggest barrier to becoming involved in school (87%). When teachers were asked about barriers, they also mentioned time (56%), as well as lack of training in how to work with parents (48%), as major barriers to working effectively with parents. (Baker, A.J., "Parent Involvement for the Middle Level Years"; DeMoss, S.E., et al., "Parental Perceptions of Long-Term Involvement with Their Children's Schooling"; U.S. Department of Education [2000], *Partnership for Family Involvement in Education*)

Think about the following questions related to barriers to parent engagement: Does the school accommodate parents' work schedules? Is transportation available for everyone? Are there interpreters for the deaf and translators for those who do not speak English? Can the school provide childcare during meeting times to help parents?

These and other possible barriers are real, and they stand in the way of productive school-parent-community partnerships. For these partnerships to succeed, the school, perhaps through a parent partnership team or other means, will have to meet these challenges in order to forge productive partnerships with parents and the larger community.

In addition, as Jeynes points out in his work, one of the most significant barriers that schools need to overcome is related to attitude and how a positive, inclusive attitude is established and communicated to parents. The school itself needs to have a welcoming, friendly atmosphere. Signs should be pleasant, readable, and useful. "Visitors must check in at the office" might be replaced with "Guests, please stop by the office for a visitor's pass." Student guides can be very helpful in this regard; for example, some schools empower students and help them build leadership skills by having them serve as greeters. (Jeynes, William H., "The Salience of the Subtle Aspects of Parental Involvement and Encouraging That Involvement: Implications for School-Based Programs)

Of course, access to the school must be balanced against safety concerns; after all, the school has a duty to provide a safe environment and to care for students. Educators can find middle ground by putting into place safety strategies such as cameras and check-in procedures, while at the same time creating a welcoming and warm tone through communications, signs, and the like.

Caring School Leadership and Parent Engagement

School administrators often remark: "But I have an open-door policy for parents. Why aren't more parents involved in our school?" Principals at successful high schools have learned that an open-door policy is somewhat irrelevant. The real issue is an "open heart." Parents can sense a lack of sincerity from a mile away.

Schools that truly want parents involved will find that parents respond best to "hands-on" principals who are actively involved with the parents. Here are some tips for school leaders from successful schools — Alan M. Blankstein, *Failure Is Not an Option* (2004, p. 167):

- Get to know parents on a first-name basis and encourage them to address you by your first name.
- Sacrifice the administrative business suit occasionally for more informal dress if that is consistent with the parents you serve.
- Work hard to demonstrate to parents that they are equal to you as human beings; you just have different roles.
- Liberal use of humor breaks down barriers. Accept good-natured teasing from parents and enjoy a good laugh together.
- Demonstrate active listening. Seek first to understand, then to be understood.
- Be aware of your nonverbal behavior and realize that this is stronger communication than the actual words you speak.
- Practice truth-telling with parents. Be candid about the school's challenges and adopt this philosophy: In this school, we tell the truth. Our problems are opportunities. What makes us different is that by recognizing these "probletunities" we have the chance to improve conditions for our children."
- If you practice authenticity with parents, you will be able to anticipate and prepare for the types of questions and concerns that parents will present.
- One of the most important personal attributes for any school leader is visibility. When parents perceive that you are everywhere — at sporting events, concerts, performances — they make a judgment that this visibility means you care about their children. Yes, this type of visibility takes a great deal of time, but the dividends pay capital gains.
- When parents sense you care, they will open up and ask questions. In addition, the authentic leader is available to work with parents on a one-to-one basis.
- In engaging parents in partnerships, the focus should always be on the children and never on the attributes or behaviors of the parents. Experience has taught many successful administrators that when parents trust you and realize you care about their children, their behavior changes unobtrusively.

- Recognize that in order to develop trust among parents you must exhibit trustworthiness. Always be true to your word.
- Finally, always remember that you and your staff work for the parents; they pay the taxes and elect the school board members who employ you.

Educational research clearly shows that the support and involvement of students' families and the community at large is fundamental to achievement in schools.

When true parent-school partnerships are established, the word gets out that the principal and his or her leadership team can be trusted. When the inevitable school difficulties occur, this trust will pay dividends in terms of a large core of parents who will support the administration. The bottom line is that authentic parent partnerships will help 9th-graders become more successful in their academic endeavors.

Communication and Parent Engagement

Effective schools recognize that there are multiple strategies to communicate with and involve parents. Although necessary, the least effective communication vehicle is often the written word: newsletters, newspaper articles, and letters.

When school leaders make a commitment to authentic, long-term, and frequent partnerships with a significant core group of parents, experience indicates that one trusted parent might communicate with 10–20 others. In other words, a core group of 25 involved parents can easily serve as effective communicators for an additional 400–500 parents who interact with the core group through various means in the community.

Ways to communicate with parents include the following:

- through daily updates from students
- at school events and community gatherings, person to person
- through incentives to students to bring their parents to school programs
- through the media, including cable television and radio
- in churches and other community organizations
- through electronic means: e-mail and school websites
- through classroom parent networks
- on the telephone

- through "key communicators," trusted community leaders who are encouraged to communicate with school leaders about issues or concerns that come to their attention
- through formal parent leadership organizations: PTA, parent councils, parent advisory organizations
- through newsletters, both all-school and one specifically intended for 9th-grade parents
- in newspaper articles, pictures, and letters to the editor.

Finally, one of the most vital yet most frequently overlooked ways to communicate is through the inviting nature of a school's practices and policies. Sometimes called the five P's of invitational education — people, programs, places, policies, and processes – the most successful schools conduct an audit related to them. How do we answer the telephone? How are parents greeted when they visit our school? Are our policies user-friendly and easily understood? How is the appearance of the outside of our school? Are our classrooms inviting places in which students truly want to learn? Is the school clean, are washrooms safe, and is graffiti removed immediately? In general, do we have a philosophy that our school should be the most inviting place in town?

> The best way to ensure parental and community involvement in a school is to welcome people into the school. Although this may seem obvious, it is actually a common stumbling block in community-school relationships.
>
> — *Barbara Eason-Watkins, HOPE Foundation Video Series, 2002*

Engaging Parents During Critical Transitions: Communication with 9th-Grade Parents

Although parent engagement is vital at all stages of education, it can be particularly important during times of transition. The information that follows examines communication with 9th-grade parents as an example of parent engagement during educational transitions.

For most parents, their first experience with high school since they were students is when their oldest child is getting ready to enter 9th grade. The initial contact with these parents is significant: The high school principal and staff members must present themselves as caring, competent human beings who truly want the best for every 9th-grade student. This orientation program for parents of new 9th-graders should occur during the spring and summer of 8th grade; often there is a special orientation session at the beginning of the new school year as well.

Part of the extraordinary effort made by schools committed to 9th-grade success is to frequently communicate positive information about 9th-graders. Educators "catch" 9th-graders doing things right and reinforce this with a quick note, e-mail, or telephone call to the parents. This is especially important for parents of students who may not have been overly successful during their pre-high school years.

When a positive communication with parents occurs first, it is far easier to involve the parents in academic intervention strategies when their youngsters experience academic difficulties. Reserving time for parent-teacher conferences on the 9th-grade level is particularly important. These conferences should be held near the start of the 9th-grade year, so that communication is established with parents early and individually.

A number of schools have had great success using the concept of student-led parent and teacher conferences. In this approach, the student conducts the conference and explains his or her academic progress (or lack thereof). David Douglas High School in Portland, Oregon, has experienced 95% parent participation at the 9th- and 10th-grade levels in student-led conferences at the conclusion of the year. Of course, schools must provide teachers with professional development to understand thoroughly how these conferences should be conducted. Students must also be briefed on their responsibilities.

For all high school parents, but especially those with 9th-graders, involvement must be meaningful. If parent involvement is not meaningful, parents will "turn-off" and may not return. These ideas can help make this involvement valued:

- Hold in-depth discussions on the curriculum offerings available to 9th-grade students and the learning expectations of teachers.
- Share instructional strategies that teachers use.
- Give frequent updates on student rules and regulations; solicit parent involvement in suggesting changes.
- Always emphasize that by being involved on a regular basis, parents will be the most knowledgeable and the first to know about school challenges, successes, and planning.

- Meaningful parent involvement means easy access to the principal, other administrators, and often one or more school board members.
- Encourage parents to visit during the school day, sit in on classes, volunteer to chaperone field trips or serve as tutors, and so on.
- It is important to sponsor programs for parents on how to make the transition to high school easier, such as "survival kit for parents of 9th-graders."
- Facilitate discussions to help parents understand that they are all in this together. Many parents of 9th-graders believe that the challenges they face with their child are unique when, in fact, they are the norm. Be sure to inject humor into the discussions.
- Encourage parents to develop mini-parent networks whereby they have easy access to the telephone numbers of other parents, develop a common set of expectations for their students, and are comfortable communicating with each other in order to know where their children are, whom they are with, and what they are doing.
- Limit or avoid fundraising. By the time their children get to high school, most parents are tired of helping to raise money.
- Above all, meaningful parent involvement should be fun and inviting. Food is normally involved. When people truly feel welcome, they will return.

The International Center publishes a handbook, *Getting College and Career Ready — Maximizing 9th Grade*, that provides much more information about strategies for working with 9th-grade students and their parents.

An Example of Parent Engagement: An Empowered Parent Voice

A high school English teacher taught juniors a one-semester course in writing. During the course, students kept their work in portfolios. About two thirds of the way through the semester, the teacher decided to involve parents directly with the students' work. She developed a simple form that included a list of questions, such as "Which piece of writing did you like best?" and "What surprised you about your child's writing?"

Students took their portfolios home and asked their parents to read their work and complete the questions. Most parents were excited and thankful to be included in the assignment. They wanted to be involved, to have their voices count. They did not hesitate to read the papers or comment in depth about what they had observed. A particularly poignant response from one parent was "I didn't know that [my son] could write so well." These parents became a part of the formal education process instead of just bystanders.

Another high school English teacher set out to involve parents in their children's work throughout the year. On Fridays, students were given 10 minutes to respond to a prompt in their writing journals. The second part of the assignment was to take the journal home for parents to respond to what the student had written. This assignment was especially empowering to parents who did not speak English, because it provided an opportunity for them to participate actively in their children's education. There was a high rate of response from all parents. The teacher observed, "My assignment imposed a particular notion of literacy and required parents to support this notion of literacy with their involvement." After using the assignment for three years, the teacher concluded that the more often parents worked on the journal with their child, the more rapidly the child improved thinking and writing skills. In addition, the assignment was a way to show parents an effective method for helping their children develop critical literacy skills. The process not only empowered parents as partners in their children's education; it also empowered the students by helping them improve their skills. Finally, the teacher claimed that the assignment helped her to forge positive relationships with the parents. It became a positive alternative to a situation in which warning notices were the only communication that she had with parents. (Frye, Damion, "Engaging Parents Beyond the Parent Conference by Using a Shared 'Parent Journal'")

Empowering Community Groups

Any community is made up of numerous pockets of different types of people. For example, there are different socioeconomic groups and various religious organizations. Some individuals will be involved with a specific interest, such as athletics or the arts. There might be an organized group of people who advocate for disabled students.

In their observations, Sanders and Harvey assert, "Community partners believed that through their contributions they were helping the school provide a richer learning environment for students." The partnership must provide satisfaction for both the school and the community organization.

Sanders and Harvey identified 10 major types of community partners (Sanders, Mavis G., and Harvey, Adia., "Beyond the School Walls: A Case Study of Principal Leadership for School-Community Collaboration"):

- businesses/corporations
- universities and educational institutions
- government and military agencies
- healthcare organizations
- faith organizations
- national service and volunteer organizations
- senior citizen organizations
- cultural and recreational institutions
- other community-based organizations
- individuals in the community

How can a school empower all of these voices? Does a representative of each of these groups receive the school newsletter and other notices? Does the school invite the groups to specific events, such as open houses or meetings relevant to their interests?

The Open House Format

A high school decided to redesign its open house format. In the past, each teacher was in his or her classroom, the parents followed a shortened form of their children's schedule, and the teacher gave a brief description of the course. One year, the school invited a number of community groups to set up displays in the hallways.

The open house then fully lived up to its name. Many of the organizations connected to the school, such as family service agencies, were present at the event. School clubs and organizations created displays and distributed information. In addition, agencies and organizations that were directly related to the school and other more tangential groups made their community presence known as well.

Respect for All

A small rural high school served many different constituencies from the towns that sent their children to its hallways. One older gentleman, who did not have children in the school but who had some teaching experience, was very vocal about his disagreement with many issues related to the school, from the budget to the administration. Though he had a few loyal followers, his tirades earned him the reputation as someone not to be taken seriously.

The school principal invited the gentleman to meet with him, extending the invitation to others who agreed with the man's opinions. To accommodate them, he set an evening meeting time at the school. They talked for about an hour. The meeting was civil and the atmosphere pleasant.

Although the principal did not agree with many of the group's ideas, their attacks — at least, those directed specifically at him — stopped. In their place were support and praise for the administrator. This near-miraculous change occurred because the principal validated the group's voice; he had empowered them.

Community Resources and Supports

In *176 Ways to Involve Parents: Practical Strategies for Partnering With Families*, education consultant and former school superintendent Betty Boult stresses how creating initiatives at the school, family, and community levels increases opportunities for families to support the success of the school and their children. (Boult, Betty, *176 Ways to Involve Parents: Practical Strategies for Partnering With Families*)

Every community can provide resources and support beyond tax dollars. Through partnerships, community groups can be empowered to be part of the education delivery system and, therefore, have a say in that system. Beyond having a say, community groups and organizations are the source for opportunities for internships, independent studies, and college courses for credit. In addition, if the school can engage the community in meaningful ways, then those partnerships may provide a solution when the school is in need of something.

Resources abound when schools accept that effective and substantive education can take place outside the classroom and can be delivered by people who may not hold teaching licenses but who do have tremendous professional and life experience. When a school loses some of its "ivory tower" quality, community organizations begin to see themselves as empowered partners in the education of the community's students. Schools can use less monolithic structures and be more welcoming and attentive forces in a community. It is helpful for schools to hold frequent open meetings, in the evening or on weekends, to discuss school issues. When these meetings are scheduled, all constituencies should be invited.

Think back to the earlier discussion about the process of developing a school philosophy, vision, and mission. Community groups should be part of many discussions along the way. Their valuable input should be solicited and seen as equally important as the voices of other groups that are more directly related to the school, such as parents, teachers, students, and the administration.

School-community partnerships are not all about the school's taking; schools can offer something back to the community, as well. On the most basic level, many schools allow community groups to use their facilities for meetings, events, or activities when classes are not in session. Many schools, especially high schools, require students to complete a certain number of hours of community service. Other schools have curricula that emphasize social justice, another lens through which students might view the community. Service learning, too, offers an empowering opportunity for students to have an impact in the community.

While both community service and service learning benefit the community and the youth who are involved, there is an important distinction between these activities. In community service, volunteers usually are connecting to an existing program to provide benefits to others. Through service learning, however, youth identify a community need, research issues, agree on a plan, take action, review progress, and showcase results. By providing some leadership opportunities, service learning offers a different level of empowerment.

Schools that focus on experiential learning often use a service learning model and place students out in the community as the basis of their learning. Again, both the community and students benefit in numerous ways. Imagine a group of students creating and implementing a project to clean up a pond in a local park, for example.

School-Community Partnerships

School-community partnerships help schools expand opportunities for teachers and students beyond the classroom. Such partnerships are not limited to any particular type of organization (Traphagen, Kathleen, and Johnson-Staub, Christine, *Expanded Time, Enriching Experiences: Expanded Learning Time Schools and Community Organization Partnerships*):

> Schools partner with community-based organizations, youth development agencies, health care and human service agencies, institutions of higher education, and cultural and arts institutions to deepen academic content, offer enrichments, train teachers, and ensure access to health, social, and other services for students and families.

Partnerships can open up opportunities that empower schools, partners, and parents. "Some partners are teaching students, engaging families, and providing professional development to teachers, resulting in a truly integrated presence and multidimensional impact throughout the school." In addition to direct service benefits, when outside agencies are working with students, teachers may find that they have additional time to work on planning and implementing instructional strategies that improve alignment of core academics, enrichment, support services, and family engagement.

For community partners, the benefits go beyond helping schools deliver content not regularly available. Through these alliances, partner agencies can "play a key role in governance, funding, policy development, and pedagogical practice of the school."

Partnerships Empower

In a case study of the power of community connections in an urban elementary school in a high-reform district and state, Sanders and Harvey note an interesting example of empowerment emerging through school-community partnerships. One partner organization was a nonprofit foundation. While the foundation representative clearly saw the significance of the principal's role in cultivating the partnership, "she also contended that it was important for the principal to *build the capacity of others in the school* to maintain the partnerships." [emphasis added] Sanders and Harvey concluded that four major factors supported the school's success in creating partnerships with community organizations (Sanders, Mavis G., and Harvey, Adia, "Beyond the School Walls: A Case Study of Principal Leadership for School-Community Collaboration"):

- a high commitment to learning
- the principal's support of community involvement
- a welcoming school climate
- two-way communication about the level and kind of community involvement desired

Empowering Special Groups

Various groups will perceive the effectiveness of their voices differently. Some will see themselves as very powerful; others, as silenced. The job of the empowering leader is to avoid giving too much sway to the loudest voices while ensuring that those who feel that they have little or no voice are truly heard. English language learners, those who have disabilities, migrant students, deeply religious families, and other special groups all must be given a voice and empowered to be part of the fabric of the school community.

Who will make sure that the parents who speak little English are informed and listened to? Who will pick up the voice of the transient population? Who will represent the disabled, members of deeply religious groups, and other special interests?

Remember, too, that students are part of the community and that their voices should count. Many schools empower students by having the student, not the teacher, present and discuss his or her work during parent-teacher conferences. This empowers both student and parent, as they become the principal evaluators of the student's academic progress.

Empowering the Business Community

One major function of schools is to prepare students to enter the workforce. Empowering the voices of local businesses is vital. Businesses, not schools, set the qualifications that they seek in the positions that they have to offer. Calculation, communications, technical reading, business writing, analytical, or group process skills are all possible necessities in the workforce. Business partnerships also play a vital role in career and technical education. The International Center publishes a handbook, *Convergence of Academics and Career and Technical Education*, which provides more information on this topic.

A 2006 study, based on an extensive survey and interviews with human resource professionals, examined whether the skills of graduates of high school and two-year and four-year colleges are adequate for success in today's workplace. The results were alarmingly negative. The skills that most schools focus on do not adequately address what most employers want and need. For example, the level of literacy required for entry-level jobs — in terms of practical and hands-on materials versus literature — is higher than that of many graduates. (Casner-Lotto, Jill, and Benner, Mary Wright, *Are They Really Ready to Work? Employer's Perspectives on the Basic Knowledge and Applied Skills of New Entrants to the 21st Century U.S. Workforce*)

The challenge for schools is to find ways to ensure that the core academics encompass more than the traditional reading, writing, and arithmetic. This is where rigor and especially relevance become important. Educators must connect classroom instruction with real-world application, and/or schools must implement strategies and initiatives to enable students to gain real-world experience that will support their professional and personal success. The International Center's handbook entitled *Supporting Instructional Excellence Through Rigor, Relevance, and Relationships* provides additional information about rigor and relevance in instruction.

A work sabbatical idea for dropout prevention is a good example of the value of linking education with the workforce demands that students will encounter. Student internships, apprenticeships, and community service provide additional pathways to connect schools with their local business community. Business partners can be a rich source of speakers, demonstrations, field trips, and other opportunities for students to explore various fields. Many schools invite members of the business community to sit on judging panels to help evaluate students' culminating projects. Some schools enlist business partners to help them develop industry-relevant standards and the course content that support the development of such skills.

Since many of the jobs that will be open to our current kindergarten students upon graduation have not yet been invented, it behooves schools to pay close attention to the voice of business. School leaders must be certain to include them in discussions of curriculum and personal skills.

Some Interesting Approaches to Engagement

Parent, community and business engagement cannot be accomplished in the same way in every school district. Each school community presents unique challenges and opportunities for engagement. The following are examples of approaches for increased community engagement.

Inservice in the Real World

In a suburb of Holland, Michigan, the school superintendent knew that the teachers were out of touch with the world of work beyond education. He arranged for each teacher to spend two inservice days before the beginning of the school year experiencing a position in the workforce. When they all came together, the teachers could not stop talking about how much and what they had learned from the experience. In particular, teachers were stunned by how individuals were operating in the workforce community. Teachers saw collaborative teams. They saw technology and connectivity that amazed them.

In the somewhat insulated realm of their schools, teachers can become out of sync with the larger changes moving through the world outside of school. If the goal of educators is to prepare students for successful lives outside of school, then teachers need to have a clear picture of what success in the world at large looks like. It is not possible to create relevant learning experiences if teachers do not know to what they are relating their lessons.

Lunch in the Factory Cafeteria

A high school in Vermont was having difficulty arranging meetings with parents because work schedules did not allow parents to come to the school during regular hours. What was the solution? School leaders arranged to have certain key teachers and counselors set up shop in the cafeterias of various local employers during lunch breaks. Working parents could meet with educators and begin to forge connections to the school without having to take time off. The school received many letters from parents who expressed their appreciation of the school's efforts to accommodate their busy schedules and to help them become move involved in their children's education.

Coffee and Donuts

One Texas high school that served a population with high levels of poverty along with a high number of families in which English was not the primary language was struggling with ways to involve parents and to make the school a welcoming place for families. Many parents worked shift jobs, so the school set out to determine out what shifts and hours parents most commonly worked.

The nearest that many parents ever came to the school was when they dropped their children off on the way to work. The principal decided to capitalize on the parents' fleeting morning presence by setting up coffee and donuts in front of the school building. Administrators and counselors staffed the tables and invited parents to come by. Parents did indeed begin to stop in for some refreshment — and a conversation with someone knowledgeable about their child's performance in school. There were always Spanish speakers available for parents who had difficulty or discomfort with English. This idea was the first step in establishing a culture of comfort for parents.

The next contact point that the school explored was the distribution of report cards. Instead of sending reports home with students, as the school always had done, the school made report cards available for parents to pick up. To make this as convenient as possible for parents, the school arranged three pickup times — including lunchtime and in the evening — each day for two weeks. The report cards of students from Spanish-speaking homes were in both English and Spanish. Parents could chat a bit with teachers and counselors when they picked up the report cards.

By taking the time to think carefully about families' needs, the school was able to launch effective initiatives to achieve the goals. By adjusting schedules, the school was accommodating parents' work schedules, rather than forcing parents to adjust to the school's time frame. Changing the report card process created an opportunity for parents to connect with the school. Creating bilingual report cards and ensuring that Spanish-speaking staff members were readily available eased communication challenges.

It is essential for schools to understand the cultures in the community, especially when working with very diverse populations. For instance, Hispanic parents often assume that the teacher, an authority figure, knows what is right. This makes parent involvement with the school unnecessary from their point of view. Parents may not actually be avoiding the school, but simply living out cultural values. Part of this school's challenge was to find ways to respect cultural beliefs and needs while creating opportunities for parents to see the value of participating in the school more actively.

Letters Home

Everyone is familiar with the traditional back-to-school letter. Teachers get one from the superintendent and principal, and many teachers send one home for students and parents. An innovative school system developed this idea into a more personal school-to-parent contact.

Every teacher agreed to write a letter home. They also agreed to go beyond the usual information that parents might expect, such as course descriptions, requirements, objectives, and expectations. They made the letters personal, sharing information about themselves to help parents relate to them on a more human level than in their official role as teachers. They included information about their hobbies, degrees held, and what they had done over the summer. Some teachers described summer courses they had taken or new skills they would be applying in the classroom. Some described their gardens or talked about their pets.

The purpose of the letters was to make the school feel less like an institution and more like a place of people and learning. Teachers hoped to begin a positive relationship and dialogue with parents immediately. The letters served to demystify school and make it less threatening to all parents, but especially to those who were reluctant to approach the system.

Points for Participation

In one economically disadvantaged southern California community, many high school students' families had difficulty paying for senior pictures, prom tickets, and other extras. The school developed an innovative system for helping with this problem while engaging parents as well.

They established a system with points that could be used to buy prom tickets, senior pictures, and other products. Whomever a student named, be it a parent or other important adult in his or her life, could earn points by participating in school events; for instance, attending a parent-teacher conference was worth a certain number of points.

The points' value fueled better parent participation in the school while opening opportunities for students. For those parents or adults who earned a particularly high number of points, there was an ultimate reward: They were invited to hand their child his or her diploma at graduation.

Meet the Movers and Shakers

Another school in California realized that minority groups were not performing as well academically as were Caucasian students. This is not a new problem, but this school found a unique answer and involved the community to make it possible. School leaders went out into the community to meet with church councils, neighborhood committees, and leaders of other organizations in which students were involved. Community leaders began to speak with the students about their performance in school. Leaders linked activities in their own realms to school academic goals. For example, a Sunday school class worked on writing essays. In essence, the school empowered community groups to empower students.

In Colorado, the Foundation for Excellent Schools helps find mentors and role models for students who most need this kind of support. The organization One Hundred Black Men, which comprises both men and women, began visiting a school in Denver regularly. Eventually, these men and women became mentors and role models for many students in the school.

Not Just a Dream, But a Goal

For many children in economically disadvantaged families, the possibility of postsecondary education is never discussed in their homes. The family goal is for the student to graduate from high school and find employment. To help students and their families turn what may seem like an unattainable "extra" into a goal and reality, schools in Hawaii began to take students as young as kindergarteners on field trips to community colleges, colleges, and other postsecondary institutions. Students had to bring an adult with them. A grandmother participating in one of these trips could not believe what she saw. She had had no idea what possibilities there were or what resources were available. She gathered brochures from every institution that she visited with her grandchild. The eye-opening experience inspired the woman to give information to her sons, all of whom eventually enrolled in community college.

What parents and students saw on these trips were people just like them taking advantage of services to improve their lives. The school's program showed them some of the resources that could be found in the community and opened them up to the idea that what once seemed impossible could be possible.

Bringing in the Community

In an effort to engage parents, one high school in the southern United States that served a large economically disadvantaged population created a community room. The room included a number of items, such as a school history, parent resources, Internet connectivity, and coffee. Parents were empowered by having their own space inside the school. They could drop in at any time during the day and spend five minutes or two hours there. Parent groups began to meet in the space. The room strengthened the community by creating, right within the school, a place for the community to emerge and take root.

Another high school hosted a naturalization ceremony so that students could watch people being sworn in as U.S. citizens. The school offered a flower to each newly naturalized citizen. Students had the opportunity to see how special citizenship, which they often take for granted, is. The new citizens and their families had an opportunity to experience the school, which is a great first step in creating a lasting interest and connection to the education community. Many schools reach out to communities by offering to hold neighborhood meetings in school facilities. Other schools give senior citizens free passes to student musical performances, plays, and sports events. One district invited senior citizens to join elementary students to create an intergenerational choir to perform for the public.

Making Your School a Community Hub

Historically, schools were at the center of communities. Though school populations have grown in size and diversity, efforts to reestablish schools as community hubs offers benefits to all.

Finding ways to involve parents and community members in your school can itself be a community activity. Challenge teachers, students, parents, and the community to generate ideas about how to make your school more accessible to members of the community. Remember, sometimes the most successful ideas come from unexpected sources, so cast a wide net. Consider these suggestions:

- using the local newspapers to invite community members to submit ideas
- appealing for suggestions through the parent newsletters and school website
- hosting community brainstorming sessions followed by a coffee hour
- including this topic periodically on faculty meeting agendas to gather ideas from staff
- creating a student committee, with membership open to all, to come up with suggestions
- creating parent/teacher/student/community member committees to help design and implement initiatives

Summary

Promotion of community engagement is an integral part of school leadership. Community engagement can be divided into three main components: engagement of parents, engagement of community groups, and engagement of the business community. Each of these types of engagement can lead to increased student achievement.

Chapter 7: Leadership and Community Engagement

Reflection Activity

1. Promoting parent engagement is an important function of school leadership. Which populations are significant in your school/district?
   - non-English speakers
   - minorities
   - specific religious groups
   - single-parent families
   - immigrant populations
   - blended families
   - families in poverty
   - households in which all adults work outside the home

   Do these groups require different pathways to empowerment? What special characteristics do you need to consider when you think about how to engage each of these groups in your school?

2. Reflect on the types of community groups in your area. Identify two specific groups with which you can imagine a mutually beneficial relationship with the school. What action steps could you take to make these relationships happen?

3. How could an increase in your school's engagement with the business community in your area benefit the school? What unique ways to implement business partnerships can you imagine?

© International Center for Leadership in Education